D0212540

1

Introduction: From Structuralism through Poststructuralism to Pragmatism

The twentieth century became the century of the sign in two interrelated respects. First, technologies of information and communication, notably the mass media, came to carry new forms of social interaction in politics, business, and leisure.[1] Second, semiotics was developed within several scientific fields to understand what Saussure had called the "life of signs within society" (1916/1959: 16), in part as a response to the mass-mediated signs of modernity. Taking stock of semiotic and other current approaches to mass communication and culture, this volume proposes a return to the semiotics and pragmatism of Charles Sanders Peirce, as well as a redevelopment of social theory in that perspective, to arrive at an integrative, social-semiotic theory of mass communication.[2]

In polemical summary, the problem with Saussurean semiology in communication studies has been a tendency to give much attention to signs as such, less to society, and hardly any to the 'life' of signs in social practices. The relative neglect of semiosis as practice in the humanities is matched by the neglect, in much social-scientific communication research, of mass media as sources of meaning. In another polemical summary, social scientists have been too busy asking who, says what, in which channel, to whom, and with what effect (Lasswell, 1948/1966), to address the more fundamental question of how communication and its 'effects' are mediated in discourse. While these disciplinary blindnesses have been recognized for at least a decade, substantial interdisciplinary convergence remains to be accomplished.

One important interdisciplinary dialogue, examining mass communication simultaneously as a social-material and a semiotic-discursive phenomenon, has occurred in the area of reception studies (for overviews, see Jensen, 1991b; Morley and Silverstone, 1991). Both theoretical and empirical work during the 1980s and early 1990s has contributed to a new conception of the reception, social uses, and impact of mass media. The classic question of effects has been reformulated to state broader issues concerning the role of mass media in the production and circulation of meaning in society and, significantly, the activity of audiences in that process. The reorientation of audience research, further, has entailed convergence between two traditionally antagonistic forms of research, namely, humanistic readings of media texts and social-scientific studies of empirical media audiences. Reception analysis has grown as a methodology of audience-cum-content analysis emphasizing qualitative inquiry into the process by which audiences interpret and apply media contents in everyday contexts. Recently, reception studies have also provoked renewed debate concerning the relative power of media and audiences. The criticism is that qualitative audience studies have become methodologically myopic and politically populist, overemphasizing the agency of audiences in the social production of meaning as part of what Curran (1990) calls "the new revisionism" (but see the response in Morley, 1992). The question focused by reception analysis, then, is not only what media do to audiences, or what audiences do with media, but how media and audiences interact as agents of the life of signs in society, with implications for both the quality of everyday life and the structure of society.

This first chapter places the argument concerning social semiotics and mass media reception in the context of current debates about culture and modernity. My point will be that pragmatism represents a third alternative in communication theory and politics, mediating between social sciences and humanities, as well as transcending the modernity–postmodernity and structuralism–poststructuralism dichotomies. The debates concerning postmodern culture and poststructuralist science are indicative of an intellectual crisis arising, in part, from a specific agenda of philosophy and theory development. Contemporary communication theory may be seen as Western philosophy in the rearview mirror.

Postmodernism, poststructuralism, and rearviewmirrorism

'Rearviewmirrorism' was Marshall McLuhan's labeling of a problematic way of understanding new communication technologies: "We still have our eyes fixed on the rearview mirror looking firmly and squarely at the job that is receding into the nineteenth-century past" (quoted in Stearn, 1967: 242). McLuhan's underlying argument was that "the medium is the message," not just that each medium carries a particular perspective on reality, but that the content of each new medium is an older medium (McLuhan, 1962, 1964). Hence, the content of writing is speech; the content of television is film. The implication is that new media seldom realize their full potential because they are made in the image of older media. For example, television news formats traditionally have been constrained within the formats of print journalism. In this respect, at least, communication technologies are similar to other forms of technology, such as early automobiles that were constructed on the model of horse-drawn vehicles.

Theories are comparable to technologies, to the extent that they represent an understanding of reality for a particular purpose, thus articulating a specific social and scientific imagination. In labeling postmodernist thinking as rearviewmirrorism, I suggest a qualified endorsement of McLuhan's position as well as a critical interest in postmodernism, which I take to be the wrong answer to the right question. On the one hand, despite McLuhan's eclecticism and rampant metaphors, his diagnosis of the literate bias of communication scholarship and his emphasis on the material specificity of other media than writing and print remain underestimated contributions to mass communication theory (for a reappreciation, see Gerbner, 1981), which offer insight into the long waves of social and cultural history. Most theorizing about mass communication today implicitly draws its models from verbal language, even when the object of analysis is film, television, multimedia, and other audio-visual communication. Moreover, the problem of theoretical validity is aggravated at the methodological level when formal models of analysis, rooted in logic or mathematics, are superimposed on verbal conceptions of communication. A more differentiated theory of signs is required to account for the actual vehicles of communication and their impact on audiences and societies.

On the other hand, I interpret postmodernism and poststructuralism as important commentaries on the Logos tradition in Western philosophy and theory, which, in one respect, has been a project of counteracting the ambiguities of everyday language. Postmodernism and poststructuralism, by contrast, have substantiated that neither everyday language nor scientific forms of representation could carry unambiguous or unified meaning. Following that diagnosis, however, they in fact perform a deconstruction of the Logos tradition within the very same conceptual repertoire. Postmodernist culture and poststructuralist science inherit the Logos tradition turned upside down.

Prefacing the brief genealogy of the Logos tradition below (see further Jensen, 1991a: 20–31), I should clarify that, for the present argument, I simply define poststructuralism as a theoretical articulation of postmodernism. I also do not dwell on the differences between (European) poststructuralism (for example, Derrida, 1967/1976) and (American) deconstructionism (for example, Fish, 1989), but treat them for all practical purposes as one position. Postmodernism may be summarized in the assumption that the relationship between signs, self, and society has been radically reshaped in advanced industrial societies during the last few decades, resulting in a culture of disintegration and recombination. Harvey (1989) has offered the important qualification that the alleged postmodern condition is perhaps best understood as an outcome of that long material and cultural process of modernization, involving industrialization, secularization, and bureaucratization, which increasingly has placed information and aesthetics at the center of political, economic, and other social developments.[3] Thus, socalled 'postmodern' culture may be one characteristic of advanced *modern* societies. The historical continuity is similarly striking when it comes to the development of theories of signs.

Logos and structuralism: From word to text

In the beginning was the Word – as the source of religious revelation, aesthetic experience, and scientific truth. The importance traditionally attached to verbal language in the history and theory of science as a medium of rational discourse may be traced, under the heading of the Logos tradition, from Greek philosophy of the fifth century BC up to, and including, poststructural- ism. The Logos tradition assumes, in essence, that there exists a "transcendental intimacy of thought, words, and reality" (Heim, 1987: 42), and it was shaped, in part, by the development of alphabetic writing. Plato's attack on the (oral) poets in the *Republic* is indicative of a gradual transition from oral to literate culture: poets could no longer be trusted in matters of social reality such as politics or the writing of history, even if their poetry could still be appreciated as personal opinion or myth (Havelock, 1963).

The Logos conception of the alphabet also had major implications for its social uses. It is likely that the alphabet helped to introduce a new under- standing of knowledge not as memory, but as a record of statements that could be disputed and verified. Reality, in the form of the alphabet, was now manifestly present as an external representation of thought that could be examined, crafted, and transformed. In fields of science, alphabetic records provide for a systematic and cumulative analysis. In public debate and poli- tics, the alphabet makes possible a governmental and social system of great size and complexity, because it offers a resource for organization and com- munication across time and space. The Word is key, then, to an understanding not just of Western arts and philosophy, but of civilization and society, as well.

It is the quasi-religious metaphysics of unity and presence associated with the Word that has become a particular target of postmodernist critique. In part as an early attempt to transcend such metaphysical implications and to pro- fessionalize textual research, the twentieth century witnessed a formalist turn in the study of language and other signs. The turn is perhaps exemplified most clearly in the shifts of emphasis within literary scholarship, from the Word of the historical author, through the autonomous Work of the New Criticism, to the structured Text of structuralism. Paralleling the linguistic turn of philoso- phy (Rorty, 1967), this theoretical and methodological development is explained, further, by its social context. New approaches were the scholarly response to the crisis of representation in the arts that had been signaled by the rise of Impressionism, which was itself a response to the spread of photogra- phy and the new fragmented, urban reality being represented, and which continued in the formal experiments of the various twentieth-century -isms (see Hughes, 1981; also Pelfrey, 1985). Realizing that the status of art as the expression of an artistic sensibility and as the representation of a reality shared in common was being called into question, scholarship may have retreated similarly to a position inside language, studying art for form's sake. The crisis of representation arguably was accentuated by the growth of factual, 'objec- tive' genres in the press from the middle of the nineteenth century, similarly highlighting the definition of social reality. Hence, new historical forms of verbal and visual representation set a new agenda for twentieth-century research on signs.

Structuralism in literary, media, and cultural studies thus began a quest for the underlying formal or deep structures of texts.[4] In keeping with Saussurean linguistics and Russian Formalism, this tradition made a final break with the Romantic understanding of literature, in Wordsworth's words, as "the spontaneous overflow of powerful feelings" (in Abrams et al., 1962: 103). However, at least in its semiological variety within the humanities, structuralism in practice did not confine analysis to formal aspects of poetic language and other signs. The ambition still was to arrive at an empathetic, introspective understanding of discourse by probing textual details from a broadly hermeneutic or phenomenological perspective.[5]

The Logos legacy is suggested by the two aspects of the semiological sign concept: the signifier, or the material aspect of signs, is only an indirect medium for the experience of "transcendental intimacy" (Heim, 1987: 42) with reality, while meaning, truth, and beauty reside in the signified, the conceptual content, as represented in some mental agency. Moreover, the retreat into this sign in the mind implies a tenuous connection to social reality. Roman Jakobson, for one, in his classic model of communication, explicitly refrained from addressing "the question of relations between the word and the world" (1960/1981: 19). If the communicators and their reality are only conceived as signs *in* communication, the explanatory value of the model for analyses of specific communicative contexts and effects inevitably is limited.

Concrete semiological studies, certainly in mass communication research, have not practiced the textual solipsism that the theory preaches, but have made farreaching extrapolations about the impact of signs on recipients. One paradigmatic case is Roland Barthes's (1957/1973) early and justly famous analysis of myth in advertising. His model of the two levels of signification, which takes a first step in the direction of Peircean, infinite semiosis,[6] implies that the primary locus of ideology is in the media discourse and, further, that particular structures of discourse may be sufficient conditions for a certain ideological impact. It was only a short step to concluding that ideological impact is due to a false or, at least, historically and situationally inadequate discursive representation of reality, giving rise to false consciousness. In conclusion, whereas much credit is due to semiological work within anthropology, literary criticism, and cultural studies for initiating and legitimating a systematic study of popular culture (for example, Culler, 1975; Fiske and Hartley, 1978), the semiological inflection of the Logos tradition in various textual methodologies, coupled with social and cultural history in broad strokes, came to suggest dubious, occasionally untenable, conclusions about the social production of meaning. Interestingly, semiological and other humanistic communication theory has joined social-scientific communication theory in posing the basic question concerning the origin of meaning in spatial and essentialist terms:

Where is meaning?

The field of communications, in addressing the origin of meaning, has reiterated the quest for some incorrigible foundation of knowledge which has preoccupied professional philosophy since Descartes (Rorty, 1979). Descartes, having hypostatized the distinction between the knowing subject (*res cogitans*) and its objects in reality (*res extensa*), committed philosophy to the project of reestablishing the lost symmetry between the subjective and objective realms, as a foundation of knowledge, human enterprise, and control over nature. At the center of the modern mental universe emerged the solitary, but perspicacious individual, just as in the areas of economic enterprise and political activity the individual presumably now reigned supreme (Lowe, 1982). The lifeline between the realms – the correlate of external reality in human experience – was defined, following Locke, as the data of sense perception. Thus, eyesight entered philosophical discourse as the major metaphor for the activity of knowing. By pointing to sense data as objective correlates of individuals' subjective knowledge, early modern philosophy arrived at a spatial and essentialist answer to the question, 'Where is reality?'

If semiology answered the question of meaning with reference to the Word as the immediate vehicle of *res cogitans*, social-scientific communication theory has referred to the manifest vehicles of information in *res extensa*. A very large proportion of international communication research is still informed, explicitly or implicitly, by Lasswell's (1948/1966: 178) formulation of "Who/Says What/In Which Channel/To Whom/With What Effect?", in which the "what" of communication is conceived of as some message entity that maintains a simple presence in the world, linking two minds with reference to an already shared reality. By contrast to the other paradigmatic communication model in Jakobson (1960/1981), the notion of a code mediating between mind and reality, and between minds in communication, is not central to Lasswell (1948/1966). Reception instead is seen to involve selective attention to certain building blocks of meaning, so that any communicant who "performs a relay function can be examined in relation to input and output" (Lasswell, 1948/1966: 186). The terminology is important in implying an analogy between human interpretation and the technology of relay stations. Meaning emerges as the entity that survived an act of interpretation.

A similarly symptomatic terminology can be found in the other foundational text of social-scientific communication theory, the mathematical theory of communication (Shannon and Weaver, 1949). Retreating further into the material vehicles of communication, this model commonly has been taken to suggest that meaning resides in signals, which are only a short step away from a concept of stimuli. Despite the disclaimers that the question of meaning is addressed in technical terms of engineering, Shannon and Weaver's original text supports the interpretation of their position as a theory of cognition and behavior, as well. While distinguishing technical from semantic and pragmatic aspects of communication, the terminology of the book conceives recipients in technical terms in suggesting that a general theory of communication "will surely have to take into account not only the capacity of the channel but also (even the words are right!) the capacity of the audience" (Shannon and Weaver, 1949: 27). Whether or not these are the right words is precisely the issue, left unaddressed. It is ironic that the several metaphorical meanings of 'capacity' and other information-theoretical terms are conflated in a model that conceives itself as formal and a-metaphorical. By assigning meaning and information to distinct categories of reality, and by assuming the hegemony of material, technical reality, the mathematical model begs the question and, like Jakobson's (1960/1981) model,[7] fails to address either the reference of communication to social and historical contexts or its reception by interpretive agents. Beniger (1988, 1990) has offered persuasive bibliometric evidence that this rudimentary model still informs what may be considered a dominant paradigm in communication research, if not in political (Gitlin, 1978), then in epistemological terms.

One of the most basic critiques of essentialist communication theory has indeed been launched by poststructuralism. Before considering an alternative question, 'When is meaning?' (Goodman, 1978: 57), defining meaning in relational, processual, and performative terms, I discuss poststructuralism as a reassertion of the dualist framework.

Poststructuralism: From text to trace

Poststructuralism conceives itself as the end of the Logos tradition, aiming for the ultimate deconstruction of the Word. Since the seminal work of Derrida (1967/1976), studies within philosophy, literary theory, and other fields have stood semiology on its head by defining the signifier as the material source of signification while rejecting the simple presence of the signified in human self-awareness as metaphysical, ideological 'logocentrism.' Poststructuralist studies do not merely expose the silent premises of specific texts, but question the first premise that texts may carry *any* stable meaning or understanding. By contrast, texts are described as chains of signifiers initiating a play of differences that constantly puts meaning into question. Moreover, poststructuralism challenges the priority given in the Logos tradition to speech as the authentic expression of mind, while writing is a secondary medium. Instead, poststructuralists refer to 'writing' in a generalized sense as the set of traces, in discourse and in the minds of communicators, which make up the vehicle of what is not quite 'communication': texts are never what they seem or say, being only the trace of an absent meaning. All communication is miscommunication.

The distinction between language as a medium of representation and as a mode of action, which was brought to the fore in recent philosophy by Wittgenstein (1958) and speech-act theory (Austin, 1962; Searle, 1969), helps to clarify both the way poststructuralism challenges the Logos tradition and the extent to which it fails to transcend that tradition. On the one hand, contemporary common sense suggests also that human language primarily enables us to describe things in the world. On the other hand, language enters into most action, orienting human purposes and transforming social realities. Saying means doing.

Resigning itself to the conception of language as a failed representation, also in scientific research, poststructuralism suggests three alternative tasks for

science. First, poststructuralist scientists should engage in what I dub 'epistemological doodling.' As philosophy has been overtaken in most domains by
specialized sciences, epistemology has become the main enterprise of modern
philosophy, examining the conditions of knowing about various domains.
Major works in the theory of science (Kuhn, 1970) and in the history of philosophy (Rorty, 1979) have concluded that epistemology cannot fulfill this
foundational mission. To the poststructuralist, the main task for philosophy
and theory of science instead becomes the documentation of how and why one
cannot justify knowing specific things about other people, texts, or institutions.
The practical outcome is unlimited self-reflexivity in a closed circuit of discourses entailing skepticism and inaction. The dualist alternative to
self-awareness thus becomes ignorance. Current debates around postmodern
ethnography, for example, include the position that ethnography is best understood not as a scientific genre, but as a form of poetry yielding ever more
interpretations (Clifford and Marcus, 1986). A similar epistemological anxiety
can be found in some cultural studies (for example, Grossberg, 1988) that in
effect denounce any will to know about the actual social uses of discourse. In
some critical scholarship, the epistemological position is confused with a political position of progressiveness when "we are informed that science is a white
male invention to maintain hegemonic rule over the 'other', and that there is
no such thing as truth" (McChesney, 1993: 101).

    A dualistic alternative also underlies the second, ontological position of
poststructuralist science. Having concluded that signs cannot serve as a guide
to reality, poststructuralism chooses a particularly emphatic, but also tri-
umphant version of antirealism which may offer a sense of ecstasy. Perhaps the
clearest statement of antirealistic ecstasy is found in the writings of Jean
Baudrillard (see Baudrillard, 1988). In suggestive prose, Baudrillard evokes the
widespread sense of a loss of authenticity in the modern world, to which neither God nor the Word is a reliable guide. While such a worldview has been
associated with a tragic sense of self and history in the arts and in cultural theory, Baudrillard rather paints a promising picture of life in a hyper-reality
consisting of simulacra – *malgré tout*. These simulacra are a reality unto
themselves, independent of any material or social reality. The Logos tradition
thus has come full circle with Baudrillard celebrating the decline of the signified and the rise of the signifier as a new autonomous reality.

    The third, political or social orientation of poststructuralist science can be
summed up as narrative laissez-faire. While much poststructuralist writing is
far removed from the concerns of both critical theory and practical politics,
Jean-François Lyotard's argument has been that scientists make themselves
socially useful by producing ever more, and more diverse, narratives (Lyotard,
1984). On the one hand, he argues, any attempt to justify political ideals or
social arrangements with reference to a system of fundamental values – a
grand narrative – entails a consensus that is closed, static, and ultimately terrorist in nature. If a political process is to result in collective social action, then
it must in the end, says Lyotard, eliminate any positions which disagree with or
actively oppose the emerging consensus. On the other hand, Lyotard suggests

an alternative, namely, an infinite series of language games involving a never-ending play of moves and differences – little narratives. The play of differences might allow dialogue to continue indefinitely, as new contributions would constantly be made by equal participants. This democratically accessible series of signifiers thus would counteract a closure of meaning around a particular signified: You can have your representation of reality, and I'll have mine.

Little narratives, however, accumulate a grand narrative of what reality is or ought to be. In political and scientific practice, certain positions prevail to the exclusion of others, sometimes by default. No social structure of some complexity could exist without procedures for ending language games, resolving interpretive disputes, and initiating collective action. There is no lasting comfort in epistemological doodling, antirealistic ecstasy, or narrative laissez-faire.

Postmodernism itself is a grand narrative, announcing the end of another grand narrative in its rearview mirror. McLuhan helped teach our field to look beyond the rearview mirror of print and Logos to contemporary popular culture. Peirce may teach us to look beyond the multiple mirrors of postmodernism to pragmatism.

Pragmatism: Signs of difference

Semiosis, action, and difference

The distinctive features of pragmatism may be summarized with reference to its conception of semiosis and action. First, pragmatism defines semiosis in general terms as a constitutive element of all human perception and cognition. Consciousness is always already mediated by signs, which thus lend form not just to cultural artifacts, but to each and every thought that enters into social life, material production, and cultural practice. Semiosis, moreover, is defined not as a system, but as a continuous process of signification that orients human cognition and action. It is this assumption that leads Peirce to suggest that "every thought must be interpreted in another, or that all thought is in signs" (1958: 34). Whereas the wide conception of semiosis calls for a typology of signs, the point is that signs, while being of multiple types, all belong to one general category mediating the interaction between humans and their natural as well as cultural environment. Mass communication, of course, is a semiotic practice central to contemporary cultural environments.

Second, pragmatism defines the representation of the world through signs as merely one form of social action. Representation, then, may be neither a privileged nor a bankrupt attempt at contemplating truth, but an act for a purpose in a context. Pragmatism further holds that signs, whether representations or other communicative forms, do not provoke a 'response' in any behaviorist sense, but may produce 'a predisposition to act.' Signs present potential courses of action. One implication for communication studies is that while complex mass-mediated signs constitute 'manuscripts' for action, they initiate a further process of semiosis in which the audience negotiates their relevance for action in context. Pragmatism thus conceives semiosis as a continuous feedback mechanism addressing the meaning of social action. Pragmatism further enables a specific emphasis on the institutionalized forms of semiosis that are designated as such – ritual, religion, and culture – and through which societies think about themselves.

The relationship between 'subjective' semiosis and 'objective' social practice is specified by a third concept of pragmatism, namely, difference. Meaning is a difference that makes a difference (Bateson, 1972: 242; Goodman, 1976: 227). Also the semiological tradition has argued that meaning is not an essential quality of a given sign, but a feature of its relations of difference with other signs. A letter, word, sentence, book, or library is defined, accordingly, by its distinctive features in contradistinction to those of other units at the same level of the sign system. The semiological focus, however, has remained on the very system of discursive differences, rather than the interpretive difference that is made by various recipients, or the social difference that their interpretation may ultimately make in other contexts of action. To exemplify, the reception of advertising discourse by audiences can be conceptualized as their interpretive enactment of discursive difference, perhaps making a social difference for their acts as consumers as well as their perspective on the social system. The understanding of semiosis as performative and of society as meaningful was pinpointed by another pragmatist, W.I. Thomas, in his explanation of why the social construction of reality in signs matters: "If men define situations as real, they are real in their consequences" (in Rochberg-Halton, 1986: 44).

Pragmatism has remained an undercurrent in twentieth-century philosophy, being mostly neglected within European research in the social sciences and humanities (but see Joas, 1993), despite its interfaces with Continental sociology and psychology as well as with cultural studies (Berger and Luckmann, 1966). In the American context, despite an abiding interest in pragmatism especially within philosophy proper, there has been little cumulative theory development and few empirical studies tapping the explanatory value of pragmatism for culture and communication (but see Carey, 1989). Recently, Bernstein (1986: 58; 1991) among others has suggested that pragmatism offers a new agenda that may engage theorists and philosophers from different origins, American and European, Continental and Anglo-Saxon, modern and postmodern (see also Nielsen, 1993). The common concern of this agenda is how to integrate a philosophy of language with a theory of society in a theory of communication that begins to explain the historical origins and social uses of meaning.

Semiotics vs Semiology

I thus approach the agenda of social semiotics according to several premises which are summed up in Figure 1.1, taken from Milton Singer's volume developing a semiotic conception of anthropology (Singer, 1984: 42). The figure contrasts (Saussurean) semiology and (Peircean) semiotics in terms of their different theoretical, methodological, ontological, and epistemological premises.

Point of comparison	Semiotic (Peirce)	Semiology (Saussure)
1 Aims at a general theory of signs	Philosophical, normative, but observational	A descriptive, generalized linguistics
2 Frequent subject matter domains	Logic, mathematics, sciences, colloquial English (logic-centered)	Natural languages, literature, legends, myths (language-centered)
3 Signs are relations, not 'things'	A sign is a triadic relation of sign, object, and interpretant	A sign is a dyadic relation between signifier and signified
4 Linguistic signs are 'arbitrary'	But also include 'natural signs' – icons and indexes	But appear 'necessary' for speakers of the language (Benveniste)
5 Ontology of 'objects' of signs	Existence presupposed by signs	Not 'given' but determined by the linguistic relations
6 Epistemology of empirical ego or subject	Included in semiotic analysis	Presupposed by but not included in semiological analysis

Figure 1.1   *Comparison of semiotics and semiology (Singer, 1984: 42)*

Whereas this volume devotes most attention to the concrete theoretical and methodological implications of semiotics and pragmatism for mass communication research, it is important to keep in mind that the various research traditions are premised on specific epistemological and ontological assumptions, as retraced in this chapter. For one thing, Peirce proposed to examine the conditions of knowledge as part of a general logic of inquiry, preparing not merely a theory of signification or communication, but a theory of science as part of a general epistemology. For another thing, Peirce's semiotics is reflexive, implying a conceptualization of the very subject who thinks through signs. Semiology, by contrast, was founded on two alternative assumptions: first, that verbal language is the model for other systems of signification and for thinking in general, and, second, that the empirical ego or subject can be presupposed as an agent centered in verbal language. In ontological terms, this further implies that semiology conceives humans and the rest of reality as constituted in and through language. Semiotics adopts a working hypothesis that is simultaneously more ambitious and more modest: different signs enable us to know about reality, even though the status of signs and the nature of reality are subject to unlimited semiosis in scientific research and public debate.

Outline of the volume

Having stated the challenge for a social semiotics of mass communication and the limitations of structuralism and poststructuralism in this respect, I turn in the rest of Part I to two sources of social semiotics. Chapter 2 presents a critical introduction to the philosophy of pragmatism originating from Peirce, identifying two lines of development for his semiotics, namely, as a theory of communication, or first-order semiotics (Part II), and as a theory of science, or second-order semiotics (Part III). While Peirce's pragmatism was limited, to a degree, by his natural-scientific, experimental conception of science, other work in this tradition has developed pragmatism as epistemology and political philosophy with direct relevance for the understanding of mass communication as semiotic action.

Chapter 3 next offers a re-reading of some seminal positions in social theory, from Max Weber to recent theories of everyday life, in the perspective of pragmatism and with particular reference to structuration theory (Giddens, 1984). My purpose is to recover some basic theoretical concepts of meaning and culture for mass communication research in order to address the production of meaning that arises, in part, from mass communication. Meaningful society is the grand total of the semiosis which knowledgeable social agents engage in as they accomplish the everyday necessities of life.

Part II brings together the pragmatist tradition and recent social theory in the outline of a theory of mass communication. I argue that a pragmatist turn holds the potential for a new theory which may give substance to the convergence under way between humanistic and social-scientific media research. Chapter 4 presents the constituents of a social-semiotic theory of mass communication, specifying with reference to four methodological dimensions of research how mass media serve as institutions-to-think-with, their discourses serving as cultural resources for audiences. I further argue that the act of reception is key to the study of how, on the one hand, mass media provide a time-out from the rest of culture and society while, on the other hand, media use is integral to many social routines as part of what I call time-in culture. With Stuart Hall (1983: 84), I suggest that both the act of reception and the wider forms of culture are subject to determination in the first instance: while the technology, economy, and organizations of mass media and other cultural institutions set the basic conditions of social semiosis, its process and outcome are open to variation and negotiation whose exact scope is an empirical issue.

Chapters 5 to 8 lend substance and empirical support to the general claims of the theory. Each chapter presents an empirical study of media reception that addresses one of the four methodological dimensions of social semiotics. Chapter 5 examines audience uses of television news, focusing on the several contexts of reception, that is, the levels and stages in which the interaction between media and audiences unfolds and takes effect. Next, Chapter 6 compares and contrasts conceptions of the audience as a demographic and an interpretive category, with reference to an empirical study of different generations of television viewers and with a critical discussion of the current notion of interpretive communities. Chapter 7, offering a study of television reception as flow, makes the argument that reception studies have come to neglect the dimension of actual media discourses in their empirical designs. Finally, Chapter 8 reviews the most common approaches to qualitative reception studies and argues, in particular, for developing systematic methods of data analysis. Part II, then, ends up reemphasizing the careful, comparative study of media and audience discourses as they enter into the life of signs within society.

Research itself is a semiotic practice working with signs in society. Part III, accordingly, turns to second-order semiotics and considers three implications of Peircean pragmatism for the theory and politics of science. While the first two parts of the volume focus on the explanatory value of qualitative approaches to communication studies, Chapter 9 more specifically considers the epistemological complementarity of quantitative and qualitative methodologies, and concludes that qualitative modes of inquiry rely on a variety of what Peirce called abduction, a third type of inferential logic different from but equal to induction and deduction. I referred above to determination in the first instance as a principle of first-order semiotics; for second-order semiotics I propose a principle of unification in the last instance, that is, *not* at the level of elementary data, but in an interdisciplinary community of researchers who recognize multiple scientific signs. Chapter 10 further examines the ontological relations between recent models of meaning and communication within semiotics and cognitive science, as exemplified by visual communication.

In conclusion, Chapter 11 explores the implications of pragmatism for the politics of communication in a discussion of the work of Jürgen Habermas and Richard Rorty. While both are prominent contemporary philosophers with affinities to pragmatism, I suggest that their inflections of pragmatism in a theory of communication and society lead respectively into the Scylla of modernism (Habermas) and the Charybdis of postmodernism (Rorty). Pragmatism offers a third way of inquiry and says, with Peirce (in Skagestad, 1981: 5), "Do not block the way of inquiry!"

2

Semiotic Action: Recovering Pragmatism

"Pragmatism survived as a philosophical position from the time of John Dewey to the late 1970s, but it did not flourish" (Prado, 1987: 1). Tracing the sources of semiotics in pragmatism and in the history of ideas more generally, this chapter suggests both the specific explanatory value of pragmatism for an integrative theory of communication and a preliminary explanation of why the pragmatist position has remained marginal not only since Dewey, but in a longer perspective of Western philosophy and science. The first main section accordingly presents a historical overview of the concept of signs, which represents a common denominator for several classic issues of epistemology and ontology that return with a vengeance in communication theory. The second section outlines the thinking of Peirce with particular emphasis on his concepts of interpretants and interpretive communities. Far from being an invention of recent literary theory (Fish, 1979), the category of interpretive communities was developed by Peirce to account for the production of knowledge in scientific communities, its analogy in recent reception studies being the understanding of audiences as discursive agents. The final three sections of this chapter examine the legacy of Peirce's pragmatism, as developed also by his contemporaries, William James and John Dewey, for current research on culture and communication.[1]

I present my argument as theory development in the mode of Peircean pragmatism, standing on the shoulders of a giant, not as a study in the historical development or specific achievements of Peirce's philosophy. Moreover, I endorse neither Peirce's scientistic inclination nor his religious beliefs. Regarding Peirce's cosmology premised on absolute chance (tychism), a principle of continuity uniting mind and matter (synechism), and the reality of evolutionary love (agapism), I concur with Johansen that "I do not feel obliged to systematically expound and comment on issues such as his tychism, synecism, and agapism, although they are essential to himself and to the study of his philosophical development" (1993: xii). Being a fallibilist, one committed to the continuous revision of scientific positions and procedures, Peirce would have approved, in principle, of an interdisciplinary redevelopment of his ideas.

A very short history of signs

The history of Western philosophy and science is not normally told as a history of signs.[2] Notwithstanding the Logos tradition described in Chapter 1, however, scholars have repeatedly returned to a broader understanding of signs as something which stands to somebody for something else, being a range of human means of interacting with reality. A sign, by this definition, is a specific quality of phenomenal experience, through which we come to know reality, and on which we may be prepared to act. Signs thus are conditions of perception, interpretation, dialogue, and action.

Whereas the explicit conception of signs as evidence of something else that is absent can be attributed to Aristotle, a similar notion is found at least a century earlier, in the writings of Hippocrates, the founding father of medical science. Considering the role of a medical doctor, he emphasized the practical benefits of interpreting signs: "I hold that it is an excellent thing for a physician to practise forecasting" (in Clarke, 1990: 11). In order to predict and intervene into the future, the physician should consider his patient's appearance, especially comparing the face to that of healthy people. Unlikenesses thus discovered, are the most dangerous sign:

> Nose sharp, eyes hollow, temples sunken, ears cold and contracted with their lobes turned outwards, the skin about the face hard and tense and parched, the colour of the face as a whole being yellow or black. If at the beginning of the disease the face be like this, and if it be not yet possible with the other symptoms to make a complete prognosis, you must go on to inquire whether the patient has been sleepless, whether his bowels have been very loose, and whether he suffers at all from hunger. And if anything of the kind be confessed, you must consider the danger to be less. The crisis comes after a day and a night if through these causes the face has such an appearance. But should no such confession be made, and should a recovery not take place within this period, know that it is a sign [*semeion*] of death. (in Clarke, 1990: 12)

Importantly, the understanding of signs as representation here is subordinated to a use of signs in orienting action. Informed by the distinction between semiosis as representation and as action, much later philosophy has given priority to signs as (imperfect) representations of reality.

Aristotle, in elaborating the classical understanding of signs as evidence of natural events or states, made a further distinction between natural 'signs' and what he referred to as 'symbols' in human communication. Simultaneously, in *De Interpretatione* (c. 320 BC), Aristotle suggested the affinity of signs and symbols, both of which may serve as evidence of either mental or physical reality:

> Spoken expressions are symbols [*symbola*] of mental impressions, and written expressions [are symbols] of spoken expressions. And just as not all men have the same writing, so not all men make the same vocal sounds, but the things of which [all] these are primarily the signs [*semeia*] are the same mental impressions for all men, and the things of which these [mental impressions] are likenesses are ultimately the same. (in Clarke, 1990: 15)

The passage identifies the three key constituents of epistemology and semiotics, namely, the objects being represented (things), the representation of these objects in the mind (mental impressions), and the media of representation and communication (spoken and written expressions). It is especially the status of the mental impressions and their bivalent relationship to signs and reality which has fed centuries of philosophical scholarship. The fundamental issue, first raised as such by Aristotle, is later summed up in St Augustine's distinction between natural *versus* conventional signs: To what degree is phenomenal experience constituted as natural signs reflected onto the human mind, respectively as conventional signs constructed within the human mind?

Precisely that distinction was elaborated in the Christian worldview: God is said to appear to humans in both nature and the Holy Scriptures. Behind the semiotic chain of things, mental impressions, and communicative expressions, a more significant reality may be recovered, just as the great chain of being in nature may be read as God's Book. While this recalls the hidden, primary reality of Plato's transcendental ideas, for which Aristotle had substituted a reality immanent and distributed in concrete things, it was St Augustine (c. AD 427) who first articulated an explicit typology of natural and conventional signs:

> A sign is a thing which causes us to think of something beyond the impression the thing itself makes upon the senses. Thus if we see a track, we think of the animal that made the track; if we see smoke, we know that there is a fire which causes it; if we hear the voice of a living being, we attend to the emotion it expresses; and when a trumpet sounds, a soldier should know whether it is necessary to advance or to retreat, or whether the battle demands some other response. Among signs, some are natural and others are conventional. Those are natural which, without any desire or intention of signifying, make us aware of something beyond themselves, like smoke which signifies fire. [...] Conventional signs are those which living creatures show to one another for the purpose of conveying, in so far as they are able, the motion of their spirits or something which they have sensed or understood. [...] We propose to consider and to discuss this class of signs in so far as men are concerned with it, for even signs given by God and contained in the Holy Scriptures are of this type also, since they were presented to us by the men who wrote them. (in Clarke, 1990: 24–5)

The contemporary implication of St Augustine's typology is that perception, cognition, and communication are all forms of semiosis, even if each process may rely on different and specific signs. Communication studies today face an unresolved issue of whether visual media such as film, photography, and television should be theorized and studied empirically as natural signs, conventional signs, or a particular combination thereof (see Chapter 10).

Elaborating Aristotle's distinction between verbal expressions and mental impressions, St Augustine further distinguished between private, mental words and the words used in public communication. Mental words, again, are poised uneasily between natural and conventional signs. While St Augustine tended to place private and public words in the same general category, later medieval philosophers began a polarization of natural and conventional signs into two reality domains. William of Ockham, for one, described mental concepts as natural and verbal language as conventional, so that "first the concept signifies something naturally, and secondly the word signifies that same thing" (in Clarke, 1990: 30). The fact that priority was increasingly given to conventional, linguistic signs is suggested by the application of the Holy Scriptures as a guide to interpreting other, natural evidence. "Natural events and states of affairs came to be regarded as God's testimony to man, and to correctly interpret them was to be able to read nature as God's 'Book'" (Clarke, 1990: 33).

An analogous conception of natural signs as primary, but rudimentary, and of conventional signs as secondary, but privileged, is found in the modern scientific approach, which came to regard natural signs, or sense data, as the minimal items of cognition, and conventional signs, or logical and interpretive frames, as the enabling conditions of scientific cognition. The first modern philosopher to conceive science in semiotic terms was neither Peirce nor Saussure, but John Locke (for overview, see Aarsleff, 1982). In his *Essay Concerning Human Understanding* (1690), Locke defined semiotics as the general theory of signs, of which logic is one subspecialty:

> The third branch may be called *semeiotike*, or *the Doctrine of Signs*, the most usual whereof being Words, it is aptly enough termed also *logike*, Logick; the business whereof, is to consider the Nature of Signs, the Mind makes use of for the understanding of Things, or conveying its Knowledge to others. For since the Things, the Mind contemplates, are none of them, besides it self, present to the Understanding, 'tis necessary that something else, as a Sign or Representation of the thing it considers, should be present to it: And these are *Ideas*. And because the scene of *Ideas* that makes one Man's Thoughts, cannot be laid open to the immediate view of another, nor laid up any where but in the Memory, a no very sure Repository: Therefore to communicate our Thoughts to one another, as well as record them for our own use, Signs of our *Ideas* are also necessary. Those which Men have found most convenient, and therefore generally make use of, are articulate Sounds. (in Clarke, 1990: 40)

While reiterating the three-fold distinction of Aristotle and St Augustine, Locke linked things and signs to abstract ideas, not mental words or impressions. Interestingly, Locke introduced a science of signs in general, only to restrict his focus to "the most usual" signs, verbal language and logic. Thus, he contributed to a crucial project in modern science which in effect excommunicated and repressed the classic, differentiated concept of signs.

Accounting for modern philosophy as the project of establishing an incorrigible epistemological basis for empirical discovery, Rorty (1979) has noted how Locke advanced the common metaphors of mirroring and eyesight to characterize the role of mind in science. On the one hand, objective phenomena have features that are registered by observers as natural signs. With the development of sophisticated techniques in various sciences, a more precise documentation of natural signs as 'sense data' became possible. On the other hand, the interpretation of sense data by human subjects lent itself to formalization in the conventional signs of logic, which further contributed to explicit and universal procedures of knowing. Scientific signs, in their reductionist and formalist varieties, made for the intersubjectivity, communicability, and applicability of findings.

This model of scientific semiosis, however, has encountered several problems in human, social, as well as natural sciences, as witnessed by current theory of science (Chapter 9). Some phenomena in social and natural reality will not be reduced to the minimal signs of sense data, just as some forms of inference and argument are not compatible with formal logic. While I do not propose to romanticize the insights of premodern theory, the transition from classical theories of signs to modern theories of science may have dissolved, rather than solved, the foundational question of what are the media of science.

If Locke, following Descartes, initiated modern theory of science, David Hume brought its first phase to a close by making the distinction between natural and conventional signs absolute. Arguing that humans have certain knowledge of logical, conceptual relations, but only contingent knowledge about empirical phenomena, Hume concluded that we cannot in a strict sense justify most of our contingent knowledge. What is in doubt, then, is several conditions of science: the principle of causality, the existence of other minds, and the continuity of 'our' own minds. The assumption that these conditions obtain may be practically but not philosophically justified, and hence they offer no foundation for sciences making universal claims. Instead, skepticism was the logical conclusion.

Modern science and philosophy were rescued by Immanuel Kant's socalled 'Copernican turn.' Kant thus reversed the perspective on how the human subject relates to its objects in reality. Whereas Hume had expected to find the laws of nature immanent in the objects of perception, Kant suggested that such laws be understood as constitutive features of human subjectivity. The point is not that either causality, time, or space is a fictitious construct of the imagination, rather these categories are *a priori* conditions of consciousness, what Kant described as transcendental forms lending shape to human experience. The transcendental forms enable concrete instances of experience. Kant did not, however, conceive his epistemology of forms as a general theory of signs, but reemphasized the centrality of "language, the greatest instrument for understanding ourselves and others. Thinking is speaking to ourselves. (The Indians of Tahiti call it the 'language inside the body.')" (in Clarke, 1990: 56).

Kant was probably *the* main influence on Peirce, whose early works read as a semiotic articulation of Kant's transcendental forms. In fact, Peirce may be said to outline a second Copernican turn, complementing Kant's recentering of the human subject by casting both the subject and its interaction with objective reality in terms of a general theory of signs and action. Being a man of modern science as well as a reader of classical philosophy, Peirce realized that science is one specific form of semiosis.

Peircean semiotics

Charles Sanders Peirce

Peirce has been described as "an offensive and disagreeable young man" (Kuklick, 1977: 104). He divorced his first wife and lived 'in sin' with another woman, had erratic work habits, and took controversial positions in science and religion (Houser, 1986: lxiii), all of which helps to explain his fate as a *persona non grata* in American academia. Peirce also is commonly acknowledged as the most original thinker to date in the United States, an eminent logician, and a talented natural scientist. With reference to Descartes's seventeenth-century *Discourse on Method*, a sequence of Peirce's early works has been described as the *Discourse* of the nineteenth century, so far superseded by no twentieth-century work (Fisch, 1986b: xxxvii), and as a logician he was even ranked by a contemporary colleague, together with George Boole, as "the second man since Aristotle who has added to the subject something material" (in Fisch, 1986a: 129).

Whereas biographical details fall outside the scope of this volume (see Brent, 1993), a brief account serves to place Peirce in historical context. Born in 1839 as the son of a famous Harvard professor of mathematics and astronomy, Charles was shaped by the social and scientific orders of his time. First, Peirce Jr had the intellectual benefits of growing up in the upper echelons of an urban society which was then being formed by political, economic, and cultural modernization. The first three decades of his life witnessed the political reforms of the Jacksonian era, the military and economic turmoil of the Civil War, and major cultural conflicts over religious, ethnic, and gender issues (see Carroll and Noble, 1977: chaps 8–10). Second, Peirce joined academia at a time when philosophy was struggling to become a profession, while simultaneously the whole academic sector was struggling to reconcile science and religion. The key event here was Darwin's publication in 1859 of his *Origin of Species* when Peirce was twenty years old. Pragmatism has been interpreted as an attempt to reconcile evolutionary science with a religious worldview (Kuklick, 1977: 26). A forum for the discussion of these issues was the Metaphysical Club in Cambridge, Massachusetts, whose members counted Peirce, William James, and other prominent young scholars, and where Peirce first presented the principles of pragmatism.

Peirce made a reputation for himself early on in the area of natural sciences as an employee of the United States Coast and Geodetic Survey, but the only long-term academic position he ever held was at the Johns Hopkins University, where he was appointed as a part-time lecturer in logic in 1879. In 1884, Peirce was dismissed; the specific reason is not known. In 1887, he moved with his second wife to the small town Milford in Pennsylvania, where he died, poor and out of touch with the rest of science and society, in 1914. For three decades, he lectured occasionally and wrote copiously in an attempt to complete his system of semiotics, logic, and science. In correspondence toward the end of his life, Peirce mentions that he was then "working desperately to get written before I die a book on Logic that shall attract some good minds through whom I may do some real good" (Peirce, 1958: 408).

Triadic semiosis

Peirce's most famous definition of signs suggests some epistemological and ontological premises of his general approach to philosophy and science:

> A sign, or *representamen*, is something which stands to somebody for something in some respect or capacity. It addresses somebody, that is, creates in the mind of that person an equivalent sign, or perhaps a more developed sign. That sign which it creates I call the *interpretant* of the first sign. The sign stands for something, its *object*. (CP 2.228)[3]

All thinking, perception, and interaction with reality, thus, is mediated by signs. Through the senses, we do not have access to any brute reality of facts. Peirce's objects include physical entities, ideas, actions, as well as discourses –

from a single word to a library or even the totality of texts in the world – and can be thought of as objects in the grammatical sense.

Interpretants are the signs by which people orient themselves toward and interact with a reality of diverse things, events, and discourses. The interpretant is neither identical with the interpretive agent, nor an essence representing the content of that person's thoughts. Being a sign, the interpretant itself calls up another interpretant, and so on *ad infinitum*. "There is no exception [...] to the law that every thought-sign is translated or interpreted in a subsequent one, unless it be that all thought comes to an abrupt and final end in death" (Peirce, 1958: 52). Interpretation, then, is a continuous process of human interaction with reality, rather than one act which, once and for all, internalizes external phenomena through a medium of signs. The argument is not that the interpretive agent is forever separated from material and social reality, since Peirce rejected the nominalist position that we can know 'only' signs. In sum, signs are not what we know, but how we come to know what we can justify saying we know. Figure 2.1 illustrates the basic triad, whereas Figure 2.2 represents the process of semiosis as a sequence of triads.

The implication of Peircean semiotics for *epistemology* is that the categories of human reasoning are not imposed on minimal sense data, as suggested by Kant; rather, all phenomena are always already conceptualized and subject to semiosis. Consciousness is not "a skin, a separate tissue, overlying an unconscious region of the occult nature, mind, soul, or physiological basis" (Peirce, 1955: 291). With his triadic model of experience, Peirce proposed to transcend the dualism persisting in Kant, by incorporating the interpreting agent into the general category of signs. Our sense of self, according to Peirce, is the indirect, cumulative result of numerous semioses whose consistency suggests a subjective center. Human consciousness can be understood as a "man-sign" (Peirce, 1958: 71).

Underlying the triadic semiotics is an *ontology* that assumes three general modes of being, namely, "the being of positive qualitative possibility, the being

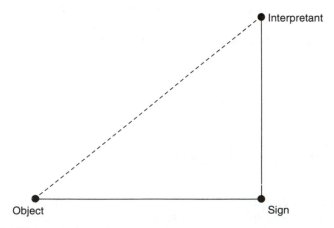

Figure 2.1   *The semiotic triad*

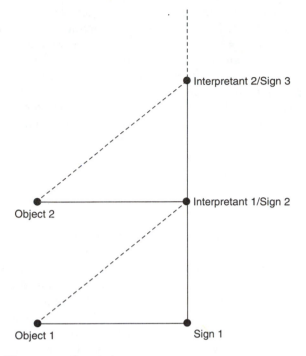

Figure 2.2   *The process of semiosis*

of actual fact, and the being of law that will govern facts in the future." The sign itself belongs to the category of qualitative possibility, Firstness, which "comprises the qualities of phenomena, such as red, bitter, tedious, hard, heartrending, noble; and there are doubtless manifold varieties utterly unknown to us." While this phenomenal experience is vague and preliminary, it remains our only concrete interface with the real world. "The second category of elements of phenomena comprises the actual facts [...] we feel facts resist our will. That is why facts are proverbially called brutal." Secondness, then, is the category of the object. It should be noted that Secondness includes non-material entities, just as Peircean objects may be imaginary or unconscious. Finally, the Thirdness of phenomena "consists of what we call laws when we contemplate them from the outside only, but which when we see both sides of the shield we call thoughts [...] the law goes beyond any accomplished facts and determines how facts that may *be*, but *all* of which never can have happened, shall be characterized" (Peirce, 1955: 75–8). Thirdness is the category of the interpretants, which mediate between discursive meaning and social action.

Interpretants

Peirce developed various typologies of his key notion of interpretants, which are explained partly by the phenomenal categories of Firstness, Secondness, and Thirdness, partly by a modern conception of different interpretants in relation to the process of communication. Johansen (1985: 250–1) identifies nine types which he describes as stages of interpretation in communication. The two extremes of the interpretive process can be seen as counterfactual conditions of understanding, namely, a minimal and a maximal state of information or "a language without a world and the total merging of reality and meaning into truth" (Johansen, 1985: 251). For the analysis of communication, the intervening Immediate, Dynamic, and Final Interpretants are of special interest. (I return below to another triad of Emotional, Energetic, and Logical Interpretants that refer to different aspects of communicative 'effect.')

The category of interpretants particularly helps to clarify the relationship between media discourses, audience decodings, and the social uses of mass-mediated signs. Mass communication comprises at least three stages of meaning which, though interrelated in a semiotic continuum, may be examined as Immediate, Dynamic, and Final Interpretants. First, the *Immediate* Interpretant corresponds to the range of potential meanings, carried by specific media discourses and identified in a preliminary interpretation, which I refer to as the *structural* meaning of media discourse. In one definition of the Immediate Interpretant, Peirce saw it as "the total unanalyzed effect that the Sign is calculated to produce, or naturally might be expected to produce" (1958: 413). Even when identifying such a potential for analytical purposes, of course, the analyst, like any other interpretive agent, is ascribing meaning to discourse from a particular interpretive stance.

The audience decoding of media discourse corresponds to Peirce's *Dynamic* Interpretant. Belonging to the realm of Secondness or actuality, this "consists in direct effect actually produced by a Sign upon an Interpreter of it" (Peirce, 1958: 413). When interacting with media in the immediate context of reception, audiences can be said to establish specific relations of difference between content structures and their available repertoires of interpretation. Interpretive agents make a difference, producing *situated* meaning. Such contextual meaning may owe less to the structure of media discourses than to the social contexts in which they attain practical relevance.

The third stage of interpretation reemphasizes semiosis as interminable process. What Peirce calls the *Final* Interpretant is "the effect the Sign *would* produce upon any mind upon which circumstances should permit it to work out its full effects" (1958: 413). While I return below to the problematic notion of a semiosis inevitably progressing toward Truth – a Sign to end all signs – an interesting implication is that the interpretive process unfolds over time and in varying contexts, so that media discourses can be reactivated outside the immediate context of reception as *performative* meaning that reorients the cognition and action of audience-publics in everyday contexts. In fact, Peirce sometimes conceived the Final Interpretant as the last link of an interpretive chain which might lead the interpreter to act:

> It can be proved that the only mental effect that can be so produced and that is not a sign but is of a general application is a habit-change; meaning by a *habit-change* a modification of a person's tendencies toward action, resulting from previous

experiences or from previous exertions of his will or acts, or from a complexus of both kinds of cause. (in Clarke, 1990: 83)

Through the Final Interpretant, a quantum change of categories may take place, from a relatively disinterested interpretation to a specific action in context. On a social scale, the transformation of potential and situated into performative meaning is one of the tasks of scientific and cultural institutions, and it is accomplished, in Peirce's terms, through 'communities of interpretation.'

Interpretive communities

Rejecting the two major premises of Descartes's philosophy – universal doubt and individual cognition resolving any doubt – Peirce, like current theorists of meaning, suggested, first, that thinking is necessarily based in prejudice in the sense of pre-understanding: "Hence this initial skepticism will be a mere self-deception. [...] Let us not pretend to doubt in philosophy what we do not doubt in our hearts" (Peirce, 1958: 40). Second, genuine doubt is resolved not by individuals, but by communities of knowers that are the only possible sanction of scientific knowledge. Each and every scientific position remains open to challenge within an ongoing, public interpretive process:

> Unless truth be recognized as *public* – as that of which *any* person would come to be convinced if he carried his inquiry, his sincere search for immovable belief, far enough – then there will be nothing to prevent each one of us from adopting an utterly futile belief of his own which all the rest will disbelieve. (Peirce, 1958: 398)

Peirce concerned himself especially with the institutionalized communities of science. Scientific communities are subject to public procedures of interpretation determining what will count as true knowledge: replication of studies, peer review, professional debate, etc. Moreover, these interpretive procedures themselves are subject to reformulation through the reflexivity of science. Even if scientific communities have no essential attributes in the form of superior insight, authority, or power, they perform the socially central function of developing and legitimating interpretive principles for examining particular aspects of reality, thus producing performative meanings that are communicated and take effect in the wider social setting. Performative meanings that address the structure of cosmos or of society can make or break individuals as well as whole societies (Kuhn, 1970; Lowe, 1982).

The interpretive communities of science have several structural similarities with the audiences of mass media, which I elaborate in Chapters 4 and 6. First, at the 'macrosocial'[4] level of institutions in a social system, both mass media and scientific institutions serve to place reality on a public agenda. In spite of their different organizational hierarchies, both these institutions are increasingly central to the maintenance of political, economic, and cultural infrastructures of society (Galbraith, 1967). In Peirce's conception, science is a context for negotiating the Final Interpretant of human knowledge. Equally, mass media provide a forum (Newcomb and Hirsch, 1984) for negotiating performative meanings which are contested, and which may be enacted through concerted, socially sanctioned action. Both science and media thus become important agents of what Giddens (1984) calls the 'double hermeneutic' of social science: by offering new interpretations of social reality, research may in the long term enable ordinary citizens to reinterpret and change that reality.

Second, Peircean semiotics clarifies the constitutive role of 'microsocial' acts of interpretation in scientific as well as communicative practice. The reproduction of most forms of social life requires not merely the availability of certain institutions and practices of communication, but also the existence of interpretive formations – social segments united by their conventions of interpretation – which may crisscross other sociodemographic formations. How interpretive formations relate to other social formations, and how such interpretive communities serve to direct the social production of meaning toward specific contexts and purposes, are still among the most underresearched issues of social science.

The concept of interpretive communities, finally, identifies a strategic juncture between micro- and macro-society, between material and discursive aspects of social semiosis, and between the various levels and processes of social structuration that I examine next in Chapter 3. While Peirce often scorned 'soft' human and social scientists,[5] his semiotics lends itself to studying the relationship between science and society in the wider framework of pragmatism.

Peircean pragmatism

The pragmatic maxim

Peirce originally proposed his philosophy of practice as a methodological doctrine of logic and science. When, two decades later, William James and others applied the term to positions in psychology and theology, Peirce responded in a 1905 article that "the word begins to be met with occasionally in the literary journals, where it gets abused in the merciless way that words have to expect when they fall into literary clutches," instead renaming his philosophy "pragmaticism", which, he added, "is ugly enough to be safe from kidnappers" (Peirce, 1955: 255). I retain the original term 'pragmatism' to emphasize the continuity of the tradition as a neglected position in the history of ideas, and I argue that a careful interpretation of Peirce's pragmatic maxim allows for a consistent and relevant application of pragmatism to contemporary culture and communication.

The pragmatic maxim was first advanced as a guiding principle of Peirce's philosophy to his co-members of the Metaphysical Club in Cambridge, and was eventually published in an 1878 series of articles. The maxim reads simply:

> It appears, then, that the rule for attaining the third grade of clearness of apprehension is as follows: Consider what effects, which might conceivably have practical bearings, we conceive the object of our conception to have. Then, our conception of these effects is the whole of our conception of the object. (Peirce, 1986: 266)

The slightly bewildering repetition of the terms "conceive," "conception," and "conceivably" suggests the point that Peirce was referring not just to material entities and experimental effects, but equally to the consequences of thought experiments. Sciences can be said to investigate what may be the case in various domains by testing the limits of conceivable existence and thus learning from both theoretical and empirical experience. Generalizing to an evolutionary perspective, Peirce, in discussing pedagogy, compared learning from experience to practical jokes: "I don't remember that any one has advocated a system of teaching by practical jokes, mostly cruel. That, however, describes the method of our great teacher, Experience" (CP 5.51). One further implication of the maxim is that the 'effects' of reality on human experience can be ascertained, 'conceived,' only at the conceptual, theoretical level, through a process of semiosis that involves a community of inquirers.

In other contexts, Peirce made the argument that also human and social domains lend themselves to systematic inquiry. Considering why research on metaphysics might be backward, he blamed the scholars, not the nature of the field:

> The data of metaphysics are not less open to observation, but immeasurably more so, than the data, say, of the very highly developed science of astronomy, to make any important addition to whose observations requires an expenditure of many tens of thousands of dollars. No, I think we must abandon the idea that metaphysics is backward owing to any intrinsic difficulty of it. In my opinion the chief cause of its backward condition is that its leading professors have been theologians. Were they simply Christian ministers the effect of entrusting very important scientific business to their hands would be quite as bad as if the same number of Wall Street promoters and Broad Street brokers were appointed to perform the task. (CP 6.2–3)

Also metaphysics, then, deals with "data." What distinguishes metaphysical research, according to the pragmatic maxim, may be that it relies on other types of signs, both in observation and theoretical analysis, and thus has different consequences than either astronomy or theology. Accordingly, I interpret the pragmatic maxim as a first principle of science recognizing multiple scientific disciplines and methods. Not least in interdisciplinary research, the pragmatist concept of conceivable consequences – differences that make themselves known in material, discursive, and other forms – has proven its explanatory value.

Differences

The concept of difference mediates between categories of *thought* and *action* in philosophy, and between *meaning* and *effect* in research on culture and communication. Beyond the understanding of semiosis as configured relations of difference in discourse, pragmatism holds that the specific discourses of both scientific theory and common sense are to be evaluated according to their practical implications for the human engagement with reality. Belief comes to be defined, therefore, not as a representation of something, but as a readiness to act in relation to that something, what Peirce thought of as a habit. The definition of belief as "that upon which a man is prepared to act" came from the mid-nineteenth-century philosopher Alexander Bain, but while Peirce was familiar with Bain's work, it was another member of the Metaphysical Club, Nicholas St John Green, who advocated the principle to the extent that Peirce thought of Green as the grandfather of pragmatism (Fisch, 1986a: 79–109). Max H. Fisch has explained the basic argument:

> Belief has no meaning except in reference to our actions. But Aristotle's distinction between potentiality and actuality applies. In respect of matters upon which we have no present occasion to act, our belief is 'an attitude or disposition of preparedness to act' when occasion offers. Under civilization and education we acquire numerous beliefs of a scientific and historical kind, upon which it is not likely we shall ever have occasion to act. But the readiness is there if the unexpected occasion should arise, and the readiness constitutes the belief. (1986a: 83–4)

For analytical purposes, I distinguish between discursive, interpretive, and social difference. These categories correspond, on the one hand, to the three types of interpretants already identified – Immediate, Dynamical, and Final – and to the structural, situated, and performative meanings of media discourse. On the other hand, these concepts allow for the analysis of meaning and effect as complementary aspects of mass communication.

First, *discursive* difference is a feature of the relational structures of media discourses. Meaning is determined by negation, that is, through a configuration of the relations of difference between the minimal features of signs. Peircean semiotics parts company with Saussurean semiology, as noted, by incorporating not just the relations of difference immanent in the semiotic system, but equally the relations of difference which are established in the practical uses of signs. Discursive difference is the condition enabling a variety of interpretations of specific discourses.

(The notion of discursive difference was prefigured in the classical logical square which positions propositions into mutual relations of contradiction and contrariety. The logical square was redeveloped in the context of Saussurean semiology by A.J. Greimas as the semiotic square which he defined as the fundamental structure of any signification [see Greimas and Courtés, 1982: 308–11]. In Chapter 10, I suggest how Greimas's semiotic square may complement the Peircean triad in a comprehensive social semiotics.)

Second, *interpretive* difference is introduced into the communicative process by interpretive agents. Mobilizing particular strategies of interpretation in their response to media, audiences can be said to match two structures of discursive difference with each other. Audiences thus literally make a difference, producing meaning that is situated in a specific historical and social context of time and space.

Third, *social* difference is defined as the contribution of cultural practices, such as mass communication, to the overall structuration of society (Giddens, 1984; see Chapter 3 in this volume). Mass media serve as a resource or enabling condition of social life. In the terminology of pragmatism, social difference is the modification, either as revision or as reinforcement, of the readiness of audiences to act in specific ways in particular social contexts.

While all three forms of difference certainly bear witness to a reality of social structures and practices, 'social' difference, as defined here, is of special interest because it emphasizes semiosis reshaping, in Peirce's sense, its object. Both mass media and their audiences can be said to reflect, and reflect upon, society. In doing so, they actively reproduce and transform, affect and effect, society.

Finally, the social differences that may arise from semiosis are specified by further varieties of the interpretant. Within the continuum of interpretation, Peirce also referred to Emotional, Energetic, and Logical Interpretants. The elements of this triad, indicating feelings, efforts, and habit-changes, are exemplified by Peirce with the soldiers' reaction to the command "Ground arms!" "The *emotional* interpretant is said to be familiarity with the words, and the bringing down of the musketts [sic] to the ground is the *energetic* interpretant" (Johansen, 1985: 244–5), whereas the Logical Interpretant conveys the law-like status of the command as a concept or proposition. While different scholars have understood this last triad as a subdivision either of the Dynamical Interpretant or of each of three main interpretants (Johansen, 1985: 247), its most interesting implication concerns the Final Interpretant, since the Emotional, Energetic, and Logical Interpretants represent three different (and not mutually exclusive) dispositions to act as a final outcome of interpretation. Communicative effect can amount to emotional experience, bodily response, as well as logical inference.

In the end, the concept of difference returns us to several classic philosophical issues, particularly what is the ontological status of the social reality that is the object of interpretation for scientists and other social agents alike, what causes or structures may explain real events, and what is our epistemological justification for the explanations. I take Peircean pragmatism to be an attempt to reconcile ontological realism and epistemological constructionism.

Ontological realism

If signs are the '*how*' rather than the '*what*' of human knowledge, a condition of rather than an obstacle to human knowledge, semiotics may be compatible with realism. Despite his ambiguities and shifting emphases from nominalism to realism (Fisch, 1986a: 184–200), the ambition of Peirce's general semiotics was to arrive at a version of realism, rooted notably in Aristotle and Kant. Like Aristotle, Peirce believed that universals, such as the quality of hardness or redness, are real, and that these universals are immanent in everyday things, what amounts, first, to a *distributed* realism.

Second, Peirce sided with Duns Scotus and other medieval realists in their conflict with the nominalists who believed that universals are merely names that summarize certain common features of a phenomenal category. One implication of this Scholastic realism is that reality comprises multiple forms of existence, from physical entities to mental constructs. Peirce (1986: 271) specified, for instance, that dreams are part of the real, thus allowing, in a post-Freudian perspective, for unconscious objects. The argument implies a *diversified* realism.

Third, like Kant, Peirce believed that the objects of our understanding are real, even if the categories, proposed by Kant and semioticized by Peirce, are conditions of possibility for such understanding. What distinguishes Peirce's realism is his assumption that the categories, along with the minds and things they mediate, are all constitutive elements of reality. Firstness, Secondness, and Thirdness are the minimal aspects of a *triadic* realism.

Pragmatism substantiates these positions with hypothetical arguments stating what would be the case if certain conditions were met. Peirce's most famous hypothetical argument is implied by the Final Interpretant: reality is what would ultimately be captured by the Final Interpretant of science if science were to go on forever. In a counterfactual-conditional argument, reality thus becomes a limit condition of any cognition or interaction, what Margolis (1986: 115) refers to as "minimal realism." In its most generalized form, the 'if–then' argument suggests that the distinctive phenomenal features of something become evidence of this something – 'if something IS, then SOMETHING is.' Peirce, however, joined Kant and modern philosophy in specifying that existence as such is not a predicate which may or may not apply to something. Instead, it is the specific qualities of something that can be taken as evidence of this something. Hence, if being (manifests a) QUALITY, then BEING (manifests a) quality, and the very structure of the 'if–then' argument establishes the RELATION between quality and being. In Peirce's early works, quality, being, and relation correspond to his mature categories of sign, object, and interpretant. In sum, triadic realism is the ontological equivalent of the pragmatic, epistemological maxim.

Realism is supported by practice, such as sitting down on a chair or doing science. The parallel between science and ordinary experience in pragmatism helps to explain Peirce's reference to his philosophy as 'critical commonsensism':

> [...] Peirce took into account differing relations to the object and argued that if the object existed, there would be a series of 'if . . ., then . . .' hypothetical statements asserting that under certain conditions of sensation, the object would have certain effects on us: if I sat down in the chair, it would not collapse under me; if I lifted it, I would find that it strained my back; and so on. By postulating the object, Peirce gave experience coherence. We could verify that we had the experience under the specified condition; he justified the postulate because it explained how we verified the series of hypotheticals. To say that a universal (quality) existed meant just that there would be a regularity in the future behavior of certain objects and that speaking of the universal explained the regularity. (Kuklick, 1977: 113)

Both the communal, hypothetical-theoretical approach and the practical approach to reality today imply an understanding of knowledge as the product of historical circumstances and social interests, even if this was not Peirce's implication. The specialization of science into ever more disciplines and the accumulation of insights through operationalization suggests a longterm process of differentiating the available interpretive procedures, thus actualizing potential qualities of reality, in a context and for a purpose. This position may be more adequate to explain specific developments in the history of science (Hacking, 1992) than the prototypical paradigms of Kuhn (1970), and it further does not necessitate faith in any absolute progress of science. Triadic realism merely assumes that different signs enable us to know and do different things under different social circumstances.

Epistemological constructionism

While realism and constructionism are sometimes seen as incompatible, this is largely due to a dualist understanding of signs as standardized elements of one subject–object interface. If diversified realism is the premise, there is a call for an equally diversified repertoire of signs to describe, analyze, and interpret the several real modes of existence. In the methodological Chapters 5–8, I explore the range of categories and procedures necessary to identify the salient features of social semiosis, and in Chapter 9 I return to the implications for qualitative and quantitative analysis and for theory of science generally. The point arising from pragmatism is that communication and culture cannot be reduced to certain *minimal* signs, but call for *multiple* semiotic categories and analytical procedures.

Despite his predominantly natural-scientific conception of research, Peirce hinted at a diversified semiotics of science, for example in his critique of early positivism as stated by Auguste Comte. In particular, Peirce attacked its narrow conception of verification:

> Auguste Comte [...] would condemn every theory that was not 'verifiable.' Like the majority of Comte's ideas, this is a bad interpretation of a *truth*. [...] Comte [and other positivists] take what they consider to be the first impressions of sense, but which are really nothing of the sort, but are percepts that are products of psychical operations, and they separate these from all the intellectual parts of our knowledge, and arbitrarily call the first *real* and the second *fictions*. These two words *real* and *fictive* bear no significations whatever except as marks of *good* and *bad*. But the truth is that what they call *bad* or *fictitious*, or subjective, the intellectual part of our knowledge, comprises all that is valuable on its own account, while what they mark *good*, or *real*, or *objective*, is nothing but the pretty vessel that carries the precious thought. (1955: 267–8)

Another ambiguity concerns Peirce's conception of the community as the final arbiter of truth. Whereas Peirce defined reality as what *everybody* will agree to in the long run, the concept of a *community* of inquiry implies the more radical notion that interpretive agents, like signs, are multiple and must engage in negotiation of truth. Even though Peirce did not pursue the social organization and historical setting of scientific communities, the very idea of community might entail a shift in the history of ideas comparable in scope to the recentering of the individual in Renaissance philosophy, science, and politics. More concretely, scientific communities entail *fallibilism*, both within and between communities, so that there is no incorrigible foundation of science, only sets of premises that are subject to error and doubt. Specific findings, analytical procedures, and interpretive frameworks all remain in question. In Chapter 11, I address the different knowledge interests of communities that necessarily introduce ethics and politics into science as social practice.

For a founding father of pragmatism, Peirce was remarkably silent on the social implications of science. He denounced the notion of applied science because, while societies tend to be conservative, science holds a radical potential that may be stifled by the social norms of particular historical periods (Skagestad, 1981: 195–228). Similarly, he had little confidence in practical men, from theologians to brokers, since "it is quite impossible for a practical man to comprehend what science is about unless he becomes as a little child and is born again" (CP 6.3). Though his communitarian notion of science has been interpreted as "logical socialism" (Fisch, 1984: xxviii), Peirce sometimes drew an opposite political conclusion:

> The people ought to be enslaved; only the slaveholders ought to practice the virtues that alone can maintain their rule. England will discover too late that it has sapped the foundations of culture. The most perfect language that ever was spoken was classical Greek; and it is obvious that no people could have spoken it who were not provided with plenty of intelligent slaves. As to us Americans, who had, at first, so much political sense, we always showed a disposition to support such aristocracy as we had; and we have constantly experienced, and felt but too keenly, the ruinous effects of universal suffrage and weakly exercised government. (1958: 402)

Other pragmatisms

Pragmatism has lent itself to alternative social interpretations, by Peirce's contemporaries and in current research. This section contains a brief assessment of William James and John Dewey, who practiced their pragmatism as pundits and activists. In the final section, I note some recent contributions to research on culture and communication, before turning in Chapter 3 to the work of, for example, George Herbert Mead and Charles Morris in the context of other social science.[6]

If Peirce was the overcommitted and underrecognized thinker of the New England wilderness, James was the self-conscious doer of the big city, popularizing pragmatism in public debate. James restated the pragmatic maxim in two distinctive respects (Kuklick, 1977: 264–74). First, he proposed studying the experiential consequences of human experience more generally, for example within psychology and religion. Difference makes a difference also in specialized empirical disciplines, and with *The Principles of Psychology* (1890/1981) James contributed to the understanding of mental processes as practical orientations. His famous "stream of thought" (James, 1890/1981: 219–78) amounts to a psychological articulation of Peirce's infinite semiosis. At the same time, in emphasizing the self-awareness of humans and their consciousness as the site of a will to believe and act, James jeopardized important nuances of Peircean pragmatism: the distinction between interpretants and interpreting agents, the community as the context of all belief and action, and the counterfactual conception of reality.

James drew a second implication from the maxim with the aim of developing pragmatism as a social and religious philosophy. As Darwinism and natural science generally served to demystify human nature, James was out to reconcile scientific rationality and religious faith. The methods of *The Principles of Psychology* today read like a curious blend of behavioral science and introspection in the service of documenting both reason and faith as instances of truth. If related to the concept of truth in an abstract sense, the pragmatic maxim might redescribe actual behavioral responses in terms of their truth value:

> Ideas and beliefs were plans of action expressed in statements. If we applied the pragmatic maxim to the concept of truth, true ideas or beliefs were those that led us satisfactorily and expeditiously through experience. Truth was what it was 'known-as' – a class name for all sorts of working values in experience. (Kuklick, 1977: 266)

Bluntly, whatever happens to work is part of a great chain of being which comprises Darwinian evolution as well as historical time, and which represents God's design being fulfilled through the sum of human actions. The 'conceivable,' potential consequences of action were narrowed down to actual consequences, thus limiting the explanatory value of Peirce's pragmatic maxim. As noted by West, while raising classic issues of science and society, "James's popular terms like the 'cash-values' of an idea or the 'expediency' of a concept suggest a vulgar practicalism or narrow utilitarianism" (1989: 67).

Dewey made an emphatic transition from the philosophy of practice to social practice, with a view to the future. The temporal aspect is important, because pragmatism can be said to focus less on what is or has been, than on what may be in the future:

> Whereas, for empiricism, in a world already constructed and determined, reason or general thought has no other meaning than that of summing up particular cases, in a world where the future is not a mere word, where theories, general notions, rational ideas have consequences for action, reason necessarily has a constructive function. (Dewey in Rorty, 1966: 210)

Fisch (1984: xxviii) has identified a related argument in Peirce as a background to his gradual shift from nominalism to realism: while the sign refers backward to the object in a particularistic and potentially nominalist relation, the sign also refers forward to the interpretant which is generated in an interpretive community considering future means for present ends.

Whereas Dewey is normally associated with social reform of educational institutions as an avenue to more public participation in politics, his activism reflected a broader concern with philosophy and science as means of social reflexivity in a variety of institutional contexts, including community groups, media, and cultural institutions (Bernstein, 1966; West, 1989: 69–111). These institutions of reflexivity serve to ask for alternatives to the prevailing forms of social organization – what society might be. In epistemology, Dewey sought to replace the familiar subject–object dichotomy with an inclusive category of 'experience' mediating between the human organism and its environment. In his social philosophy, Dewey emphasized the practical side of philosophy in ethics, poetics, and politics, and he developed an aesthetic conception of science and human thinking, just as he defined art as a practice.[7]

Despite sympathetic social schemes, Dewey's philosophy relied on a dated tradition of conceptual analysis, more characteristic of a philosophy of consciousness than of a philosophy of language or political practice (for example, Dewey, 1927). It is ironic that Dewey still performed his conceptual analyses with the aim of transcending the very tradition of conceptual analysis (Rorty, 1982: 35), caught between theory and practice, philosophy and politics. In a comparison of Dewey and Ludwig Wittgenstein, Murphy (1990: 79) has summed up the point: "In contrast to Wittgenstein who, although he was the paradigmatic twentieth-century *philosopher* was in many ways a nineteenth-century *man*, John Dewey was a twentieth-century man although he was in certain ways a nineteenth-century philosopher."

Toward social semiotics

If pragmatism has not flourished since Dewey, it survives as an undercurrent of ideas in both social sciences and humanities, and key figures of twentieth-century interdisciplinary research such as Roman Jakobson and Noam Chomsky credit Peirce as a major influence on their ideas (Fisch, 1986a: 430–1). Taking stock, Richard Bernstein (1991) identified five enduring features of pragmatism: anti-foundationalism "exposing what has come to be called 'the metaphysics of presence'" (p. 326); fallibilism;[8] the radical contingency of both human existence and nature (here Peirce anticipated recent discoveries in quantum physics [Bernstein, 1991: 329]); the community as the social agent certifying knowledge; and plurality as a guiding principle for science and politics. This legacy has been developed in three different bodies of work with implications for mass communication research.

First, within *philosophy* proper, the pragmatist tradition is maintained by a small circle of scholars around such journals as *Semiotica* and the *Transactions of the Charles S. Peirce Society*. In related disciplines, Peircean pragmatism and semiotics have been the explanatory framework of studies by Sheriff (1987) in literary studies (see also Thibault, 1991), Colapietro (1989) in psychology, and Singer (1984) in anthropology. Moreover, Johansen (1993), Rochberg-Halton (1986), and Rosenthal (1986) have outlined the general relevance of pragmatism for studying culture as discourse. In linguistics, Halliday (1978) refers to his pragmatic approach to language use in context as social semiotics; I return in Chapter 8 to this approach as a methodology for qualitative communication studies.

The second group of studies comes under the wider, interdisciplinary heading of *semiotics*. Although Saussurean semiology remains the dominant tradition, Peircean semiotics has been mediated by, for example, Ogden and Richards (1923/1946), and is increasingly included in textbooks and anthologies, hence informing recent theory development. Umberto Eco, for one, has adapted the concept of unlimited semiosis to his comprehensive theory of semiotics (Eco, 1976), and like Peirce, Eco proposes to develop semiotics as a philosophy of language (Eco, 1984) (but see the critique in Colapietro, 1989: 27–47). Thomas A. Sebeok (1985), for another, has contributed to a home-grown, American redevelopment of Peirce in a pan-semiotics studying also animal and intra-organismic 'communications.'

Less reliable sources, such as the film theory of Gilles Deleuze, have collapsed Peirce's sign typologies with a Bergsonian phenomenology to support the argument that cinematic signs emerge from reality as such and impress themselves directly onto audience consciousness (Deleuze, 1986, 1989). The argument becomes untenable when Deleuze (1989: 32) frankly notes that Peirce's terms are used, but their meanings changed. A similarly dualist, essentialist, and nominalist recasting of the Peircean alternative is the post-structuralism of Jacques Derrida. "Derrida's method is to deconstruct, to confuse and confound a way of looking at the world that is solely dyadic, binary, by using the very principles it deconstructs – the dyadic sign and binary oppositions" (Sheriff, 1987: 130). For several critics of semiology and structuralism, Peircean semiotics and pragmatism represent the road not taken.

The third, small body of work is found in *mass communication research proper*. While specific references are few, James Carey has argued that contemporary cultural studies of mass media make up a felicitous formation of American pragmatism and European theories of signs, subjectivity, and society (see Carey, 1989: 13–68), and he acknowledges the particular influence of Dewey on his own influential definition of communication as ritual. In a history of American mass communication theory, Peters (1989) found that Dewey in particular influenced the theories of both Walter Lippmann and Paul Lazarsfeld. In *Social Semiotics* (1988), Hodge and Kress assessed the Saussurean heritage critically, recovering a dynamic semiotics implicit in Saussure and suggesting the relevance of Peircean semiotics in combination with, for example, Volosinov's (1929/1973) materialist linguistics. In fact, the concrete studies in Hodge and Kress (1988) rely on conventional, semiological text analysis, and the volume does not offer an integrative theoretical or methodological framework. One of the few specific proposals for a Peircean semiotics of mass media is Tomaselli and Shepperson (1991a, 1991b), who argue for its critical as well as theoretical potential.

Having recovered aspects of pragmatism, I turn in the next chapter to a possible reconstruction of social science in the context of mass communication research. Semiotic action is a constitutive element of meaningful society.

3

Meaningful Society: Recontextualizing Social Science

If Aristotle was the first social scientist (Bazerman, 1993: 4), defining the human being as a a *zoon politikon* or social being, his four forms of causality identify structuring principles whose relative importance remains undecided in contemporary social theory. Aristotle distinguished between the efficient cause, the material cause, the formal cause, and the final cause of phenomena in reality. While Aristotle conceived the final cause as an immanent feature especially of natural phenomena, in a post-Renaissance perspective the final cause is commonly interpreted in terms of human intentions and purposes. In the case of a law court being built, the building has the entrepreneur and workers as its efficient cause, wood and stone represent the material cause, the plan of the building-to-be serves as the formal cause, and the purpose of constructing a setting for legal actions is its final cause. Admittedly, underlying each cause is a more complex set of social determinations, such as the ownership and organization of the building industry, the technological form of available building materials, the cultural level of architecture, and the political-administrative process establishing a particular law court. Moreover, the causes interact in producing what is known as a social institution. Indeed, it is far from clear what we *mean* when we say that the building 'houses' or 'symbolizes' the institution. This chapter addresses society as a category of meaning and examines a few major theoretical statements on how the reproduction of meaningful society is accomplished by institutions and publics.

Aristotle assigned special importance to the final cause, being an indicator of where the world might be moving. Much social theory has focused instead on possible efficient causes of social order and conflict, attributing final causes to individual and institutional agents, and leaving formal and material causes as enabling conditions of modern society. One question shared across different theories is how the interchange between final and the efficient causes takes place, as society is being structured and transformed. Because society is material-social as well as discursive-semiotic, social science has traditionally drawn on both natural-scientific and humanistic forms of analysis. In his classic definition of sociology, Max Weber summarized the two aspects of the social-scientific enterprise as a "science which attempts the interpretive understanding of social action in order thereby to arrive at causal explanation of its course and effects" (1964: 88).

I approach these issues, as they relate to mass communication, with reference first to the structuration theory of Giddens (1984), applying his framework in a comparison of social structure as conceived by Weber and Durkheim. In the middle section, I examine structural functionalism, as anticipated by Durkheim and articulated by Parsons, and contrast it with interpretive theories of everyday life, which have highlighted interpersonal and mass communication as complementary elements of semiosis. This section also reestablishes a link to the pragmatism of Mead, Morris, and symbolic interactionism. The final part of the chapter outlines a conception of meaning as emergent in social contexts, locally generated, and historically situated. While several research traditions have read society as a textual *system* with a central perspective (Barthes, 1957/1973; Lévi-Strauss, 1963), a more fine-grained analysis of semiosis as discursive *processes* in social *practices* is needed to integrate the social-scientific and the humanistic study of society.

Structuration theory: Meta-theory of society

Dualism revisited

Structuration theory is relevant primarily as a meta-theory of social science, reflecting on dichotomies of interpretive and causal, subjectivist and objectivist, hermeneutic and materialistic, micro- and macro-approaches to studying society. "If interpretative sociologies are founded, as it were, upon an imperialism of the subject, functionalism and structuralism propose an imperialism of the social object" (Giddens, 1984: 2). While several contemporary theorists, such as Pierre Bourdieu (1984) and Clifford Geertz (1973), have tackled the general problem, I take Anthony Giddens' (1984) work as one of the most systematic, reconstructive frameworks, although I quarrel with certain aspects below.[1] Three components have particular relevance for the study of culture and communication: the general relationship between structure and agency, the category of reflexivity, and the technological and institutional reconfiguration of modern societies across time and space.

The core of structuration theory is the notion of a '*duality of structure*' which defines human agency and social structure as enabling conditions for each other. Structure is no more material or permanent than agency; agency is no more mental or transitory than structure. Human action, accordingly, is not the manifestation of any individual free will, nor is social structure a set of external constraints on the individual: "[...] the structural properties of social systems are both medium and outcome of the practices they recursively organize" (Giddens, 1984: 25). Agency and structure intersect in practices which are continually structuring the contexts of action as well as producing relatively stable social systems:

> [...] social systems, as reproduced social practices, do not have 'structures' but rather exhibit 'structural properties' and [...] structure exists, as time-space presence, only in its instantiations in such practices and as memory traces orienting the conduct of knowledgeable human agents. [...] The most deeply embedded structural properties, implicated in the reproduction of societal totalities, I call *structural principles*. Those

practices which have the greatest time-space extension within such totalities can be referred to as *institutions*. (Giddens, 1984: 17)

To exemplify, politics does not reside in delimited institutions and actors, but in the practices of legislation and debate they facilitate; mass communication does not reside in media organizations or their discourses, but in the social and cultural practices that constitute their production, transmission, and reception.

The duality of structure, moreover, operates *on* something like the raw materials of social life and *through* certain procedures, called resources and rules. *Rules* are defined as "'methodical procedures' of social interaction" relating both "to the constitution of *meaning* and [...] to the *sanctioning* of modes of social conduct" (Giddens, 1984: 18). Rules need not, however, be explicit or intentional in order to affect practice, as suggested by the category of practical consciousness below. *Resources* are of two kinds – allocative and authoritative:

> Allocative resources refer to capabilities – or, more accurately, to forms of transformative capacity – generating command over objects, goods or material phenomena. Authoritative resources refer to the types of transformative capacity generating command over persons or actors. (Giddens, 1984: 33)

Mass media serve as both authoritative resources, circulating meanings that legitimate particular forms of conduct, and allocative resources, producing economic value like other means of production. Equally, media production and reception are subject to specific rules of interpretation and conduct.

The second component of structuration theory is *reflexivity*. Giddens argues that reflexivity ascribes meaning to the transactions of daily life, even if such meaning may not be consciously articulated. "'Reflexivity' hence should be understood not merely as 'self-consciousness' but as the monitored character of the ongoing flow of social life" (Giddens, 1984: 3). Challenging Freudian and Lacanian psychology and adapting a version of Erikson's ego psychology, Giddens distinguishes three levels of consciousness: discursive, practical, and the unconscious. The unconscious, comparable in most respects to the Freudian unconscious, is defined as "those forms of cognition and impulsion which are either wholly repressed from consciousness or appear in consciousness only in distorted form" (Giddens, 1984: 4–5). Discursive consciousness, next, has the capacity to verbally express perspectives on reality, justify action, and engage in argument. Most important, *practical consciousness* is the innovation and middle ground of the model, comprising a substantial 'grey' area in between focused intentionality and the classic unconscious. Positioned in the border area of humanistic and social-scientific research, it represents the main challenge for studies on everyday uses of media and culture generally.

The central role of reflexivity not only in social science but throughout social life entails what Giddens terms a 'double hermeneutic.' The hermeneutic is double because it involves both "the meaningful social world as constituted by lay actors and the metalanguages invented by social scientists; there is constant 'slippage' from one to the other involved in the practice of the social sciences" (Giddens, 1984: 374). Social theory must, in part, represent the lay participants' perspective on social life. In doing so, social science intervenes in both the participants' lives and political and cultural agendas. A case in point is the work of Freud, which today is part of Western common sense; equally, opinion polls and commissioned studies are constitutive of the modern political process. Structuration theory thus incorporates social science as a social practice in its own right.

The final element of structuration theory for present purposes is the conception of society not as a quasi-biological or physical system, but as *overlapping practices and integrated institutions* in politics, economics, and culture. Whereas social scientists have commonly taken the neatly bounded nation-state as their model society, other social systems may be "by far the more numerous in history" (Giddens, 1984: 164). Alternatively, a society can be thought of as "a specifiable overall 'clustering of institutions' across time and space" (p. 164), being integrated through procedures of interaction and legitimation which contribute, as well, to a sense of common identity in its subjects. Identifying two forms of integration, Giddens defines *social* integration as "reciprocity of practices between actors in circumstances of co-presence," whereas *system* integration is "reciprocity between actors or collectivities across extended time-space, outside conditions of co-presence" (pp. 376–7). The modern mass media may be reconfiguring the two forms of integration and contributing to new forms of social interaction between public and private spheres (Thompson, 1990; see also Horton and Wohl, 1956; Meyrowitz, 1985).

Triadic society

Two aspects of structuration theory require redevelopment in the perspective of social semiotics. First, despite his broadly hermeneutic inflection of social theory, Giddens gives little concrete attention, in his own analytical practice, to the signs and interpretive frames mediating between agency and structure. While referring to three structural dimensions of social systems, namely, signification, domination, and legitimation (Giddens, 1984: 29), the theory of structuration is least specified regarding signification or semiosis. Second, the conception of subjectivity in ego-psychology terms also implies a dualism of coherent subjects and well-delineated social objects which does not do justice to the contradictory features of consciousness, be it discursive or practical, in social contexts. Semiosis serves to articulate both specific subject positions and the conflicts through which subjects and societies are reformed. Meaningful society is triadic.

Figure 3.1 sums up the understanding that social *structures* are enacted through human *agency* with continuous reference to a *medium*, resulting in the 'social construction of reality' (Berger and Luckmann, 1966). Through signs, reality becomes social and subject to reflexivity. While verbal language presumably remains the primary medium, the place of different semiotic systems in social practice calls for further theoretical and empirical research. This

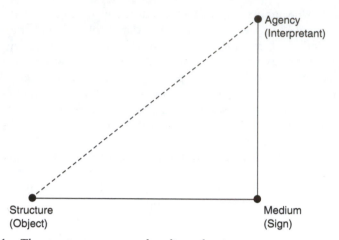

Figure 3.1   *The structure, agency, and medium of society*

meta-framework sets an agenda for examining previous social-scientific statements on the life of signs in society.

Micro- and macro-society

The meaning of ideal types

> Although superseded and, to some extent, transformed by classical sociological
> ideas, the micro–macro distinction ranks with the core oppositions in Occidental
> thinking, at least since the late medieval differentiation between the individual and
> the state. Entering academic discourse and political debate as part of the nominal-
> ism versus realism dispute, it helped form the background for such enduring
> controversies as whether the whole is more than the sum of its parts, whether state
> and society can claim ontological and moral primacy over individuals, and whether
> the meaning of concepts can be reduced to their empirical referent or involves some
> transcendental ideal. (Alexander and Giesen, 1987: 3)

Weber's ideal types represent one of the two main metaphors (Johnson, 1987)
designed to overcome the micro–macro distinction in modern social theory,
the other being the conception of society as an organism. Ideal types may be
understood as a 'deep structure,' a heuristic device constructing "certain elements of reality into a logically precise conception" (Gerth and Mills,
1948/1991: 59) in a vocabulary which, importantly, would be recognized as
meaningful by social agents and social scientists alike. Grounded in historical
cases, ideal types occupy a middle ground between natural, nomothetic law
and cultural, idiographic coincident (see further Chapter 9).

One classic example of an ideal type is 'the spirit of capitalism' – the ethical
principles of Protestantism as applied in the economic and cultural practices
of capitalism. Religious doctrines have secular, socially relevant consequences
as rules of conduct:

[...] it is not the ethical *doctrine* of a religion, but that form of ethical conduct upon which *premiums* are placed that matters. Such premiums operate through the form and the condition of the respective goods of salvation. And such conduct constitutes 'one's' specific 'ethos' in the sociological sense of the word. For Puritanism, that conduct was a certain methodical, rational way of life which – given certain conditions – paved the way for the 'spirit' of modern capitalism. The premiums were placed upon 'proving' oneself before God in the sense of attaining salvation – which is found in all Puritan denominations – and 'proving' oneself before men in the sense of socially holding one's own within the Puritan sects. Both aspects were mutually supplementary and operated in the same direction: they helped to deliver the 'spirit' of modern capitalism, its specific ethos: the *ethos* of the modern *bourgeois middle classes*. (Weber, 1948/1991: 321)

It is the dialectical relationship, the religious constitution of social rules, which is made explicit in the ideal type. In the terminology of Giddens, religion serves as an authoritative resource, interpreted according to rules which equally serve to structure social interaction. In the terminology of pragmatism, the 'spirit' of capitalism is a particular predisposition to act.

Whereas Weber developed the concept for scientific analysis, ideal types can be said to inform everyday practice generally, being semiotic categories that identify a range of possible social actions. In fact, the double hermeneutic noted by Giddens may work, in part, through ideal types whose relevance for specific contexts is recognized by ordinary social agents. In their introduction to Weber's work, Gerth and Mills (1948/1991: 57) had referred to the tension between Weber's structural form of explanation in his empirical studies and his theoretical emphasis on individual agents and interpretive sociology; the ideal types offer a mediation between structure and agency, macro- and micro-society. Contrary to the argument in Gerth and Mills (1948/1991: 59), however, that Weber's "attempt to avoid a philosophical emphasis upon either material or ideal factors, or upon either structural or individual principles of explanation," led to nominalism, the ideal types begin to suggest the semiotic forms of a shared social reality.[2]

From organisms to systems

In the preface to the second edition of *The Rules of Sociological Method* (1895), published in 1901, Émile Durkheim responded to criticism of ontological collectivism in the first edition, implying the existence of a reified body social. While Durkheim suggests that his critics disagree with the realist argument "which presents social phenomena as external to individuals" (1901/1982: 38), the real issue may concern the understanding of this supra-individual reality in terms of the second metaphor, namely, the self-regulating, anthropomorphic system or organism. In *Rules*, Durkheim abandons the seemingly cautious distinction between physical, psychical, and social facts that are said to have different "substrata" (p. 40), arguing repeatedly that more complex 'entities' follow from these elementary facts: "Whenever elements of any kind combine, by virtue of this combination they give rise to new phenomena. One is therefore forced to conceive of these phenomena as residing, not in the elements, but in the entity formed by the union of these elements" (p. 39).

The further purpose of sociology is to develop "rules for the distinction of the normal from the pathological" (Durkheim, 1901/1982: 85), so that the 'health' of the social entity as such may be established in a central perspective, by objective, decontextualized criteria: "For societies, as for individuals, health is good and desirable; sickness, on the other hand, is bad and should be avoided" (p. 86). Accordingly, Durkheim returns to Aristotle to characterize society as an entity subject primarily to efficient causes:

> [...] the widespread character of collective forms would be inexplicable if final causes held in sociology the preponderance attributed to them. *Therefore when one undertakes to explain a social phenomenon the efficient cause which produces it and the function it fulfils must be investigated separately.* We use the word 'function' in preference to 'end' or 'goal' precisely because social phenomena generally do not exist for the usefulness of the results they produce. We must determine whether there is a correspondence between the fact being considered and the general needs of the social organism, and in what this correspondence consists, without seeking to know whether it was intentional or not. All such questions of intention are, moreover, too subjective to be dealt with scientifically. (Durkheim, 1901/1982: 123)

While Durkheim is at pains here to distinguish "the general needs of the social organism" from final causes, the ambiguity of collective 'needs,' versus 'goals' and 'ends,' still suggests the conceptual difficulty of 'social organisms,' which is solved only in a metaphorical way. The concept of 'functions' rather collapses efficient and final as well as collective and individual causes, thus obscuring the issue of social agency.[3]

Later work, notably the structural functionalism of Talcott Parsons and Robert K. Merton, has rearticulated the organismic metaphor in systemic terms, retaining the assumption that social systems may be both self-regulating and structured according to a central perspective.[4] *The Social System* (Parsons, 1951), for one, attempts a comprehensive account of the relationship between individuals' motivation for action and the embedding social structure, the entire system revolving around the category of roles, which is defined as "translations of macro, environmental demands onto the level of individual behavior" (Alexander and Giesen, 1987: 24). Individual agents thus become carriers of underlying social structures, and their interaction reproduces a system "in the scientific sense," for which social theory must develop "the same order of theoretical analysis which has been successfully applied to other types of systems in other sciences" (Parsons, 1951: 3). The premise, in Parsons as in Durkheim, is that the systems are essentially homologous across ontological domains. Despite the meticulous specification of roles and subsystems by Parsons (1951), however, it remains unclear how, specifically, causality and meaning interact as constituents of social action.

Parsons was painfully aware of the complexity of these social processes, but hoped to develop "a second best type of theory [at] the structural-functional level of systematization" (1951: 20) that would claim a place for social science at the bottom of the hierarchy of systematic sciences. In a next, methodological step, Parsons and particularly Merton proposed to systematize the middle range between micro- and macro-society.

Theories of the middle range 1

If classic social theory from Durkheim through structural functionalism asked how social *order* is possible, recent social theory has restated the logically antecedent question, 'How is social *structure* possible in the first place?' Presupposing a 'law of inertia' in social processes that is similar to homeostasis in physiology, Parsons suggested that "The essential point is that for there to be a theory of *change* of pattern, under these methodological assumptions, there must be an initial and a terminal pattern to be used as points of reference" (1951: 483). It is significant that Parsons formulates the question in *methodological* terms as a matter of conferring "an initial and a terminal pattern" and thus examining possible external influences on the initial pattern in order to explain and predict developments. In order for there to be a theory of pattern change, presumably there will also have to be a general *theory* of social patterning or structuration.

Merton (1968) specified theories of the middle range as a way of mediating in empirical inquiry between grand theories of society as such and working hypotheses about delimited contexts. Whereas 'the middle range' thus refers to analytical procedures at an intermediate level of abstraction, middle-range theory equally emphasizes the interrelations between overarching, macro-structures and distributed, micro-processes. The concept of 'functions' is at the center of this attempt to conceive micro–macro links in practical, methodological terms. Realizing the ambiguity of the concept, Merton emphatically distinguished between "subjective dispositions (motives, purposes)" and "objective consequences (functions, dysfunctions)" (Merton, 1968: 104–5). Further, he argued, the common confusion of the two categories

> requires us to introduce a conceptual distinction between the cases in which the subjective aim-in-view coincides with the objective consequence, and the cases in which they diverge. *Manifest functions* are those objective consequences contributing to the adjustment or adaptation of the system which are intended and recognized by participants in the system; *Latent functions*, correlatively, being those which are neither intended nor recognized. BASIC QUERY: What are the effects of the transformation of a previously latent function into a manifest function (involving the problem of the role of knowledge in human behavior and the problems of 'manipulation' of human behavior)? (Merton, 1968: 105)

Although the query is indeed basic and the distinction between latent and manifest functions relevant, Merton curiously does not recognize that, in addition to being both intended and recognized, or neither intended nor recognized, functions may be intended by a specific group of participants, or they may be recognized merely by a particular group. For example, an arguably unintended, but widely recognized function of the judiciary system in Western societies is its tendency to privilege those who can afford the best legal counsel. Merton's implicit premise, however, is that functions can be defined according to one central perspective on what Durkheim had called "the general needs of the social organism" (1901/1982: 123). Hence, Merton leaves out those functional categories which may never take the shape of an effective,

institutionalized consensus – the *potential* forms of social interaction and conflict being negotiated in distributed contexts.

In sum, structural functionalism has tended to collapse Aristotle's efficient
and final causes in the notion of functions by assuming, first, that social
agents share a common interest in a project called 'society,' and, second, that
both the efficient causes of, and the obstacles to, this end may be established
from an Olympian perspective. Contrary to Merton's argument, human
knowledge is not so much a specific "problem" in explaining the transformation of latent into manifest functions, but rather a general condition of social
practices as they lend shape to both final and efficient causes of society. While
Merton recognizes an "ideological tinge" (Merton, 1968: 108) in functionalism
favoring the social status quo, the more basic, theoretical problem of the struc-
tural-functionalist position is that it may neglect the conflicted variety of
'functions' and the processual nature of the resulting 'structure.'

Functionalist theories of the middle range have an afterlife in the widespread understanding of societies as quasi-natural, functional systems that
lend themselves to formal methods of analysis as developed in natural-scientific fields. This is witnessed, for instance, in the credo of a standard handbook
of methods, the fifth edition of the *Handbook of Research Design and Social
Measurement* (1991): "*Social data are natural data. Their study can and should
follow the contours of the scientific method*" (Miller, 1991: xii).[5] Most recently,
neofunctionalism (for example, Alexander, 1987) has attempted to rehabilitate
structural functionalism to develop a systematic theory of society (but see
Joas, 1993: 188–213; Turner, 1991a). Distanciating himself from the concept of
reflexivity in, for example, Garfinkel, Gouldner, and Giddens, Jeffrey C.
Alexander suggests that 'reflexivity' is altogether too vague (and too focused
on what Giddens [1984] has called 'existential' as opposed to 'structural' contradictions of life) to address the contingency of human agency in particular
social contexts: "'Reflexivity' is too Sartrean [...]" (Alexander, 1987: 299).
Reflexivity, however, has proven central to a different, triadic conception of the
middle range.

Theories of the middle range 2

Everyday society

Both Weber's ideal types, as reinterpreted above, and Giddens' conception of
reflexivity suggest that meaning is continuously being ascribed to society by
humans as a constitutive aspect of their interaction. As part of a general turn
toward the category of everyday life, outlined below, recent social science has
witnessed both a renewed theoretical emphasis on how reflexive social agents
coproduce their larger contexts and a specific empirical focus on the local
processes that reproduce a global social system. The production of meaning in
everyday practices represents an empirical as well as theoretical middle range
of analysis.[6]

Everyday practices may be conceptualized with reference to time, space, and agency. First, everyday life is located in a particular social *space* in which events and encounters take place in the presence of those involved (Giddens' [1984] 'social integration'). Importantly, the everyday is not confined to the private sphere of consumption or leisure, but equally comprises work, political and cultural practice, and other public activities. The everyday is a physical space where individuals intervene directly into events; it is also a set of 'places' where social encounters recur, thus contributing to a specific sense of identity. I am, in a sense, where I am, at home, at work, and in the community. The everyday thus is both a lived experience and a context of action, for individuals who are simultaneously subjects and agents in society.

Second, everyday *time* is characterized by its socially organized, regularized structure, repeated across days, weeks, and years. The specific regularity, while being rooted in the seasons and similar natural cycles, arises from the economic or religious institutions of a particular historical setting. Whereas the modern mass media serve as an interface between the everyday and other social spaces, the temporal structures of mass communication – broadcast schedules and the frequency of print publications – also lend structure to everyday life as such, punctuating daily routines and mediating between different spheres of activity (Scannell, 1988). If time and space hence set the limiting conditions of everyday life, it is the exercise of agency that accumulates specific forms of experience and interaction.

Third, then, the everyday is constituted through the *agency* of countless anonymous individuals whose interaction is coordinated through complex practical, tacit knowledge and extensive communicative practices, including mass communication. One central task for social theory is to account for both conflictual and consensual elements of this agency, beyond predefined categories of 'functions' and 'roles.' Another task is to specify how the agency of institutions and individuals is maintained across time and space through different forms of semiosis. This last question has been a major issue addressed by three bodies of social science on the everyday.[7]

Researching the everyday

First, *anthropological* theory and methodology have had a general impact on other social science, in part as a critical response to the dominant conception of middle-range theories above. On the one hand, anthropology has helped to refocus research on culture as meaning production permeating and orienting all of social life, also in the context of contemporary industrialized societies. As noted by Mukerji and Schudson (1991), while one anthropological tradition, notably the structuralism of Lévi-Strauss (1963), has approached cultures as *systems* of meaning, the more influential approach in current research on society and culture is the interpretive study of distributed *processes* of meaning production, as proposed in the 'thick description' of Geertz (1973). In communication and cultural studies, the shift of emphasis has been from culture as distinctive, high-status artefacts and rituals to culture as "a whole way of life" (Williams, 1977). On the other hand, this refocusing on semiosis has entailed renewed critical attention to the status of social-scientific discourses,

their knowledge interests and articulation of personal and political commit-
ments (Clifford and Marcus, 1986; Van Maanen, 1988).

Second, not least interdisciplinary research in areas such as cultural and
gender studies has been informed by the undercurrent of *qualitative* social
science which runs from early classics in sociology including the Chicago
School, through symbolic interactionism, to the current interest in discourse
analysis and 'grounded theory' (for overview, see Jankowski and Wester, 1991).
An important recent influence has been work on the frames of everyday cognition and interaction by Erving Goffman (for example, Goffman, 1974), who
is central also to Giddens' meta-theory of social science. Much work in this
tradition has a background in pragmatism, particularly George Herbert
Mead. Whereas William James applied Peirce's pragmatic maxim to experiential consequences within psychology, Mead (1934) introduced the maxim to
interpersonal communication and socialization, defining the individual subject
as a practical consequence of social interaction in context. The social self thus
emerges by incorporating the external perspective of a 'generalized other' and
by mastering roles and symbols implicit in that relation. What is less clear in
Mead's model of ongoing socialization is the linkage of self and other to specific institutions and relations of power, a problem recurring in the third body
of research.

The third tradition can be summed up under a heading of the *phenomenology* of human experience in social context. The works of Georg Simmel and
Alfred Schütz have been influential in conceptualizing everyday life with reference, for example, to social encounters and the experience of time. Schütz
(1973), for one, examined everyday experience as a "vivid present" unifying
inner and outer time, providing Giddens with the notion of concurrent reflexivity. Simmel, further, outlined a sociology emphasizing the multitude of
concrete interactions that make up society (see Featherstone, 1991). One problem, however, of phenomenological social theory has been a tendency to
retreat from the middle range of society into an empathetic, aesthetic understanding of familiar phenomena, from which universalistic implications may
be drawn with little reference to situated social agents or practices. This recalls
"Weber's charge that in Simmel's works 'problems of being' are often treated
as 'problems of meaning,' and that the latter thereby give expression not only
to a *metaphysical* but also to an *aesthetic need*" (Lichtblau, 1991: 53).

The 'meaning of life' is a different category of analysis than the meaning of
social being. The difficult task of middle-range theory remains one of walking
the fine line between imperialisms of the social object and subject (Giddens,
1984: 2), between structural and existential contradictions, between functional
explanation and interpretive understanding. The difficulty is suggested by two
sources of social semiotics addressing socialization.[8]

Nummy-num vs hunger

Charles Morris had hoped to develop semiotics into a hard behavioral science
which would include "behavioristics" (Morris, 1971: 21) as well as syntactics,
semantics, and pragmatics. His *Foundations of the Theory of Signs* (1938) was

published in the 'Encyclopedia of Unified Science,' a book series of logical
positivism. Morris, accordingly, introduced a subtle, but significant rearticulation of Peirce's concepts. For example, the interpretant is redefined as a
"disposition to react in a certain way because of the sign" (Morris, 1964: 3);
action becomes reaction. Moreover, the sign becomes a stimulus, the interpretant a response, and methodologically Morris conceptualizes the
'disposition to react' in probabilistic terms. Thus, several different types of natural and conventional signs are collapsed into relatively uninformative
categories of stimulus and response. Occasionally the semiotic nature of the
interpreting agency (Peirce's mansign) is forgotten altogether (for example,
Morris, 1971: 21).

To exemplify, discussing how children are socialized through signs, Morris
says:

> [...] if a mother tries to get her child to swallow a teaspoonful of castor oil by saying
> 'nummy num,' the child is set for something that he will favor. Since he does not like
> it when he tastes it, and if the mother continues to talk like this in a variety of situ-
> ations, the term 'nummy num' will change from a positive [...] sign to a negative [...]
> sign – or the child will come to regard his mother as a liar. (1985: 181)

The relevant point, however, is not so much that the child may reevaluate the
term, or label his mother as a 'liar,' but that the term is constitutive of a basic
form of social interaction which may now take a different course. The sign is
not primarily a representation of a specific, positive or negative quality, a
stimulus entailing a specific response; it rather serves to reorient future action.

V.N. Volosinov, working in the circle around Mikhail Bakhtin that emphasized studies of the specific uses of language in social context as an alternative
to (Russian) formalism, had outlined a different, materialist theory of communication and society (Volosinov, 1929/1973) which has influenced
contemporary cultural and media theory (Fiske, 1987; Hodge and Kress, 1988;
Williams, 1977).[9] While the word for Volosinov remained the sign *par excellence*, used also in 'inner speech,' he rejected Saussure's systemic approach to
language as abstract objectivism, arguing instead that language is constituted
in and through social practice. An ambiguous key statement reads, "*The immediate social situation and the broader social milieu wholly determine – and
determine from within, so to speak – the structure of an utterance*" (1985: 53).
His concept of multiaccentuality, to which 'polysemy' is heir (see Chapter 5),
suggests that even though, for example, different classes in society rely on the
same signs, each class may interpret and enact such signs differently. Social
conflict is carried on, in part, through signs.

Exemplifying what is not a "referential message (communication in the narrow sense) but the verbal expression of some need – for instance, hunger"
(1985: 53), Volosinov discusses the social form and possible effect of communication:

> The immediate social context will determine possible addressees, friends or foes,
> toward whom the consciousness and the experience of hunger will be oriented;
> whether it will involve dissatisfaction with cruel Nature, with oneself, with society,

with a specific group in society, with a specific person, and so on. Of course, various degrees of perceptibility, distinctiveness, and differentiation in the social orientation of an experience are possible; but without some kind of evaluative social orientation there is no experience. Even the cry of a nursing infant is 'oriented' toward its mother. There is the possibility that the experience of hunger may take on a political coloring, in which case its structure will be determined along the lines of a potential political appeal or a reason for political agitation. It may be apprehended as a form of protest, and so on. (p. 54)

In sum, while Morris's human organisms merely happen to be situated in a society as they react to semiotic stimuli, Volosinov's argument begins to suggest how signs constitute social networks of meaning and action, being an early example of the generative model of social semiosis below.

The semiosis of society

Meaning as recontextualization

Ascribing meaning to other people, everyday events, and social structures, humans articulate and rearticulate society. With reference to scientific inquiry as a special form of meaning production, Richard Rorty has characterized this process as recontextualization:

> As one moves along the spectrum from habit to inquiry – from instinctive revision of intentions through routine calculation toward revolutionary science or politics – the number of beliefs added to or subtracted from the web increases. At a certain point in this process it becomes useful to speak of 'recontextualization.' The more widespread the changes, the more use we have for the notion of 'a new context.' This new context can be a new explanatory theory, a new comparison class, a new descriptive vocabulary, a new private or political purpose, the latest book one has read, the last person one has talked to; the possibilities are endless. (1991a: 94)

Leaving the problematic postmodernism of Rorty's "endless" possibilities to Chapter 11, I take Rorty's account of meaning, action, and context to offer a useful semiotic conception of the middle range of society.

Figure 3.2 illustrates four prototypical forms of action involving semiosis in distinctive ways. Whereas *cognition* is most basically understood as a subject relating to an object through some contextual category of understanding, semiotics conceives the interpreting subject as an interpretant whose orientation toward an object is mediated by a sign, perhaps complemented by a second subject. It is only through *communication*, however, that the two interpreting subjects engage each other in a social process of semiosis with reference to a common object of interest, thus negotiating the status of different signs to arrive at a degree of (scientific or public) intersubjectivity. In *interaction*, this process is generalized so as to include the status of other subjects on the agenda of semiosis: social agents may redescribe each other – and their purposes and contexts – as both subjects and objects of action, ends and means of society. Others' description of who or what I am, in which context of action, implies what I can do. *Reflexivity* in individuals is solitary

Cognition

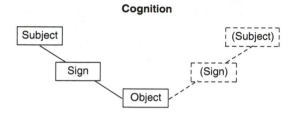

Communication

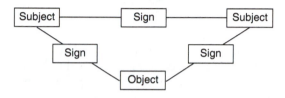

Interaction

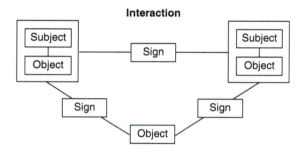

Reflexivity

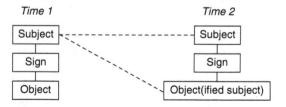

Figure 3.2   *Semiosis and forms of action*

recontextualization, implying what I may be able to do in the context of others.

Transitions between discursive consciousness, practical consciousness, and the unconscious provide a major example of recontextualization. By discursively describing what you are doing, I indicate that I know what you may be up to, unconsciously or in effect. On a social scale, the mass media are institutions of recontextualization. The recontextualization of other social agents, events, purposes, and contexts, in sum, constitutes the semiotic dimension of social structuration.

Four models of social semiosis

Because semiosis is complex and distributed across social structures, it is necessary to specify several models that may capture its different aspects and make them accessible for empirical research. Figure 3.3 suggests that models of meaning vary along two dimensions, regarding their constituents and structure. The horizontal dimension distinguishes models depending on whether they comprise a predefined, finite inventory of final units or events. The vertical dimension indicates whether there exists a predefined structure for the final configuration of the units or events. I refer to units *or* events of meaning to allow for both systemic and processual conceptions of meaning in empirical methodologies.

Deterministic models, first, assume that their elements are linked by universal relations of causality, as epitomized by laws of nature. They are commonly taken not to have major explanatory value for social phenomena such as meaning and culture, hence the parentheses in Figure 3.3. Conversely, indeterministic models hold that social agents are free individuals, interacting with relative autonomy according to their specific interpretation of social reality. Indeterministic models may be especially suited to produce pilot studies capturing the range of meanings which are associated with particular forms of social action, to be researched systematically with reference to either stochastic or generative models.

The generative and stochastic models are both central to social science, even while the latter predominate. The main principle of a stochastic model is that it "refers to a probability construction in which a sequence of behavioral events occurs in time and to which are assigned probabilities for the joint

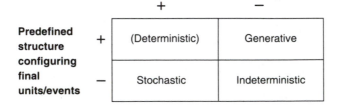

Predefined inventory of final units/events

		+	−
Predefined structure configuring final units/events	**+**	(Deterministic)	Generative
	−	Stochastic	Indeterministic

Figure 3.3   A *typology of models of meaning*

occurrence of such events" (Miller, 1991: 53). The standard political opinion poll can be said to tap the meanings which arguably orient the behavior of the electorate at the polls. Stochastic models thus predefine the possible inventory of variables, values, and correlations and predict their actual configuration. A generative model, finally, predefines the configuration of meaning elements, particularly in terms of standardized genres and similar discursive forms. The analytical aim is to identify the specific constituents or units of meaning by interpreting each with reference to its social as well as discursive context of use. I return in later chapters to the notion of interpretive communities (Fish, 1979), or, better, interpretive repertoires (Potter and Wetherell, 1987), as instances of a generative model. The further implication for empirical research is that historically and socially specific deep structures of meaning can be examined as thick, cultural categories (Geertz, 1973) complementing the abundant, thin knowledge about, for example, audience demographics.[10]

Models, theories, and empirical methodologies

Figure 3.4 relates each of the three models of meaning in mass communication research to its main empirical domain, its concept of meaning, and its epistemological focus in terms of Peircean semiotics. By way of preface, I should emphasize that I approach the models and concepts of meaning as ideal types that complement each other in both theoretical analysis and empirical studies. In particular, practices are inscribed and recontextualized through discourse, and they accumulate as institutions of society.

First, the focus on signs in their own right has been characteristic of humanistic studies of communication and society, which have singled out media discourses in empirical studies, to be interpreted as articulations, for example, of a culture or historical epoch. Hence, scholarship tends to approach meaning in intentional, phenomenological terms as the irreducible experience of texts that arises from empathy. As I suggested in Chapter 1, this emphasis also informs much structuralist research on culture and communication. While some critical media studies have explored the textual determination of the audience response, the predominant theoretical model in humanistic scholarship remains indeterminist and implies a methodology that conceives meaning as the creative accomplishment of a singular, insightful interpretive agent, the analyst.

Second, the conception of society as an objective structure conditioning

Epistemological focus	Theoretical model	Empirical domain	Concepts of meaning
Sign	Indeterministic	Discourses	Intentional
Object	Stochastic	Institutions	Causal
Interpretant	Generative	Practices	Performative

Figure 3.4 *From social science to social semiotics*

human action and experience shifts the empirical emphasis to the entrenched institutions of society. Stochastic models can identify specific social institutions by documenting their permanence as social facts, as witnessed by human agents, across time and space and across units and contexts of analysis. For example, stochastic models usefully inform research on the relationship between media output and market conditions, the representation of public events in media content, as well as audience perceptions of media institutions. Whereas handbooks of social science warn that correlation does not equal causation, the implicit concept of meaning in this tradition, nevertheless, is frequently a causal one: if social agents are informed by this opinion – meaning, agenda, idea, or similar concepts – their thinking and action in relation to particular institutions can be predicted as a consequence with a certain probability.

Third, generative models enable empirical research to study the social practices in which, simultaneously, discourses are articulated and institutions reproduced. The Peircean interpretant suggests that meaning is performative, carries a predisposition to act, and makes a social difference. In order to identify the principles informing meaning production, there is a special call for empirical studies which relate the analysis and interpretation of meaning to a specific context of action, within a theory of social semiotics.

PART II
COMMUNICATION THEORY: FIRST-ORDER SEMIOTICS

4

A New Theory of Mass Communication: Constituents of Social Semiotics

This chapter outlines a theory of mass communication, drawing on the reper-toires of semiotics and social science retraced in Part I, and developing a framework for the empirical studies of reception presented in the following chapters of Part II. The understanding of mass communication as a variety of social semiosis represents a new departure in communication studies, to the extent that it provides conceptual specification and methodological substan-tiation of how to study mass communication as a discursive practice in social context.[1]

Starting from the general definition of mass communication as a techno-logical, institutionalized form of reflexivity producing and circulating meaning in modern societies, the theory situates mass communication in relation to other cultural forms, social institutions, and the everyday life of audiences. The first section of the chapter explores two distinctive aspects of *culture* – what I refer to as time-in culture and time-out culture – that help to clarify the sense in which mass communication is both a form of representation and a social practice. In the second section, I reinterpret Jürgen Habermas's classic model of the public sphere and other social *institutions* (Habermas, 1962/1989) as a discursive as well as a material-economic-legal fact, while the third section defines the institutions as determinations in the first instance of the social pro-duction of meaning. The fourth section of the chapter then links modern culture and social institutions in a triad with the everyday *practices* of mass media audiences, who are simultaneously citizens, publics, and private indi-viduals. The fifth and final section sketches the methodological conception of these constituents of social semiotics which is developed in the empirical analyses in Chapters 5–8.

Time-in culture and time-out culture

Two concepts of culture

Whereas a history of the concept of culture falls outside this volume, two of its traditional senses serve to introduce the focus of my argument.[2] On the one hand, culture has been conceived as a *process* that is continuous with and constitutive of, in phenomenological terms, the human lifeworld. Deriving from the Latin *colere*, to cultivate, the term 'culture' was originally associated with cultivating the earth and its animals in a relatively neutral sense, but over

time it acquired two distinctly normative senses, one religious, the other secular. The religious sense is found, for example, in St Augustine, who derived the
concept of *cultura animi*, cultivation of the human spirit, from Plutarch and
Cicero, and rearticulated this to mean the cultivation *of* God *by* the human
spirit, suggesting the common blurring of 'culture' and 'cult.' The secular
sense of culture was recovered during the Renaissance and revitalized by the
new middle classes of the modern period. Aesthetic or rhetorical competences
could serve, literally, as a sign of distinction in contrast to both the uncultured
working class and the superficial sophistication of the aristocracy. The
Romantic Age, however, contested the conception of culture as a scarce
resource, implying rather that culture is the distinctive feature of all humans,
civilized or not, Christian or not. The definition of culture as that which both
unites and differentiates humans into cultures in the plural became influential
especially through the work of the German philosopher Johann Gottfried
Herder (*Ideas for a Philosophy of the History of Mankind*, 1784), and it later
informed anthropology as founded by E.B. Tylor's *Primitive Culture* (1871).
The processual and egalitarian understanding of culture is half the legacy of
contemporary research on (mass) communication and (popular) culture.

On the other hand, culture came to be understood increasingly as specific
products of the human spirit, or containers of culture. Williams' (1983) semiotic history of 'culture' and other everyday concepts suggests that the new,
pervasive emphasis on culture as artifacts, and as a separate sector of society,
grew out of the wider process of modernization that served to segment social
life into domains of arts, sciences, politics, and so on. The reification of culture
is explained, in part, by the modern institutionalization and bureaucratization
of human activities. Cultural institutions, nevertheless, might offer a
metaphorical garden to be cultivated and contemplated as a reality apart from
the society that was becoming second nature. Modern high culture could be
seen as the self-defense of humans against a society of their own making.

The structural conception of culture as a realm apart has frequently been
combined with a normative preference for a contemplative aesthetics, excom-
municating the mundane processes of culture and insulating arts from the
realm of practice. And insulation has proven only a step away from absolutization, as expressed in Matthew Arnold's classic definition of culture (1869) as
"the best which has been thought and said in the world." Popular culture,
accordingly, became the excommunicated other of modern high culture
(Huyssen, 1986), comprising multiple forms of experience and pleasure that
provided a different realm apart, with a different relation to other processes
and practices of society.

The duality of culture

Any theory of mass communication must come to terms with these
dichotomies of modern culture. Whereas social-scientific research has given
priority to popular culture in social processes, and while humanistic studies
have emphasized mass communication as a textual analogy to the high-
cultural realm apart, the duality has remained central to the field as such. If

the duality of structure is key to social theory (Giddens, 1984), the duality of culture is key to mass communication theory.[3] Mass communication constitutes both a set of aesthetic products and an everyday process, a realm apart as well as a social practice, a potential vehicle of both high cultural and popular cultural norms. I develop the notions of time-in culture and time-out culture not as new ideas in themselves, but as complementary elements of an integrative theory of culture and communication. The analytical distinction is anticipated in classic theories of Fourth Estate institutions (Habermas, 1962/1989; Sennett, 1974; Siebert et al., 1956), in anthropological theory of the liminal realm (Turner, 1967), and in mass communication theories conceiving the media as agenda-setters (McCombs and Shaw, 1972) and as a cultural forum (Newcomb and Hirsch, 1984). Mass media, then, are industrialized institutions-to-think-with, being modern equivalents of the objects-to-think-with (Schudson, 1987: 56) identified by anthropology.[4]

The origin of the time-in, time-out terminology is in popular culture, in sports. For example, in ice hockey and basketball coaches can call for a break during which to discuss strategy and tactics with their teams. The point is that such a time-out, while apparently suspending action during a moment of reflexivity, addresses and occurs within the total time-in of the game. Similarly, institutionalized cultural activity such as mass media use may suspend other everyday activity, but still takes place in the context of the everyday with reference to specific social institutions.[5]

I define *time-in culture*, first, as the aspect of semiosis which is continuous with and constitutive of other social practices. Comprising the many premises and procedures that serve to orient social interaction, time-in culture is the medium representing and incorporating agency and structure within a context of action. Such situated social semiosis, drawing on face-to-face interactions, mass communication, and other communicative encounters, is a necessary condition for the reproduction of meaningful social relations. Time-in culture is a practice of representation enabling other social action.

Second, I define *time-out culture* as the aspect of semiosis that may be designated as a separate social practice, and which can be identified by social agents as such. It places reality on an explicit agenda as an object of reflexivity, and provides an occasion for contemplating oneself in a social, existential, or religious perspective. While such contemplation has traditionally been associated with religious rituals and fine arts, mass communication, certainly in a quantitative sense, is the main ingredient of time-out culture in the modern age. Time-out culture is a practice which reflects upon the nature and representation of social reality.

I emphasize that time-in and time-out culture are both constitutive and emergent aspects, not separate elements, of the concrete instance of mass communication and, indeed, of most conceivable cultural practices. A particular configuration of time-in and time-out culture, within a specific technological and institutional infrastructure, helps to account for the central cultural characteristics of different historical periods. To exemplify, an interdependence between church and state institutions, or between artists and their benefactors,

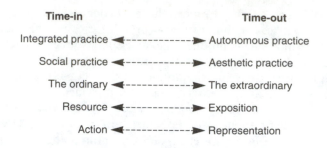

Figure 4.1   *Dimensions of time-in culture and time-out culture*

or between media and political parties, gives rise to different cultural products and processes.

Figure 4.1 summarizes some main dimensions of the distinction between the time-in and time-out culture. Time-out cultural practices lay claim to a relative autonomy as aesthetic practices in their own right, beyond practices reproducing the social system. Moreover, in rehearsing ideas and worldviews, time-out culture may introduce an experience of the extraordinary into the everyday. Perhaps the crucial distinction is made between resources and expositions, such as narratives or arguments (Bruner, 1986), and, by implication, between action and representation. Cultural events, texts, and artifacts become resources for time-in culture when they serve to orient action in social contexts. Conversely, an exposition – a literary narrative, a political poster, or a scientific argument – represents a possible world that may or may not be enacted in practice. Time-out culture prefigures social action; time-in culture configures social action.

The theory of social semiotics thus defines mass communication as an institution producing and circulating meaning in society through the interrelated practices of time-in and time-out culture. The semiotic processes are conditioned in the first instance (Hall, 1983) by technological, economic, and organizational factors of the particular historical context, to which I turn in the next section. Further, the theory entails an emphasis on 'reception' as a strategic juncture between communication and action, to which I return in the third section. In sum, the distinguishing feature of mass communication in relation to other social institutions is the semiotic process and cultural practice through which mass media participate in the articulation of meanings that audiences act upon, both in the immediate context of reception and in the wider social context.

The public-sphere model revisited

Jürgen Habermas's *Strukturwandel der Öffentlichkeit* [The Structural Transformation of the Public Sphere] (1962), published in English in 1989, remains the best framework for a comprehensive analysis of culture and communication in modern Western societies.[6] The key point of the volume is that the modern social system can be conceived as a set of interconnected, if in principle autonomous, spheres, namely, the private sphere (subdivided into social and intimate spheres), the public sphere (political and cultural), and the sphere of the state (see Figure 4.2). The model suggests that the central, economic activity occurs within the social sphere of production; the role of state agencies is primarily one of providing a stable legal and fiscal framework for industrial and other production. The intimate sphere of family life, equally, is conceived as a haven insulated from the demands of either the market or the state. The mediating element of the system is the public sphere, which comprises the major political and cultural institutions as well as the Fourth Estate, presumably setting the terms of cooperation between the state and individuals through rational, democratic communication. Thus, the model conceives public communication as a central locus of power in industrial capitalist democracies. Whereas Habermas (1962/1989) emphasized the liberating, utopian potential of the model, even while deploring its contemporary decline, other communication theory has described it as a historically- and class-specific conception of ideal public communication, an ideology in the inclusive sense (Mortensen, 1977; Negt and Kluge, 1972/1993).

One explanatory value of the theoretical model is its differentiation between the political and cultural public spheres, their constitutive genres, and the implied social uses by the audience. The political public sphere addresses classic social issues of power and privilege, and conceives the audience as citizens participating in a political process. The cultural public sphere, in its turn, addresses what are thought to be universal issues of human existence, conceiving the audience as subjects in civil society. Hence, for example, current soap operas and situation comedies construct perspectives on family life

	Society		State
	Private sphere	**Public sphere**	
	Intimate sphere	*Cultural public sphere*	
Object	Religion, sexuality, emotion, friendship, etc.	Preaching, art, literature, music, etc.	The (agencies of the) state ensure(s) the material infrastructure, overall economic stability, law enforcement, and regulation of capital-labor conflicts by economic, coercive, legal, and ideological means
Institution	Family	Organizations, clubs	
	Social sphere	*Political public sphere*	
Object	Private economic activity, production and sale/purchase of commodities, including labor	'Politics' and 'the economy', including social issues	
Institution	Private enterprise and stores	Parliamentary organs, representing political parties, and the press	

Figure 4.2   *The public-sphere model (Jensen, 1987a: 10)*

within the intimate sphere; news arguably provides a basic resource for political activity; and talk shows can be said to trace the borders between private and public domains, offering public perspectives on private issues, and vice versa. Moreover, the model identifies a specific compartmentalization of society, as articulated in media genres, which may either fragment the public's understanding of the social totality, or naturalize a particular separation of spheres and powers, or both.

In the present context, my main interest is in the double status of the model, being both a material, institutional fact and a semiotic, discursive fact. On the one hand, the model presents a real configuration of the major institutions in modern society. Because the model informs the very organization, for example, of socializing agencies, from schools to mass media, and because we constantly encounter the institutions of each sphere in everyday life, the public-sphere model tends to be reproduced as part of common sense. The model, then, cannot be rejected as false consciousness in classic Marxist terminology, even if it may set the outer limits of the political imagination.

On the other hand, the model is effective, in part, as a dominant discursive construction of the social order that is founded on a number of controversial assumptions. For one thing, it does not allow for the possibility that certain corporate economic decisions may preclude certain other political decisions, which will be enforced by a less than neutral state. For another, specifically the mass media in the public sphere are, for the most part, private enterprises whose operations are guided not merely by political, but equally by economic logic. By overstating the autonomy of the spheres, and by implying the inevitability of their present organization as a neutral means of regulating social conflict, the public-sphere model articulates what is known as a 'hegemony' in the tradition originating with Gramsci (1971). Hegemony gives rise to "a sense of absolute because experienced reality beyond which it is very difficult for most members of the society to move, in most areas of their lives" (Williams, 1977: 110).

The public-sphere model, accordingly, provides a prototypical case of Giddens' (1984) duality of structure as well as the double hermeneutic. First, it is both a source of agency, orienting interpretation and action vis-à-vis social institutions, from the family to the mass media and parliament, and an institutional structure which is the outcome of continuous social action. Second, the model states a particular hermeneutic of social reality, arising from liberal political theories in seventeenth- and eighteenth-century Europe, and adopted as an offensive tool by the rising middle class to assert specific political and economic interests as universal human rights. In both respects, the public-sphere model constitutes a performative meaning and an ideal type of a society.

Most important perhaps, this reinterpretation of public-sphere theory allows for an understanding of the social relationship between meaning and action, and, in present terms, between time-out and time-in culture, which breaks with the rhetoric of origin, fall, and decline in Habermas (1962/1989). Habermas fell victim to the type of communicative utopia that the critique of ideology was designed to deconstruct. The most farreaching implication of the historical public-sphere model, and of its systematic counterpart in the 'theory of communicative action' (Habermas, 1981/1984, 1981/1987; see Chapter 11), is that society might, after all, be contemplated and evaluated from a position outside any social context of interest-driven action. The public sphere thus tends to become reified in the historical perspective, and ontologized in the systematic perspective, as an autonomous domain of time-out meaning production. The social-semiotic alternative is to conceive time-out meaning as constituted in conjunction with time-in meaning, by necessity enacting a social purpose with reference to a historical context. Communities of communication and inquiry cannot step outside of society or history, but in embracing that condition of semiosis, they participate in the construction of both history and society.

Determination in the first instance

If the distinguishing feature of mass communication is the semiotic process and cultural practice arising from the interaction between mass media and audiences, then the reception, social uses, and cultural contexts of media take on a special, strategic importance for research. At the same time, the public-sphere model identifies a whole set of structural determinations on the process, that is, preparatory conditions of semiosis of at least three kinds. First, the available *technological* resources determine the potential form of the public sphere, enabling a particular organization of communication across social time and space. As noted in Chapter 1, scribal, print, and audiovisual technologies in turn prepare new forms of social interaction, while ruling out others. Second, the *economic* basis of mass communication, as anticipated in political, legislative frameworks, shapes the diversity and specific historical form of mass media. Third, their *organizational* level of development, including the degree of professionalization and bureaucratization of the institution, affects the concrete discourses and practices of individual mass media, and hence their place in the cultural domain as a whole. Each of these factors have been, and must be, the subject of specialized studies in what will likely remain, for the foreseeable future, an interdisciplinary field rather than a unified discipline (Levy and Gurevitch, 1994). Organizational, economic, and technological studies are indispensable elements of mass communication research to the extent that they address such factors as determinations in the first instance (Hall, 1983) of semiosis.

Furthermore, I take as an initial premise, at the *theoretical* level of analysis, that societies come before media as generators of meaning. Meaning flows from existing social institutions and everyday contexts, via media professionals and audiences, to the mass media, not vice versa.[7] For most people most of the time, mass communication is hardly the factor determining their personal or social orientation and action. Meaning is ascribed to the discourses and practices of mass communication with reference to the social contexts which they represent and address. In sum, the center of mass communication, and of mass communication research, lies outside the mass media as such (Negt and Kluge, 1972/1993)[8] – within the discourses, practices, and institutions in whose reproduction the media participate.

It is in *methodological* terms that research must focus on the specific contribution of mass media to social semiosis – the difference they make in social contexts. In order to document the processes of mass-mediated semiosis, empirical studies are called for of the economic conditions and professional norms shaping particular media organizations, of the content structures resulting from legislative rules as well as programming policies, and of the modes of socialization that produce the historical audience. Equally, it is in methodological terms that reception offers a strategic site of research. Not only is the reception of mass communication the cultural practice most widely engaged in by the contemporary general public. Reception in the basic sense of exposure, moreover, initiates a process of interpreting and enacting multiple potential meanings; reception is not a single act producing a unified meaning. Audiences reactivate meanings deriving from mass media in multiple social contexts of action. Media reception, thus, feeds into a semiosis that is distributed across time and space, and which must be studied through several phases of impact. This interchange between time-out and time-in culture constitutes a form of Peircean, infinite semiosis.

Mass communication as cultural practice

Constituents of social semiotics

Figure 4.3 relates the main theoretical concepts, drawn from the humanities and social sciences as necessary constituents of social semiotics, to their epistemological correlates in semiotics and to their methodological correlates in mass communication research.[9] In the movement toward an integrated set of concepts and methods for interdisciplinary communication studies, common denominators may be found at a meta-theoretical level of analysis, as represented by semiotics and structuration theory. While I return in Chapter 9 to theory of science as a form of second-order semiotics, a brief examination of the meta-theoretical level is necessary to link the theoretical argument in this section with the methodological argument in the final section of the present chapter.

Meta-theoretical analysis is a bridging activity, linking specific theories of communication with epistemological issues and methodological operationalizations. It is instructive to think of research as scientific semiosis which operates through the use of language and other forms of discourse. Research is a reflective practice, performed through signs, and assigning explanatory value – relevance and meaning – to findings at various levels of analysis. Figure 4.4 suggests five discursive levels of scientific analysis (see Egebak, 1972: 134; Greimas and Courtés, 1982). The discourses of mass media, and of audiences about the media, are the objects of analysis at the first level of *everyday discourse*, to be grasped and documented in the categories of *analytical discourse*,

Epistemology	Theory		Methodology
	Humanities	Social sciences	
Signs	Discourses	Contents	Media constituents
Interpretants	Subjectivities	Practices	Audience constituents
Objects	Contexts	Institutions	Context constituents
			(Analytical constituents)

Figure 4.3   *Constituents of social semiotics*

for example linguistic discourse analysis or content-analytical coding. The third discursive level specifies a *methodological discourse* in terms of research designs, analytical procedures, and bases of inference. Further, the findings about media and audiences are necessarily interpreted in the framework of a *theoretical discourse*. Finally, the status and explanatory value of the other discourses must be justified at the level of *epistemological discourse*. Each level makes up an interpretant in the chain of scientific semiosis. The scientific study of communication is only a case in point, illustrating that all science is, among other things, a semiotic enterprise.

The further implication for research is that scientific theory is neither a detached, deductive activity in a context separated from empirical inquiry, nor an immediate, inductive activity to be 'grounded' in empirical reality without (explicit) theoretical preconceptions, as Glaser and Strauss (1967) come to suggest. Scientific semiosis is a continuous process of validating empirical findings and generating new theory. Referring back to Figure 4.3, I note that the methodological column to the far right introduces self-reflective or recursive semiosis into the model. While the media constituents, audience constituents,

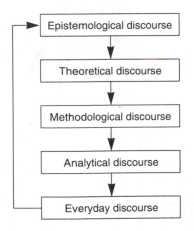

Figure 4.4   *Discursive levels of scientific semiosis*

and context constituents provide conceptual interfaces between the theoretical discourse and empirical reality of concrete studies, the analytical constituents posit particular aspects of these three domains as objects of analysis, interpretation, and reflection. Because the analytical constituents represent the next level up in abstraction, producing representations of the media, audience, and contextual constituents, they are placed in parentheses in this figure and considered in detail in the next section.[10] First of all, I turn to the two theoretical registers that contribute to an understanding of how media, audiences, and contexts interact in the cultural practice of mass communication.

Discourses, contents, and media constituents

The concept of 'discourse' is the legacy of textual scholarship in Western philosophy, humanities, and the Logos tradition generally (Chapter 1). The assumption has been that language is the primary medium of interchange between humans and reality – in processes of perception, cognition, and action. Contemporary semiotics transcends this position, first, by placing an equal emphasis on other semiotic systems, and, second, by studying not just religious, scholarly, or literary 'works,' but equally the contextual, social uses of signs. Discourse, then, is said to include everyday interaction and forms of consciousness, constituting the medium of the social construction of reality (Berger and Luckmann, 1966). Hence, I define discourse as the use of language and other semiotic systems in social contexts, including reflective practices such as science and time-out culture. It is through discourse that reality becomes intersubjective as an object of scientific analysis and social conflict.

A social turn in linguistics and other humanities, complementing the linguistic turn in philosophy and current social science, has taken place under the heading of discourse analysis. While I return to the systematic procedures of discourse analysis in Chapter 8, the approach emphasizes a theoretical conception of language use as a form of social action. Originated by Austin (1962), and developed by Searle (1969) and others, speech-act theory defines a statement literally as an instance of linguistic action. Through language, people do not primarily make a description *of* the world; they perform actions *in* the world. The classic examples include rituals (a marriage ceremony) and other institutionalized procedures (a sentence pronounced in a court of law) in which the very enunciation accomplishes a socially binding act. However, also by stating promises, questions and answers, or arguments, we perform speech acts continuously. Even statements that appear to be purely descriptive are performed mostly to produce an effect on a recipient in a shared context. Speech-act theory is perhaps the most important humanistic theory development since Wittgenstein (1958), specifying his dictum on language that meaning is use. The notion of discursive action also offers a methodological bridge between social-scientific and humanistic approaches to culture.

Social-scientific approaches to the discursive vehicles of communication have been handicapped because of a rudimentary theory of meaning (Beniger, 1988, 1990). As noted in Chapter 1, the founding texts of social-scientific communication research (Lasswell, 1948/1966; Shannon and Weaver, 1949) have been taken to imply a spatial, essentialist conception of messages as signals or vessels carrying 'contents.' In content analysis and survey research, categories for coding and scaling meaning capture the most familiar, discursively articulated aspects of meaning production concerning, for instance, recall, cultural indicators, and 'opinions' about media, that is, unit meanings of communication that are comparable to the unit acts which Parsons (1951) had identified in social life. For many purposes of research, such categories of meaning are the appropriate, economical tools of analysis. Problems arise, however, particularly in the study of the contextual meanings that are implicit, but necessary conditions of all communication. The reference in a mainstream history of the field (Lowery and DeFleur, 1988) to the rise of a new 'meaning paradigm,' acknowledges a crisis in the field, what was diagnosed in the symbolic 1983 issue of the *Journal of Communication* as 'ferment in the field.' What social-scientific communication theory needs to preserve is the conception of communication as social action, contributing to a middle ground between the empathetic exegesis of representation and the measurement of behavior. The rush to studies of social life in terms of 'narratives' (for example, Polkinghorne, 1988) runs the risk of throwing the baby of action out with the behaviorist bathwater.

The category of *genre* incorporates both discursive and performative aspects of communication. As argued by Williams (1977), genres must be defined not merely by their formal composition, as in aesthetics and literary theory, but equally by the type of subject matter or social sphere referred to, and, most important, by their mode of address. Genres invite audiences to take particular stances that imply their social roles as actors in the possible world being represented. Being vehicles of representation, expression, ritual, as well as transmission (Carey, 1989), genres offer a promising avenue for studying mass communication as a cultural practice. The classic examples from communication history include the novel, the mass press, and the encyclopedia; I turn next in Chapter 5 to a study of the social uses of the news genre.

The discourses of mass media make up the *media constituents* of social semiotics. In semiotic terminology, media discourses are the signs which, in addressing audiences, generate interpretants that predispose audiences to act in their social and historical context. (Chapter 7 considers in more detail the several analytical levels of media discourses.) While content and reception studies have frequently focused on single discourses and media, or on particular genres, neither the pervasive intertextuality of mass communication nor the existence of integrated media environments has been subject to much systematic research from the perspective of the cultural practices of audiences. These characteristics of contemporary mass communication highlight the importance of studies of the relationship between time-in and time-out culture.

Practices, subjectivities, and audience constituents

Practices can be defined as meaningful activities, or, to be precise, forms of social action that are recontextualized as meaningful in specific contexts. Practices constitute the everyday and regenerate the institutions of the social system, sometimes with a difference. Social action thus both articulates agency and enacts structure in meaningful forms that lend themselves to generative models of research. The social semiotics of mass communication examines the specific contribution of mass media to the practices of time-in and time-out culture which, to varying degrees, both orient and defamiliarize everyday life. Mass communication is a cultural practice enabling other social action.

Humanistic theories of culture have emphasized subjectivity as a condition of social agency (Coward and Ellis, 1977). Agency requires a position, closure, or sense of identity in relation to particular social ends and means. In contrast to a philosophy of consciousness that would conceive subjects as autonomous agents exercising moral and aesthetic judgment, current theories of language and subjectivity characterize the subject as a position *in* language, in semiosis. Subjectivity, thus, is not a contamination of scientific knowledge to be avoided, but a condition of all knowledge to be embraced reflexively. One argument has been that mass media and other cultural institutions serve to 'interpellate' (Althusser, 1971) or 'hail' the subject to occupy particular positions. A further argument has been that this positioning of subjects implies their excommunication from certain other positions – the unconscious – a process which is said to structure the unconscious as a language (Lacan, 1977). Whereas the nature and extent of the determination has been subject to much debate (Hall, 1980), the general line of argument elaborates the pragmatist conception of the relationship between signs, beliefs, and actions. In Peirce's (1958: 71) word, mass communication contributes to the maintenance of a "mansign," or (wo)mansign, that centers social action, including unconscious and practical forms of consciousness.

Interpretants, moreover, provide a category mediating between subjectivity and social action. In Chapter 2, I argued that the category of interpretants helps to distinguish *as well as* relate three moments of semiosis: the potential, structural meaning of media discourses; the actualized, situated meaning produced by audiences; and the performative meaning with consequences beyond the immediate context of reception. I argued further that the triad of Emotional, Energetic, and Logical Interpretants suggests how Peirce's semiotics may support a *social* science of signs and action, even though he did not himself pursue the implications for society and culture. Social semiotics may specify the slogan of pragmatism, that 'meaning is a difference that makes a difference,' with reference simultaneously to discursive structure, interpretive variation, and forms of interaction.

Advertising is one major genre that helps to discursively mediate particular forms of social interaction. For one thing, the genre implies the practices of buying and selling in an economic market, even while recognizing a range of potential interpretations of specific advertising discourses. For another, advertising discourses, in representing the institutions of different social spheres with concrete reference to the goods and services on display, enable audiences to negotiate the roles of consumer, employee, and citizen. Much historical research has documented this multi-step semiosis of advertising, circulating commodities as well as conceptions of society (Barthes, 1957/1973; Berger,

1972; Schudson, 1984). Raymond Williams and Michael Schudson have both referred to advertising as constitutive of a widespread cultural practice, what they describe respectively as the official art of capitalism (Williams in McGuigan, 1992: 120) and as "capitalism's way of saying 'I love you' to itself" (Schudson, 1984: 232).

Other genres and media equally contribute to the practices of everyday life, for example in the home. In a modern classic examining the place of television in family life, Lull (1980) developed a typology of the uses of television in the immediate social context, including both 'structural' uses that help to organize everyday routines, and 'relational' uses of the medium as a point of reference for interaction. Television schedules are used structurally, among other things, to establish firm bedtimes, and the portrayal of families in fictional television series has relational uses as a source of arguments in disputes about family matters. Thus, the socializing impact of television over time stems both from the representation of society on TV and from the social act of watching. In a longer historical perspective, media may redraw the boundaries between private and public spheres of society. As argued by Meyrowitz (1985), television has brought new images of social life into the home, thus establishing a new cultural practice, namely, the private consumption of public images of previously private lives.

The cultural practice of mass media use – the reception, interpretation, and application of mass communication in the context of other social practices – is addressed by the *audience constituents* of social semiotics. (Chapter 6 explores conceptions of the audience as both a socioeconomic and a discursive formation in a study of old and young television viewers.) While evidence is constantly being accumulated on audience demographics, little is in fact known about the concrete interpretive repertoires with which audiences approach media, or about the complementarity of the demographics and semiotics of audiences.

Institutions, contexts, and contextual constituents

Institutions can be defined, in a triadic conception of society, as recurring forms of social action to which human agents ascribe meaning. In another common sociological definition, Peter and Brigitte Berger have suggested that

> everyday life is crisscrossed by patterns that *regulate* the behaviour of its inhabitants with each other and that, at the same time, relate this behaviour to much larger contexts of meaning (such as, in our instance, canons of acceptable etiquette, the moral order and sanctions of law). These regulatory patterns are what are commonly called *institutions*. (1976: 20)

These authors go on to specify that institutions have certain characteristics, that is, external and intersubjective reality, coercive power, moral authority, and a history (Berger and Berger, 1976: chap. 4), and they further suggest that language is *the* fundamental institution of society. By contrast, I have argued that language is a *different* category of 'institution' than either markets, families, or parliaments, namely, a semiotic, enabling condition of social institutions, and that other semiotic systems besides language serve this purpose.

The relationship between semiosis and social institutions has been treated in humanistic communication theory with reference to a discursive conception of contexts (see Jensen, 1991a). One point is that the social setting of mass media is literally a con-text – a configuration of texts or discourses that also must be 'read' in the process of making sense of media. Studies of discourse have taken their cue partly from the structuralist tradition generally, partly from Michel Foucault (1972), who approached 'discourse' as an intermediate level of meaning production, between individual texts and culture as a whole, which carries certain dominant registers or worldviews. This perspective further entails a generative turn of the analytical focus, from the 'works' of particular authors and media, to the deep structures or discursive foundations of societies and cultures emerging, for example, in the discourses informing media planning and public debate about media (Ang, 1991). Both authors and audiences are conceived in that tradition as media, or servants of a master discourse. While the discursive foundation is said to be riddled with ruptures through which new discourses may emerge, the Foucauldian approach has tended to ontologize discourse, overemphasizing the discursive determination of social action. A relevant empirical question for communication studies, however, remains the form and degree in which meaning is generated – by mass media, audiences, and other major social institutions – according to a specific discursive logic. The methodologies of social semiotics may address the relationship between concrete media discourses and the entire discursive field embedding media and audiences, through a comparative discourse analysis (Chapter 8).

The relevance of a discursive conception of social institutions is illustrated by the place of contemporary mass communication in everyday life. Increasingly, mass media serve to structure a day in the life of Western, urbanized societies, as they represent institutions in the political, economic, and cultural spheres of society as continuous points of reference for everyday routines. Thus, listening to news on a (clock) radio when waking up is a way of linking up with the temporal structure of, and the latest events in, community and nation. Next, a newspaper read over breakfast is, among other things, a guide to planning leisure activities later in the day. As one goes to work, a walkman or a car radio may create a customized media environment which fills the gap between two well-defined contexts of home and work. In different work settings, media occur as continuous mood-setters canceling, in part, the reality of labor (music in offices or shops), as constitutive elements of an institution (economic news in the financial sector), or as cultural resources for a specific purpose (funnies during a lunch break, radio traffic reports for the journey home). Shopping malls, department stores, and supermarkets, visited on the way home, offer a carefully structured sequence of experiences of merchandise, music, advertising, announcements, and more merchandise to complement and orient the sequence of purchases. The electronic household, cinemas, arcades, and entertainment centers offer occasions to reconsider and transcend some of the previous routines. In each case, mass media contribute to the process of semiosis which sustains the everyday of individuals and reproduces the institutions of the social collective.

Chapter 5 takes up the *context constituents* of social semiotics, focusing on news reception as a practice that is oriented toward the political institutions of the public sphere. Whereas the social context of each instance of mass communication, in principle, includes the entire public-sphere model, previous research has identified strategic points of the communicative process as methodological foci.

Methodological constituents of reception analysis

Figure 4.5 lists the four sets of methodological constituents from which selections are made in the empirical reception studies of the following chapters. Whereas mass communication studies, to varying degrees, address the discourses, practices, and institutions of social semiosis, it is through reference to the methodological constituents that empirical studies are able to delimit a particular aspect or moment of the process, to be interpreted with reference to a theory of the entire process. Further, it is primarily the specific methodological conception of discourses, practices, and institutions that distinguishes various areas of specialization and scientific traditions. One common problem in different audience research traditions, drawing on either social sciences or humanities, has been a failure to incorporate selections from both the media, audience, and context constituents of mass communication into research designs.[11]

Context constituents

Each element of the contextual dimension corresponds to a stage of the communicative process that has been identified in previous research. Hence, it

Context constituents	Audience constituents	Media constituents	Analytical constituents
Gratifications sought	Demographic categories:	Media environments	1 *Collection* Survey
Consumption	1		Experiment
	2	Flow	Depth interviewing
Context of use	3		Participating
	etc.	Media	observation
Gratifications			'Encounters'
obtained	Interpretive	Genres	Records
	categories		
Decoding	A	Texts	2 *Analysis*
	B		Coding
Recall	C	Discursive elements	Thematic exegesis
	etc.		Discourse analysis
Effects on cognition and action			

Figure 4.5 *Methodological constituents of reception analysis*

represents a methodological construct of a particular research tradition, not a link in a chain reaction that adds up to one consistent conception of mass media reception. Methodologically speaking, as argued, meaning can be traced as it flows from media to audiences and into various social contexts, even if, theoretically speaking, meaning should be interpreted as flowing from social practices, publics, and institutions to the media. In a social-semiotic perspective, research on each context constituent contributes different insights into the distributed process of semiosis – insights that may be unified in the last instance, at the epistemological level of discourse (Chapter 9).

Uses-and-gratifications research (Blumler and Katz, 1974; Rosengren et al., 1985), in asking what audiences do with media, has produced taxonomies particularly of the *gratifications sought* from different media (Katz et al., 1973), suggesting audiences' general orientation toward media as social resources. Research on the availability of media and genres, and on audience segments' actual *consumption*, next, produces the most continuous form of evidence, as in ratings for electronic media (Nielsen, 1989) or national cultural and time-use statistics (Szalai, 1972), even if incompatible categories between studies, regarding different media, social contexts, and historical periods, counteract a more general understanding of mass communication as a cultural practice. Studies of gratifications-sought and of media consumption, in sum, outline the public's conceptions and uses of mass media as constitutive elements of everyday practices and social institutions.

Complementing this predominant survey evidence, two bodies of research have examined audience interaction with media in different social settings. First, ethnographic studies of the immediate *context of use*, particularly of television in family life, have supplemented and questioned other findings about audience sizes, 'secondary' media exposure, and the social uses of media in everyday life (Hobson, 1980; Lull, 1988a; Moores, 1993; Morley, 1986; Silverstone, 1994). Second, qualitative interview studies during the 1980s and 1990s, focusing on the audience *decoding* of media discourses, have documented the variability of reception, depending on the contexts and interpretive repertoires that audiences bring to bear on media (for overviews, see Jensen, 1991b; Lewis, 1991). Both bodies of work have begun to explore the semiotic process in which audiences contribute to the social production of meaning.[12]

Finally, many heterogeneous studies have examined stages of cognitive, emotional, and behavioral impact (for an overview, see Jensen and Rosengren, 1990; also Comstock et al., 1978; NIMH, 1982). For example, research on audience *recall* offers indicators of how media may orient audience action in relation to a range of social issues and institutions, while a subgroup of studies on knowledge gaps (Donohue et al., 1987; Tichenor et al., 1970) has addressed cumulative inequalities in the distribution of knowledge in society. Research about *effects on cognition and action*, with multiple specializations, is in fact one of the few areas of mass communication research that has a long history of identifiable phases with characteristic concerns (McQuail, 1983: 175). Interestingly, current research both on agenda-setting (McCombs and Shaw, 1972) and on media as cultural fora (Newcomb and Hirsch, 1984) has come to suggest a communicative model which allows for the efficacy of media in framing and conditioning the audience response, while recognizing the relative autonomy of audiences, both in the immediate context of use and in other contexts of social action.

Audience constituents

Demographic categories – comprising gender, age, economic status, political affiliation, and other background features – characterize audiences in relation to entrenched social *institutions*, and may predict the nature and extent of their mass media use. In this respect, the audiences for mass media tend to be well-documented in earlier research. Moreover, characteristics such as cultural activity and organizational affiliation help to explain audiences' perceptions and interpretations of media in both quantitative (Piepe et al., 1975, 1978) and qualitative (Morley, 1980) studies. Recent social-scientific research on 'life styles' represents a further attempt to capture some of the interpretive frames differentiating audiences (Rosengren, forthcoming), whereas Bourdieu's (1984) theory of social tastes suggests a system of correspondences between specific cultural competences and social segments.

The more elusive characteristics of audiences – the *interpretive categories* informing their discursive and practical consciousness, predisposing them to act – have not been documented in the same comprehensive and continuous manner. Traditionally, these categories of experience have been studied in aesthetic and historical disciplines with reference to the texts, artifacts, and other *discourses* of high culture, less so with reference to situated cultural *practices*. Social-scientific and humanistic communication research together have produced much less empirical insight into the practices than into either the institutions or discourses of mass communication. Building on reception studies of interpretive categories relating to social status and gender (for example, Ang, 1985; Hobson, 1982; Morley, 1980; Press, 1991; Radway, 1984; Schlesinger et al., 1992) and to cross-cultural variation (for example, Biltereyst, 1991; Liebes and Katz, 1990; Lull, 1988a), further research is needed to develop comprehensive interpretive typologies complementing the demographic typologies.

Media constituents

The everyday contexts of media use, as noted, increasingly make up integrated *media environments*. The term suggests that the available media set the conditions of cultural practice, by analogy to the natural environment, but in a specific historical and social form. In part because of the difficulties of operationalizing their complexity, media environments have been the object of few studies to date (but see Bennett and Woollacott, 1987; Pearson and Uricchio, 1991; also Kubey and Csikszentmihalyi, 1990). Furthermore, *flow*, or interrelated discourses, may be a distinctive feature of modern mass communication, not just in broadcasting (Ellis, 1982; Williams, 1974; Chapter 7 in this volume), but within and across other media (Jensen, forthcoming). By contrast to earlier cultural forms, such as books, films, theater plays, and performances having a relatively unified message, the audiences for radio, newspapers, magazines, and recorded music typically receive several programs, articles, and compositions.

Individual *media* have been studied extensively, as aesthetic forms of representation, as behavioral stimuli, and, less frequently, as resources in social action. *Genre*, as suggested, offers a strategic, medium level of analysis (Larsen, 1991: 129), integrating social and discursive aspects of communication and implying how particular media discourses may be approached by audiences. Indeed, it is the level of genre conventions, rather than the single artwork with 'aura' (Benjamin, 1977), which must be the primary concern in research on mass communication and popular culture, even if reception studies necessarily address specific texts as exemplary instances of genres. In a few cases, because of their social impact, single media *texts* call for case studies, as in mass-mediated public spectacles (Halloran et al., 1970; Lang and Lang, 1953) or media events (Dayan and Katz, 1987), the classic example being Orson Welles' 1938 radio production of the *War of the Worlds*, which reportedly produced a panic among listeners (Cantril, 1940).

Finally, some studies particularly of recall and of the socializing impact of media have taken *discursive elements* as their media constituent. While addressing one basic aspect of reception, the approach tends to assume that the meaning of elements is stable across different media discourses and contexts of use. Social semiotics emphasizes further research on genre, flow, and media environments as cultural resources whose relevance and meaning are tied to their context of use.

Analytical constituents

While methods of data *collection* and *analysis* commonly go together in pairs, it is nevertheless instructive to consider their respective emphases. Regarding data *collection*, the *survey* interview remains probably the predominant instrument of mass communication research, notwithstanding meter systems in television (Ang, 1991). Premised on an unambiguous relationship between the verbal form of questions and the meaning that different informants take from them (Hyman, 1954: 192; Miller, 1991: 163), survey research is well-suited to address the aspects of reception that are already discursively articulated, sociocentral, and relatively uncontroversial. *Experimental studies*, further, have uncovered fundamental regularities of communication, comprehension, and action, within a controlled set of conditions, with reference to carefully orchestrated variations of the audience characteristics, signs, and contexts of mass communication (for references, see Lowery and DeFleur, 1988; NIMH, 1982).

The second group of methods, by contrast, explore meanings that are emergent in the cultural practice of mass communication. *Depth interviewing* – also referred to as free, open, focused, qualitative, and informal (Belson, 1968: 18–19) – seeks to document audiences' interpretive procedures with reference to their contextualized categories of understanding, thus tapping the process of articulating meaning. *Participating observation*, next, is suited particularly to examine the social and cultural contexts of reception with reference to several semiotic systems, from statements and silences to artifacts and actions (Morley and Silverstone, 1991; also Ellen, 1984). *Encounters*, further, are group interactions, as employed in product development in the preview houses of American television networks (Gitlin, 1983) and socalled 'confrontations' between producers and audiences in Scandinavian broadcasting – a neglected method that I elaborate in Chapter 6.

Records, finally, also present discourses with a bearing on reception, as argued by Gripsrud (1994) regarding letters from audience members to media institutions and public debates on the social purpose and cultural quality of mass communication. Reception analysis, having reemphasized the relevance of interviewing and observation in interpretive audience studies, may thus broaden its scope as comparative discourse analysis.

The discourses of research lend themselves to three main forms of data *analysis*. First, *coding*, as developed in social-scientific communication research, assumes that different signs, or codes, may be assigned to units of meaning whose recurrence across audience and media discourses is then measured and processed through quantification. Despite much confrontation since Kracauer's (1953) attack on Berelson's (1952) conception of discourse as "a closed, segmented object with determinate, composite meanings" (Larsen, 1991: 122), coding is an indispensable, efficient method that documents discursively articulated aspects of semiosis. Second, a form of literary, empathetic, or *thematic exegesis* has frequently been presented, from Barthes (1957/1973) to Fiske (1987), as an alternative to coding. Third, in Chapter 8, I argue that linguistic *discourse analysis* offers, not so much an alternative as a systematic complement to coding that may fill in the analytical deficit in current qualitative reception studies.

5

The Politics of Polysemy:
Context Constituents of
Social Semiotics

News may be the prototypical genre of modern mass communication. By disseminating political, commercial, and other information to the general public, and by enabling that public to engage in reflexivity about society, the news media potentially contribute to the democratization of knowledge beyond the narratives and rituals of traditional societies. Symbolizing as well as serving new political practices from the eighteenth century onwards, the news genre thus offers a lowest common denominator for public debate, providing to the ordinary citizen, in Robert Park's (1940) terms, an 'acquaintance-with' events and issues that modern science produces 'knowledge-about.'

This chapter presents a study examining the use value of present-day American television news from the audience perspective. Currently identified in polls of the US public as the central news medium, television news is a cultural resource with major political uses and implications. The interaction between news and viewers constitutes one step of a communicative process that is also a political practice, and the immediate context of reception implies other contexts of action addressing the political institutions which are centrally located in the news discourse. The study, while emphasizing the audience conception of possible social uses of television news, also analyzes the visual and verbal discourses of American television news and their background in the institutions of a particular media system.[1] The comparative analysis of media and audience discourses suggests that, whereas television news stories are polysemous, that is, open to various legitimate and pleasurable interpretations by the audience, the reception of news is subject to a specific form of polysemy that bears witness to a divided form of everyday consciousness arising from contradictions at the level of social institutions. It is the polysemy of reception, I submit, that should be studied in order to assess empirically the political promise of the news genre.

In terms of the methodological constituents of social semiotics, the study focuses on the *decoding* of the television news genre as a *resource* for political and other social action by audiences differentiated by *socioeconomic* status, as documented and analyzed through *depth interviewing* and *discourse analysis*. The discussion of findings emphasizes the contextual aspect of how news relates to political practices and institutions in the eyes of its audiences.

Polysemy and the politics of research

Polysemy of reception

At the beginning of the 1990s, academic research on culture and communication had reached a juncture at which the critical faculties and sensibilities of the mass audience came to be celebrated. The accumulating evidence on the decoding of media content increasingly has been taken to imply that audiences appropriate and transform meaning for their own ends. Yet, whether audiences may be resistant to the mass-mediated constructions of reality and thus presumably to any ideological impact of mass communication is a question that needs to be critically reexamined. As argued by Schudson, "The fact that audiences respond actively to the materials of mass culture is important to recognize and understand, but it is not a fact that should encourage us to accept mass culture as it stands or popular audiences as they now exist" (1987: 66).

The empirical findings below suggest that socalled 'oppositional decodings' of news texts, for example, are not in themselves a manifestation of political power in any relevant sense. The wider ramifications of opposition at the discursive level depend on the social and political uses to which opposition may be put in contexts beyond the relative privacy of media reception. For analytical purposes, this entails moving beyond the decoding of individual texts and focusing on genres, their historical origins and designated social uses. A genre is both a conventional form of expression and a means of situating the audience in relation to a particular subject matter (Williams, 1977: 183), thus implying its relevance as political information, cultural event, pastime, and so on. In the case of news, it is important to ask whether the implied political relevance of the information is accepted or negated by viewers, and whether they establish other forms of relevance. I argue below that several such relevances coexist in the reception of television news in a form that articulates a contradictory form of everyday consciousness. The political implications of polysemy appear from a comparative analysis of the discourses of news and those of its audiences.

Polysemy of media discourses

The concept of 'polysemy' refers to the interpretive scope of media texts, the argument being that several interpretations coexist as potentials in any one text, and may be actualized differently by different audiences, depending on their interpretive conventions and cultural backgrounds. Drawing, in part, on the seminal work of Bakhtin (1981) on 'heteroglossia,' and of Volosinov (1929/1973) on 'multiaccentuality,' Fiske (1986, 1987) has argued that polysemy is the source not only of the popularity and pleasure of watching television, but of a progressive political potential, as well. While emphasizing the active role of television audiences, Fiske focuses attention on the discursive structures of media that may explain different interpretations. Television discourse, he suggests, must be polysemic in order to be popular with a heterogeneous mass audience, and he supports his point with some insightful readings of television programs. In addition, whereas the pleasure of reception may work either as a "motor of hegemony" or as an essential component of "the ability to shake oneself free from its constraints" (Fiske, 1987: 234), "its typical one is the playful pleasure that derives from, and enacts, that source of all power for the subordinate, the power to be different" (p. 236). The conclusion, then, is that television discourses are not only potentially, but tendentially, progressive in political terms because they provide audiences with the means to resist the dominant social order still implied by the media. It is the constitutive polysemy that enables audiences to move beyond what may have been "the preferred reading" (Hall, 1973) in order to construct their own alternative reading. In sum, polysemy might be an inherently political concept, and reception in itself could thus be a political act of resistance.

Fiske (1987) is careful to qualify his argument in various ways, lest he be thought to overestimate what might be a "pseudo-power" (p. 318). Still, although it is certainly true that "social or collective resistance cannot exist independently of 'interior' resistance, even if that is given the devalued name of 'fantasy' " (p. 318), this makes fantasy a necessary, but not a sufficient, condition of social change. When Fiske deduces the further point that "paradoxically, diversity of readings may best be stimulated by a greater homogeneity of programming" (p. 319), he implies a defense of whatever programming proves economically most profitable, thus entrusting cultural policy to market forces. Whereas there may be no populist intention behind the argument, the analysis tends to lose sight of the forest of political implications amidst all the polysemic trees. In fact, I know of no research evidence that supports Fiske's conclusion, because most reception studies have not been comparative, and have most often focused on programs that have been popular in market terms.

It is surprising to find, a few pages later, that a very different argument applies to reception in the context of developing nations:

> A lot more work needs to be done on the international reception of both news and entertainment programs and ways that the developed nations can help the less developed to produce their own cultural commodities that can genuinely challenge Hollywood's in the arena of popular taste rather than that of political or economic policy. (Fiske, 1987: 323)

While more international research certainly is needed, and while the tribute to cultural specificity elsewhere is always a nice gesture, it is not clear why the subcultures of the socalled 'developed nations' do not need "their own cultural commodities," but are well served by those of Hollywood. Theoretical inconsistency may be the first casualty of the wars over political correctness (Levy, 1992). Ultimately, even if popular cultural forms may offer sources of resistance, in part because of their polysemic structure, the implications of polysemy need to be assessed by social standards. Resistance is always resistance by someone, to something, for a purpose, and in a context.[2]

News as a political genre

The news audience is addressed as recipients of factual information, primarily about the political process and economic matters. The specific relevance of this information, however, may be conceived in two different ways. On the one hand, the news discourse can be thought of as a narrative or *exposition* that reports particular political events and issues as a way of keeping the audience up to date as citizens and voters. In this respect, news works as an agent of representative democracy, documenting as well as legitimating this specific form of political life as a working reality.

On the other hand, news may be seen as a *resource* for the audience in a different, participatory form of democracy. At least ideally, the information can become the basis of political intervention, an ideal anticipated by the political revolutions of the Western world (Habermas, 1962/1989; Schudson, 1978), and surviving today in the rhetoric of much political discourse and some social theory. If audiences do not perceive news as a specific resource for political awareness and action, then, arguably, the legitimacy of the political process and its institutions is called into question. It is these social implications of news which make it a central political genre, communicating in and about a particular historical context.

Methodology

A total of twelve news programs and twenty-four interviews were recorded in a metropolitan area of the Northeastern United States during three randomly selected weeks in the fall of 1983. On a given night, a particular news program was recorded, and on the following day the recording was shown to two respondents individually, who subsequently were interviewed individually. Since one aim of the analysis was to explore the profiles of public and commercial TV news as perceived by viewers, the newscasts comprise an equal number of programs from a network, a local commercial station, and a local public station. One further aim was to reassess the finding of research on news recall that different socioeconomic groups approach news with different competences (Katz et al., 1977; Tichenor et al., 1970), asking also whether the social uses of news are perceived differently by specific audiences. The sample drawn from a local university directory constitutes two groups of twelve male full-time teaching and research staff and twelve males in various service or administrative positions; in order to focus the analysis, gender and age factors were not considered.[3]

Whereas television may not be the main source of news for Americans in terms of information recalled (Robinson and Levy, 1986), it is nevertheless perceived as the most credible and comprehensive source (Roper, Inc., 1985). Moreover, television has become a cultural forum (Newcomb and Hirsch, 1984) in which major social events and issues can be negotiated by the audience. While the respondents go into some detail about individual news stories, this chapter focuses not on the decoding of stories as expositions, but on the viewers characterization of television news as a resource of everyday and political life. Taking the particular program as a point of reference, each interview followed a semi-structured guide that had been constructed with the assumption, shared by critical and mainstream research (Blumler, 1979; Holzer, 1973), that media have at least three different relevances for recipients. First, media may be a source of information and a means of surveillance of the social context, suggesting a course of action, or at least a readiness for action. Second, media may be a source of social identity or self-legitimation, providing a sense of belonging to a community, (sub)culture, or political order. Third, media are a means of entertainment or diversion, offering relief for anxiety and escape from boredom.

Discourses of news reception

Qualitative audience research approaches the reception of mass communication as a *process* in which meaning is actively negotiated and constructed. The verbatim interview transcripts, totaling about 800 single-spaced pages, can be thought of as the discourses by which the respondents constructed their conceptions of the news genre. Specifically, the process of making sense can be traced in the linguistic details of the interview discourse. Linguistic discourse analysis has particular relevance for mass communication research (see Chapter 8 in this volume), offering a systematic approach to the analysis of qualitative data. Thus, discourse analysis may avoid some constraints of formal content analysis, while at the same time establishing some characteristic linguistic structures in a relatively large interview material.

Whereas a variety of phonetic, grammatical, and semantic features may be taken as keys to the analysis, it is the *pragmatic* level of linguistic description that is particularly relevant for the present study. Drawing on speech-act theory (Austin, 1962; Searle, 1969) and functional linguistics (Halliday, 1973), pragmatic analysis focuses on the *uses* of language in discourse, examining how people interact in everyday conversation and other social contexts, including mass communication (Coulthard and Montgomery, 1981; Crystal and Davy, 1969; Halliday, 1978; Leech, 1983; van Dijk, 1985). In reception interviews, it is especially rewarding to establish the central arguments of the respondent, their interrelations in the context of the whole interview, as well as the substantiations and implicit assumptions that are taken by the respondent to support the arguments. In linguistic terms, the three major analytical categories are coherence, presuppositions, and implicit premises. Below, the interview data are reported, first of all, with reference to the linguistic categories, which are exemplified with specimen analyses. In the following sections, the audience uses of television news, as they emerge in the interview discourses, are categorized and interpreted further.

Coherence

Everyday talk produces more or less coherent discursive universes, and the precise form of coherence (Arndt, 1979; Halliday and Hasan, 1976; van Dijk, 1977) bears witness to what may be inconsistencies with social implications. One may test the respondents' generalizations concerning their media use with reference to the examples they introduce to support the generalizations. For example, asked whether he would be more inclined to also watch the news if he were watching the program immediately preceding it, an assistant professor of comparative literature says:

No. I don t think so, because I have a real thing. When I was living at home my sister is one who just always has some appliance on, and I really, something deep in me, I really dislike that, so that, no, if I get up, and if the first story didn t catch me, or maybe even if I was done with that program I'd turn it off and not keep it on just because it had been on the hour before.

The respondent here begins to project an image of himself as a rational, goal-oriented viewer. The initial "no" as well as the summarizing "so that [no]" signal his generalized self-conception, namely, that he does not watch television as a flow, but individual programs, which he contrasts with his sister's media use. However, the two examples that are employed to substantiate this self-report are quite dissimilar. In some cases, it is hastily added, he may just turn off the set when a program is over, but his initial suggestion in the first if-clause is that the appeal of the first news story may be the determining factor. The implication is that this professor may also watch television and its news programs as a flow.

Elsewhere the same respondent emphasizes that he will not turn to television as a major source of information, watching it only very "occasionally" and "selectively." Still, the relevance of newsviewing as a *habit* emerges several times:

[...] if I was there alone, you know, I would very often maybe turn it on while I make dinner or was eating dinner or something like that.

The implication appears to be that, for this respondent, newsviewing is, above all, a habit of everyday life with certain contextual uses.

Presuppositions

In some cases, the respondents also advance concrete definitions of the news genre. Such definitions sometimes emerge in the presuppositions (Culler, 1981; Garner, 1971; Leech, 1974) of the interview discourse. A presupposition is what is taken for granted and not otherwise elaborated in the coherence of an argument. Presuppositions "are what must be true in order that a proposition be either true or false" (Culler, 1981: 111). Talking about the time at which the news is broadcast, a printer finds it convenient:

[...] it's a good time just to sit there while you're still kind of hyped up from the work, from the busy workday, and you get in and you see the news, and then you, after that you, whether you relax or you decide to go out, you did get that news in, right along with *the rest of the workday*. (emphasis added)

Newsviewing is categorized as something belonging to the various daily duties of the workday. It is an activity which must be attended to before one can "relax" or "go out." The fixed news times could, then, be seen as rather convenient because, as the same respondent says later on, "there's the news right there before you get a chance to do anything else." Newsviewing has its place in the context of evening life and constitutes a habit within a daily routine. Compared to the literature professor above, however, this respondent emphasizes that the news genre in particular allows him to perform a social *duty*. Being a newsviewer, he is able to exercise his responsibility as a citizen.

Implicit premises

In other cases, the premises on which an argument is based are not manifest
in the interview discourse. Instead, a premise may be implicit but deducible
from the statement-in-context, or from the very fact that the statement is
made. Everyday conversation is permeated by such premises, and they are
variously referred to as 'expectations' (Leech, 1974) and 'pragmatic presuppositions' (Culler, 1981). Conversation is made possible by the assumption
that speaker and hearer will attempt to cooperate and, further, that the hearer
can be expected to reconstruct the speaker's premises (Grice, 1975). From an
analytical perspective, it is necessary to establish the implicit premises in
order to identify the points made by the respondents. For example, in the
interview with the printer above, he was asked whether he would have liked to
see some other pictures or news items in the program he had just watched, but
he finds nothing to criticize in this respect: "If it didn't happen for that day, I
can't really think of any outside thing that I would really wanna see." Since
the first clause is conditional, it does not in a technical sense presuppose that
nothing else happened on that day. Still, the clause makes the point that presumably whatever is in the news is what has happened. In addition, the clause
appears to make the point that the news should concentrate on day-to-day
occurrences, adding the notion of timeliness to the notion of news as something which has ostensibly happened. According to this argument, ultimately
news is news, and hence it is difficult to imagine "any outside thing" that
should be included. The news may be conceived, then, as a naturalized element of everyday consciousness.

   Summing up the findings of the discourse analysis, one can say that the
structures of coherence, presupposition, and implicit premises are the linguistic 'media' by which the respondents reconstruct their conceptions of the news
genre. It is true, of course, that the discourses do not derive from the natural
viewing context, and should be interpreted accordingly. However, since the
object of analysis was not the recall of information under everyday circumstances, but rather the audience conception of the news genre as such, the
interview data suggest a categorization of the news as received.

The social uses of television news

The term 'uses' is introduced here to refer to that broad range of social, famil-
ial, and individual relevances which viewers ascribe to news and other media
genres. It goes beyond most formulations of uses-and-gratifications research
(Blumler and Katz, 1974; Rosengren et al., 1985) by insisting that not just the
origin, but also the gratification of communicative needs through media use is
a complex process that is embedded in a specific social setting and cultural
context. In his reconception of media uses and gratifications, Lull (1980)
showed how the immediate context of use in the family setting comes to shape
the reception of mass communication. The characteristic contextual uses of
different program categories, however, as well as the wider political and

cultural relevances of specific genres, have been given less attention in previous audience studies.

Contextual uses

Media are, in several respects, integrated elements of their context of use, not least in the family environment, where they serve to punctuate daily life (for example, Hobson, 1980; Lull, 1988a; Modleski, 1984; Moores, 1993; Silverstone, 1994). The present interviews show that television news may play a special role in this respect, being scheduled at the juncture between the workday and the free time of evening. The respondents repeatedly note that newsviewing and cooking or eating are parallel activities that sometimes interfere with each other. As suggested by the literature professor above, however, the activities may be thoroughly integrated as elements of one routine. An ice-hockey coach who is only at home and thus able to watch the news for part of the year describes this period as an occasion for being together with his wife as well as watching the news:

> [...] in the springtime, sometime, a lot of times we sit in the living-room. We have a nice table, then we just sit on the floor and eat dinner and then watch the news, but there will be times when we start talking about one of our own happenings that happened here in the course of the day, and before you know it you've missed 5 minutes or 6 minutes of the news.

At the same time, it comes out that family members do not have an equal opportunity to watch the news, because the gendered roles and relations of power in the family also apply to media uses. This respondent, for one, is well aware that he is more likely to watch the news than is his wife:

> [...] we will be cooking dinner and I'm constantly [laughs], hold on a second, I'm gonna run in here and watch it, not while eating but while she may be making it. I'm the one who'll sneak away because she's more in charge of making the food. I help out and stuff.

Newsviewing may, then, be seen as inscribed into the roles and routines of family life; it is an integrated element of the evening context in the home. Simultaneously, news is labeled as a particularly important or privileged form of communication. Several respondents mention that they will make a special effort to be able to concentrate on the news. An assistant professor of astronomy describes how he will very often read a book while listening to the stereo and watching television with the sound turned off. He emphasizes, however, that he does not do this for news, which he categorizes as a contrast to "run-of-the-mill television shows" or "background." Similarly, a professor of drama finds that he tries to schedule evening appointments after eight o'clock, so that he seems to "organize my life around the news moments on television."

It is further striking that the scheduling of news is accepted by the respondents as natural. There are no arguments, for example, that the evening news might be scheduled differently, fitting news to everyday life rather than vice versa. A professor of music who frequently travels across the country has noted that the daily rhythms associated with news times in other regions are very different, but asked whether he prefers what he finds in his home region, he says: "Well, I'm just used to it, I don't know I have [laughs] [...]."

Moreover, news is normally available several times during an evening from different channels, so that viewers have a choice of times. Particularly the stations affiliated with the Public Broadcasting System tend to broadcast their own news program at a different time than the commercial stations, and then in a different format. While several respondents praise the news of the public station in the area as well as the MacNeil–Lehrer network program for their depth and background, they nevertheless suggest that they will not specifically choose these programs over the commercial news programs. Some respondents mention that despite their preference in principle for in-depth news such as *The MacNeil–Lehrer Newshour*, they do in practice watch the news programs of the commercial stations, which are broadcast simultaneously with the MacNeil–Lehrer program. Other respondents explain that they may watch news from the public station in the area if they are already tuned to this channel. One professor of English literature describes his context in the following way:

> [...] I would be watching, oh, say, *Great Performances* or something like that between 9 and 10, and then at 10 o'clock that, that news program, it would probably if, you know, if I were in a weakened moment [laughs], probably continue to hold my interest and I would watch it through [...].

In a similar vein, an accountant describes his viewing of the public news program thus:

> [...] usually a movie or a sporting event goes from like 9 to 11, so if it's halftime or something of a football game I might turn over and watch it.

In both cases the upshot is that television, including news programs, tends to be watched as a flow (Ellis, 1982; Williams, 1974). Since the commercial channels dominate the spectrum, or super-flow, of American television, they also tend to dominate the flow of viewing. (See Chapter 7 on the reception of television flow.) While the news programs from the public station thus are praised for their quality, not least by the professorial group of respondents, this quality may not motivate an actual choice. Still, the respondents insist that the quality of information is decisive: news presumably has a range of specific informational uses.

Informational uses

One may define the informational aspect of news, in preliminary terms, as factual knowledge of political issues and events that is relevant to viewers in contexts of social action. The respondents substantiate the relevance of television news in this respect with the argument, first, that one needs the information in one's roles as a consumer, employee, and, above all, a citizen and voter, and second, that it is necessary to check this vital information, both over time and with reference to several media.

As far as the argument regarding 'checking' is concerned, the respondents find it difficult to present any concrete examples of issues about which they might have to verify information. Instead, they support their argument with lists of general areas of news coverage as well as further lists of the news media that they read, watch, or listen to as a matter of habit. Having argued that one should always rely on more than one source and, further, that he does do so for the day-to-day coverage of some issues, a security assistant exemplifies the issues thus:

> I don't know, maybe, there's always the political issues and the economic issues, and they run hand in hand usually, I guess, too, though. Social issues.

Furthermore, discussing whether, in fact, they ever get conflicting information from different news media, the respondents find it difficult to point to concrete examples, and they do not focus on the conflicts or take them as the point of departure for consciously preferring one medium. This response serves to question the validity of the standard opinion polls on news media (Roper, Inc., 1985), which start from the assumption that audiences evaluate the news media consciously with reference to such conflicts. A professor of English finds that, rather than choosing one account, "I'd just leave it until I got more evidence," and in response to whether he would, then, seek more evidence, he says:

> I would probably seek more evidence. You've got, it's kind of an interesting idea that, that two news, news sources, two, two medias who are in conflict in their reporting. It would be kind of interesting to see how, you know, how it works out, how it comes out.

After the initial generalization that he would "probably" seek more evidence, the second sentence carries the implicit premise that the issue is not just interesting, but new to him. The more interesting point is that at least this professor is only concerned about the quality of information in an abstract sense; in practice, he would not be likely to seek more evidence. The lexical choices are significant, in that "evidence" is something that one might "get," just as a conflict is something which "works out" and "comes out," rather than something which is actively resolved. The further political implication is that the respondents' reference to several news sources is a way of proving their competence as a political subject or, in other words, a democratic ideal rather than an actual practice of everyday media use. Asked what he would do about conflicting information, a professor of music spontaneously responds: "[laughs] You mean besides chuckle?"

These arguments raise additional questions of why, for what purpose, viewers might want to check their information and why, in practice, they do not. As the interviews turn to specific social uses of the information, the respondents suggest what appears to be a basic ambiguity of news reception. On the one hand, news is indeed categorized as an instrument or resource for political dialogue and action. On the other hand, the political uses of news which are brought up primarily have to do with a general form of political awareness between elections, or voting information, rather than any active participation in the political process. Addressing this ambiguity of news and politics, the respondents express both frustration and embarrassment. For example, an assistant professor of economics notes that the editorials of news broadcasts can be points of entry for the public into political debate, an opportunity which, however, does not materialize:

> [...] sometimes I see one of those and I think, I could make a much more balanced or, you know, what I think is a desirable view, point of view on that issue, but I don't do it. I mean, and it could be done, but I don't do it [laughs].

More fundamentally, the printer feels that in practice the opportunity for political participation has not materialized for him:

> Well, I can vote. As far as taking any further, I don't know. I guess the opportunity will have to arise. Being, you know, I feel I'm just the average person out here [...]. As a young person I always wanted to be in the, you know, the public view, I always, I don't know, my mother and, tried to push me to get into politics, and I, I did at one time wanna be a part of it, and I guess deep in the back of my mind I still want it too, even though I didn't pursue it, but, you know, it still affects me, and I, I'm very, I'm a very vocal person [...].

A discrepancy is evident between the potential and actual relevance of news for this individual in politics. There is no institutionalized precedent or point of access for such social uses of news.

One additional, concrete use of news – in everyday conversation – is frequently mentioned. However, judging from the way that the respondents characterize their conversations about news, their political relevance may be limited, being restrained in two different ways. First, the respondents indicate that they primarily engage in a brief exchange of comments, where "you say, hey, did you see such and such," or "you say, how about so and so," rather than some form of sustained interaction. In this respect, news appears to be different from other genres, so that fictional genres such as soaps or other television series may, in fact, be debated more intensively for the issues they raise than is the case with the explicitly political genre of news. This appears to be because, second, news is delicately political, so that the respondents will refrain from discussion in different contexts, both at social occasions and at work, "where your political opinions can affect you." A video engineer states that he would hesitate to initiate a discussion about issues in the news, and he contrasts this with the relevance of news for forming one's own opinion:

> [...] I watch the news. I just form my own opinion, just for myself. If someone happens to bring up the subject, then I'll, you know, I usually discuss it with somebody if they bring it up. I don't normally, you know, run around asking other people their opinion of the news.

In sum, a tension emerges clearly in the interview discourses between, on the one hand, the active and public uses that are associated with the news genre in a political perspective and, on the other hand, its more limited practical relevance for audiences in terms of "keeping up" with issues for the purpose of conversation or voting in political elections. Interestingly, there is no manifest difference between the two groups of respondents as they articulate their uses of news. The interview discourses vacillate between the two positions and point toward a general contradiction in the social definition of news, which amounts to a polysemy of reception. By reasserting the competence of viewer-citizens as political agents within a specific social order, news audiences implicitly contribute not just to their own self-legitimation, but also to the reproduction and legitimation of the social order as it currently exists. Such legitimating uses of news emerge as a constitutive feature of the news experience.

Legitimating uses

It is commonly assumed that the media have a personal identity function (Blumler, 1979), providing a point of reference for self-reflection. The respondents specify that, in the case of news, the media address the recipients' *social identity*. Newsviewing is not so much a way of exploring one's personal identity in the abstract, but an act of situating oneself in relation to a particular range of concrete political concerns. This suggests one mechanism underlying the agenda-setting role of news, which has been identified as a major form of impact by previous research on political communication (McCombs and Shaw, 1977). The experience of checking one's information on current issues over time and with reference to several media may, further, provide an important ingredient of the recipient's political self-conception. According to a professor of communications, "[...] I think that's the democratic ideal, and I try to aspire to that [laughs] [...]."

Elaborating on the political relevance of news for the individual, the respondents rely on the twin concepts of *control* and *distance*. The news may give its audience a sense of control over events in the world that would otherwise appear as distant. This is especially clear in the case of local political matters, which the respondents repeatedly refer to. The professor of communications thus contrasts local news with the "far away" national and international news:

> Sometimes on the local level it's, if you can't do anything about it, at least it's more, it's closer to you, you know, and, you know, you feel like you can do something more about it maybe when it comes to voting or to some other activity.

The important implication here is that, in practice, the local news may not be very different from other news in terms of what the viewer-citizen can control. Instead, it is the *feeling* of control which is crucial, even if "you can't do anything about it." The sense of distance is underscored by other respondents when talking about the mechanisms of political influence. The printer says in this connection:

> [...] anything that would happen in the news that I would have to hear on the news I don't think I could control. If I could, maybe I would have knew about it before it got on the news.

Political events, then, are characterized as distant from the specific concerns of the audience, and the news is not conceived of as a mediator between the realms of politics and everyday life. Rather, the news offers a generalized sense of community, of *contact* rather than control or influence. A computer operator notes that he is normally preoccupied with his own affairs, and that the news provides an occasion to "feel some sort of community with the rest of the people." One important prerequisite for being part of a social or political community is having an awareness of a particular range of issues; in this context the respondents refer to issues ranging from housing to high-school achievement. This recalls the understanding of media as a cultural forum (Newcomb and Hirsch, 1984), offering self-legitimation by enabling viewers to at least ask and be concerned about the same questions.

A news story may, in certain cases, have very concrete implications for the viewer's sense of social identity and integration. A security assistant argues that economic information is relevant to his own life, and refers to a report of high unemployment figures as an example:

> [...] you may be less disgruntled and then keep your job as opposed to being unemployed, if you've got one [laughs]. If you're unemployed and you see those figures, I'd say it might be very depressing personally [...].

The implied premise is that an economic story can bring home to the viewer the pragmatic, socially specific need to become integrated, subordinated, even pacified. Rather than assuming a general political viewpoint on the problems of employment and economy, the respondent appears compelled to focus on basic material issues from a personal perspective, which is thus entrenched in the prevailing social order.

The concept of legitimation is not meant to imply that the respondents unquestioningly accept the legitimacy of the television news medium itself. As indicated below, there are several specific criticisms, for example, of the lack of depth or the "glittering generalities" of local news, as one respondent puts it. As far as the genre of news and the social institutions of politics are concerned, however, there is no argument or implicit assumption that a reform of the news would be relevant as a means of making it serve its purported political function. The argument shared in common is that, in the context of everyday life, television is a convenient mechanism for keeping up with what is, in any event, crucial political information. When an assistant professor is asked repeatedly whether he would change anything in the program he watched, he suggests embarrassment since this is an issue on which he ought to have a critical stand, but does not: "I probably would, but I said that I haven't thought about it. I just haven't thought about it." In the same context, the professor of communications criticizes the drama of news in the form of "fires" and "poor people who're suffering," but asked what one might do about it, he says:

> Oh, I might choose fires myself if my job depended upon it and, you know, in a commercial situation, because, you know, you, you don't work in a vacuum, you work in a system that's controlled by certain factors of economic and so forth [...].

The implied premise here is, first, that news must be dramatic in order to be successful and, second, that the "system" of socioeconomic factors must be taken for granted. Similarly, the ice-hockey coach is willing to accept the fact that especially "high-ranking" people are given access to the news as interviewees since they will "sell the advertising and keep the television going." While the respondents thus hint at alternative social forms of communication that appear conceivable and might even be preferable, they do return to the socio-economic constraints on any change in the news, thus reasserting the limits of the political imagination.

Both groups of respondents give television news high marks for credibility. While survey evidence indicates that viewers with a relatively long education are more likely to also rely on print media and public television for their information (Comstock et al., 1978; Gans, 1979), television news may be perceived generally as the most credible source of news (Roper, Inc., 1985). One professor of music finds that "I do trust the newspapers and the TV to dig out the important facts." It is perhaps more striking that the professors, who have been trained to critically gather information for research purposes, including the professor of communications, characterize television news pictures as direct representation, implying that they may be particularly credible. Thus, the communications professor:

> Sure, you like to see things, you like to see pictures of things that are happening and you think of it as sort of first-hand information [...].

I should emphasize, finally, that the concept of legitimation does not imply that the respondents necessarily endorse the legitimacy of particular political positions. As shown by previous research on the decoding of news (Jensen, 1988a; Lewis, 1985; Morley, 1980), there is a relatively great scope for selective and socalled 'oppositional' interpretations of the individual news stories as *expositions* that may dismiss the dominant or preferred readings. It is in this capacity, as narrative, that the news provides a forum for public issues to be articulated, enabling different audiences to situate their particular concerns in a political perspective. When it comes to the social uses of information, however, these respondents suggest that the news genre is not conceived as a resource in political practice.

Diversional uses

The legitimating and integrative audience uses of television news have led some critical researchers to argue that news is a political form of entertainment (Bogart, 1980; Dahlmüller et al., 1973), a spectacle diverting the attention of the audience, not just from boredom or anxiety, but also from major issues of social conflict and power. From a different theoretical and political position, gratifications research has assumed that, in principle, entertainment might be as relevant a use of the news genre as any other (Levy, 1977; McQuail et al., 1972; Palmgreen et al., 1980).

Questioning these positions, the findings of the present study suggest that because news is defined socially as a political genre, it offers a specific scope for diversional uses. The respondents, to be sure, repeatedly note the importance of an appealing performance of news. An engineer who works in local radio draws the line between "flash," which is excessive, and "sparkle," which to him is a necessary element of the TV news mode of address. Other respondents point to the appeal of "nice, trivial information," and the assistant professor of comparative literature suggests that diversion and pleasure may be integrated aspects of newsviewing; he describes his ideal news program thus:

> It would be more in the direction of something like MacNeil–Lehrer but with more pizzazz to it, with more visuals.

Various qualities of "pizzazz" appear, then, to be an important additional or subsidiary gratification of news reception.

Diversional qualities are especially associated with two aspects of television news. First of all, the respondents emphasize that anchors must have both journalistic competence and personal appeal. A professor of drama, among others, talks at length about the stylistic qualities of the news teams at the various local stations, and a computer operator refers to one variety of happy talk, the banter of the anchorpeople (Altheide, 1976), which leads him to prefer a particular program. Two local female anchors, named Natalie and Liz, are referred to by two respondents, in Freudian slips of the tongue, as Natalie Wood and Liz Taylor. And, a chemistry professor who criticizes at length the "self-conscious" effort of the female anchors to "flirt with the camera" nevertheless likes to look at the "pretty skirts" of the news teams. Recasting the anchors as glamorous objects, rather than subjects of a discourse on politics, the male respondents evidently derive a variety of visual pleasures from watching TV news.

Second, the respondents refer to the visuals of news events as an attraction in their own right. The images offer great variety, and may be used as an occasional diversion from house chores and other work. The diversional aspect of news seems to be interlaced with the contextual uses of television in the home during the early evening. Moreover, the visuals communicate a sense of experiential immediacy which the respondents characterize with such adjectives as pleasing, enjoyable, easy, vivid, and exciting. An accountant sums up the quality as a contrast to print: "it's black and white compared to color."

The sense of immediacy sometimes blends into a sense of reality, particularly in the case of dramatic stories where the visuals carry the narrative. Talking about a story of an airplane which had technical problems before landing, an administrative assistant remembers paying particular attention to the pictures:

> [...] I was looking at the airplane to see if there was any explosion. It turns out that there weren't. [...] I was a little bit curious, interested or curious to find out that it was actually broadcast that way. It could have been a near fatal catastrophe, and it was just, it would have been broadcast on national TV. That would, that caught my attention.

While the main argument in context is that these kinds of pictures should not be broadcast, the underlying premise of the penultimate sentence is that the story was aired *before* it was known whether it would result in a catastrophe.

The implication of "that way" in the preceding sentence is that this was live coverage, which ostensibly it was not. The "mistake" suggests the holding power of the visual narrative.

Whereas the respondents thus refer to inherently aesthetic, pleasurable aspects of the news experience, they nevertheless make a categorial distinction between news and entertainment. The news is distinguished from other, factual and fictional genres which have similar stylistic qualities or which, in certain respects, offer similar types of information, for example talk shows and commercials. An associate professor of engineering notes that news is not "just another" form of entertainment, rather "it's the kind of entertainment that contains some information," and he contrasts it with the "*Dukes of Hazzard*, if you know what I mean." A video engineer establishes the distinction in more absolute terms with reference to his own motives for watching the news: "No, I'm not entertained, I'm informed. I watch to be informed and, like I say, there's really no entertainment there." The implication is that the designated social uses of news and entertainment are different. If nothing else, the distinction between news and other genres is a social fact which is established in reception, and which has specific consequences for the way in which audiences conceive the information as an aspect of everyday life.

Conclusion

Whereas a range of diversional and contextual uses are thus attributed to American television news, the respondents place a particular emphasis on the traditional political relevances of news. The interviews serve to identify a contradiction in the audience definition of 'political relevance.' Even though the concrete information of events and issues is characterized as, in principle, a resource for political participation and action, the respondents' discourse suggests that the central relevance of news be thought of in terms of *legitimation*. Television news provides a daily forum for the viewers' reassertion of their political competence within a representative form of democracy, but it is not conceived as a point of departure for action in relation to the institutions or current organizations of political life. The contradictory nature of news reception bears witness, in a wider perspective, to a divided form of everyday consciousness that derives from contradictions at the systemic level of social organization. On the one hand, the news media are potentially a tool for political influence and change; on the other hand, such social uses of news by the audience-public are not institutionalized, and do not have a precedent in the practice of American politics. It is a contradictory *social* definition of news which manifests itself at the level of media use and audience discourse.[4]

The interviews indicate, moreover, that, at least with respect to the social uses of news, the differences between various socioeconomic groups may be negligible. While earlier research documents major differences between such groups in terms of media consumption as well as their decoding of specific texts, it is plausible that viewer-citizens generally are informed in their uses of news by the dominant social definition and institutional framework of politics.

The reception of television news, accordingly, can be seen as an agent of *hege-mony* which serves to reassert the limits of the political imagination. As the theoretical literature on hegemony argues (Gramsci, 1971; Sallach, 1974; Williams, 1977), even though the social production of meaning may be seen as a process in which the prevailing definition of reality can be challenged and revised, the conditions of that process are established within particular historical and institutional frameworks of communication. The polysemy of mass media discourses is only a political potential, and the oppositional decoding of mass communication is not yet a manifestation of political power.

Reception studies, to some degree, can contribute to articulating the political and cultural interests of the audience-public. Though the conclusions of the present study apply to American television news, it carries the general implication that neither the availability of political information nor a particular level of formal education will ensure substantive social uses of news. Beyond the availability of political information, an institutionalized system of public access to the means of communication would be a constitutive element of a participatory political system, also in any 'information society' to come. And beyond formal education, which traditionally has focused on print literacy, a broader form of media literacy is presumably required. Since the political process is increasingly conducted through the mass media, popular participation depends on a new functional literacy comprising critical comprehension skills as well as concrete production skills (Masterman, 1985). Ultimately, only the audience-public can insist on the substantive uses of media, both within the political system and in other areas of social practice, by transcending the ambiguous role of recipient. As they currently exist, the news media do not realize their potential, as stated also by the two respondents in the sample who do not follow the news on a daily basis. In response to whether he does not, then, feel left out of society, a professor of physiology says:

> Well, let me ask you, what's the point of keeping up? [laughs]. I mean, you know, the reason for keeping up in many cases is so that you can carry on intelligent conversations about what's going on in the world and so on and, so it's nice to be able to talk to people about what's going on, but I'm not sure that, you know, that that's really critical. I think that it's important that those things which a person feels are important to him, that he should try to find out about them, but most of the things in news are not things that I think are important to me.

6

Television Futures: Audience Constituents of Social Semiotics

Do mass media audiences, after all, constitute potential political and cultural publics that share a common interest in particular forms of media content and particular ways of organizing the institutions of communication? If so, do the predominant methodologies of mass communication research help to articulate audience interests in a form which could serve as feedback to communicators, regulators, and to the publics themselves?

While a great deal of research refers to the audience as a 'public' (McQuail, 1987: 219), methodologies are not normally designed to empower audiences in any political or other social context. This is due, in part, to a restricted theoretical conception of audience studies. The purpose of much previous research – both in the commercial and in the academic sector – has been to explain audience behavior in terms of demographic and, to different degrees, social-psychological variables, rather than to explore the interpretive participation of audiences in social communication processes, or to elicit actual audience assessment of media. As a result, research has failed to tap significant audience perspectives on the mass media, including possible alternative forms of mass communication. This chapter presents a methodology for exploring audience interests and an empirical study addressing its explanatory value.

The empirical study focuses on the context constituent of *gratifications sought*, on the audience constituent of *age* and its associated interpretive categories, and on the television *medium* as such, employing the analytical constituent of an *encounter* session, which is specified below with reference to the methodology known as 'workshops on the future.' The resulting data are documented and interpreted in the categories of *discourse analysis*.

From interpretive communities to interpretive repertoires

The concept of interpretive communities has become a focal point for research debates on a discursive, interpretive conception of mass media audiences (Lindlof, 1988). The issue, in summary, is the precise sense in which audience segments may be understood as 'communities,' constituted primarily through a predisposition to generate meaning through similar interpretive acts. The implication is that interpretation, broadly speaking, is a form of social action which articulates a specific orientation toward the social reality being represented, and interpretation thus can be said to express interests of an ultimately political and cultural nature. Lindlof (1988), for one, calls for a comparative analysis of genres of content with what he calls 'genres of interpretation' and 'genres of social action.'

While the notion of interpretive communities originates from Peirce and pragmatism, current studies of mass communication frequently credit Stanley Fish (1979) as the source of the argument in its radical form, namely, that the readers, not the texts, are the source of all (literary) meaning. In a response to his critics, Fish (1989: chap. 7) has summarized his position as a solution to the classic problem of interpretive authority: those who see the text as the final arbiter of meaning are embarrassed by the fact of disagreement, while those who see the reader as the final arbiter are embarrassed by the fact of agreement. To Fish, the notion of an interpretive community solves the problem by transcending it:

> What was required was an explanation that could account for both agreement and disagreement, and that explanation was found in the idea of an interpretive community, not so much a group of individuals who shared a point of view, but a point of view or way of organizing experience that shared individuals in the sense that its assumed distinctions, categories of understanding, and stipulations of relevance and irrelevance were the content of the consciousness of community members who were therefore no longer individuals, but, insofar as they were embedded in the community's enterprise, community property. It followed that such community-constituted interpreters would, in their turn, constitute, more or less in agreement, the same text, although the sameness would not be attributable to the self-identity of the text, but to the communal nature of the interpretive act. (1989: 141)

It is crucial, however, to note that Fish's further aim is not the study of actual communities with social and historical identities, but rather the deconstruction, on theoretical and epistemological grounds, of any notion of a 'correct' reading of texts and, by implication, a debunking of the idea that professionals in different domains may arrive at some Olympian truth of the matter. To Fish, then, theory does not provide any privileged position of understanding or reflexivity. Indeed, theory has no consequences for practice (Fish, 1989: 14), and, hence, there is no place of insight outside of practice. His alternative is not to engage in, for example, advocacy research, but to question the grounds of scientific research as such. Fish shares this inflection of interpretive communities, and of pragmatism as anti-foundationalism, with Richard Rorty (Chapter 11). In the present context, it is sufficient to note that Stanley Fish stops short of the kind of theoretical and methodological specification that might make the framework relevant for studies of culture and communication or other domains of research, staying instead within the discursive loops of epistemological doodling.

Specification of the category of interpretive communities has been provided in other research, notably Janice Radway's (1984) study of romance readers. She explicitly notes Fish's work as a major source of inspiration, while referring also to work in sociolinguistics as being compatible with the notion of interpretive communities (Radway, 1984: 242–3). Radway's informants qualify as a community also in a classic sociological sense, because they make up a network of actual individuals interacting around a bookstore, newsletter, and what another research tradition would label an opinion leader (Katz and Lazarsfeld, 1955). The more difficult question is how to delimit such interpretive formations for empirical study, theoretically and methodologically, when it comes to the more numerous audiences that are not even informally organized.

An alternative conception of the relationship between social and interpretive categories of analysis has been outlined in the context of social psychology by Potter and Wetherell (1987). Criticizing the theory of 'social representations' developed by Moscovici, the authors note that the fundamental premise of this theory, namely, that social groups are constituted by their shared social representations, leads into "a vicious circle of identifying representations through groups, and assuming [that] groups define representations" (p. 143). In the terminology of reception analysis, the premise would be that demographic segments correspond to a specific subset of interpretive procedures, which in their turn serve to identify demographic subsegments. The implication of a neat, one-to-one relationship may be theoretically attractive, but empirically unjustified. More likely, the mapping of demographic and interpretive categories onto each other is highly complex, and it is not justified to define reception from the outset in terms of the stable structure implied by 'communities.'

Potter and Wetherell (1987), drawing on research about the discourses that different scientific communities employ in debating findings and theories, introduce the concept of interpretive repertoires to allow for complexity: "Rather than make the somewhat unlikely assumption that *all* these people – biochemists, social scientists, and lawyers – are members of the same social group, it is much more fruitful to accept that repertoires are available to people with many different group memberships [...]" (p. 156). The point is that particular interpretive repertoires may or may not be available to different demographic segments, and the specific combination of interpretive repertoires with social background variables is, in any event, a matter for empirical inquiry (see also Schrøder, 1994). Over the last three decades, for example, sociolinguistics has begun to document major social variations in language use (van Dijk, 1985). For interpretive communication studies, equally, there is no way around the long empirical haul.

Methodologies and knowledge interests

The different methodologies for studying audience interpretive repertoires and interests may be reassessed in the light of their specific philosophical legacies. The modes of inquiry which predominate within various scientific fields and traditions are characterized by different constitutive 'knowledge interests' (Habermas, 1968/1971). The term suggests that any scientific analysis is a means of generating knowledge that always already implies the social interests informing the subsequent applications of knowledge. Scientific research, being a social practice, bears witness to the premises and purposes of science in a particular historical context.

Habermas (1968/1971) distinguishes three forms of knowledge interest in the modern sciences.[1] First, in the natural sciences, the purpose of inquiry generally has been that of technical *control through prediction*. This understanding emphasizes that, by developing criteria for predicting natural phenomena and processes, modern science has been able to control the natural environment to an unprecedented degree. This control makes possible extensive social planning through the management of resources, notably in agriculture and industrial production.

Second, the purpose of scholarship within the humanities traditionally has been one of *contemplative understanding*. This is the scientific domain covering philosophy and the arts, addressing, among other matters, existential issues facing the individual. In many ways, the purposes of humanistic inquiry, focusing on the private sphere, are complementary to the public purposes of natural science.

Third, the knowledge interest of the social sciences can be traced to several origins. Being a product of the late nineteenth and early twentieth centuries, contemporary social science has drawn its notions of scholarship from both the natural sciences and the humanities. This legacy helps to explain a number of the fundamental divisions within social science disciplines, the paradigmatic case being the distinction between quantitative and qualitative forms of analysis. Nevertheless, Habermas suggests that different types of social-scientific inquiry share a common knowledge interest, namely, emancipation. The purpose of social-scientific inquiry, accordingly, is one of *critique* that seeks to identify emerging alternatives to the prevailing forms of social organization. Social-scientific critique does not imply advocacy of specific positions, stipulating *what should be*, only reflexivity exploring *what might be*. Social science thus might serve as a public forum for the social imagination.

Whereas the three forms of knowledge interest are ideal types, subject to variation in scientific practice, Habermas emphasizes the extent to which the natural-scientific, technical variety has come to inform also the study of social phenomena. One characteristic feature of the contemporary social-scientific mainstream is that it generates knowledge facilitating predictive control over social agents and institutions. In mass communication research, such a technical knowledge interest is most evident in studies that broadcasters and advertisers use to predict the behavior of audiences (Nielsen, 1989). But, a similar conception of audiences has been reflected, for example, in the flowchart models of standard reference works in academic research (Comstock et al., 1978). The purpose is, again, explaining – predicting with a statistical significance – the cognition and action of media users with reference to their demographic characteristics.

The other mainstream of research, rooted in the humanities, can be said to offer a contemplative understanding of media texts as cultural expressions (for overviews, see Fiske, 1987, and Jensen and Rosengren, 1990). Even though the text-centrism of much of this research has limited its explanatory value, frequently leaving the concrete institutions and audiences of mass media to be examined at the level of abstract theoretical analysis, a critical or emancipatory knowledge interest can be seen to underlie classic studies of both media institutions (for example, Gitlin, 1983; Tuchman, 1978) and media content (for example, Barthes, 1957/1973; Eco, 1987; Fiske and Hartley, 1978). Such works have identified alternatives to the current organization of mass media as well as alternatives to the dominant construction of social reality in mass media content. Particularly for the critical tradition proposing to articulate audience interests vis-à-vis media that has been central to humanistic communication studies, there would appear to be no way around the empirical audience. As noted by Fejes (1984), however, audiences until recently remained a blind spot of empirical work in the critical tradition. If mass communication research is to contribute a critique of media in the interest of their audiences, it must develop methodologies that engage audiences in a process of reflexivity about the social purposes of mass communication.

A final qualification of critical research is in order, since the relationship beween science and critique is frequently misconstrued. A critical knowledge interest arises *not* from the political stance of individual researchers, but from the procedures and theories guiding their work. Researchers may feel committed to influencing an ongoing political process or supporting particular socioeconomic groups through their work, but such a commitment is not the defining characteristic of a critical knowledge interest, neither a necessary nor a sufficient condition of critical science. The knowledge interest of any given study is, instead, constituted through the practices, institutions, and epistemologies of a specific scientific tradition. Because the exercise of knowledge interests is an inescapable condition of all science, the point is *not* to first establish 'the facts' and then perform a critique with reference to their social implications. What critical researchers *can* do is to make explicit the status and potential applications of the knowledge which their methodologies produce. Workshops on the future produce a form of knowledge which lends itself to social and political uses by the participants.

Workshops on the future

The setting might be the meeting-room in your local library. The time, Saturday afternoon. Your state of mind, lightly euphoric. For more than five hours now, you have been brainstorming with fifteen neighbors about current problems in your local community. The walls around you are covered with large posters that express the group's ideas in words and drawings; the floor is littered with coffee cups, soda cans, and more notepaper. Welcome to a workshop on the future!

Workshops on the future originated as a tool for organizational work in Western European political movements and communities (Jungk and Müllert, 1981). Growing out of grass-roots organizations and labor unions in the Federal Republic of Germany, the technique was developed over the last couple of decades through a dialectic of political practice and theorizing. Recently, some private companies have employed workshops on the future as a group-dynamic method for bringing out and solving problems of organizational communication and structure. Workshops have also been conducted in other cultural contexts, with topics ranging from urban planning to pollution and international détente (Jungk and Müllert, 1981: 17).

A workshop on the future initiates a process of group interaction in order to examine a problem or issue facing the group as a whole. All participants are created equal in the context of the workshop. This means that neither officials nor presumed experts are allowed to set the agenda of debate. The underlying assumption is that socalled 'ordinary citizens,' having expert knowledge of their own problems, collectively may arrive at the most relevant solution to them. From the individual participant's perspective, the workshop offers a context for airing frustrations and criticisms. From a systemic perspective, workshops may function as a Fourth Estate, depending of course on the actual power that is vested in them. Ideally, then, workshops empower people to participate more actively in the social and political processes that lead to decisions affecting them in fundamental ways.

A workshop comprises three interrelated phases, each addressing the theme of the workshop from a specific perspective. A round of all-out *criticism* opens the session, noting everything that participants dislike about the topic (in this case, American television). All statements are written down verbatim on large posters by the workshop leader, who encourages participants to speak out and generally serves as master/mistress of ceremonies. The posters are taped onto the meeting-room walls and remain in view during the entire session. Participants take turns, but each person is only allowed to make brief statements so as to keep ideas flowing from the group as a whole. Crucially, participants are not allowed to debate the pros and cons of a particular viewpoint at this stage, because discussion tends to disrupt the process of elaborating and taking cues from previous criticisms. Moreover, participants are told that criticism need not be 'constructive' or 'responsible.' The aim is to elicit as much and as diverse criticism as possible. As a last step of this first phase, participants select the most important issues, either through discussion or by each assigning points to particular criticisms. These main criticisms are then summarized by the group with reference to general concepts or themes.

The pivotal *utopian* phase starts out by reconsidering the main criticisms and restating them in positive terms. For example, the criticism, "There are too few foreign films on American TV," might be restated as, "There is unlimited access to foreign films on American TV." The aim is to allow the group to consider in detail an ideal state of affairs. Again, individual interventions are not discussed. Participants are asked to disregard any practical limitations – in terms of either economics or technology – as they recommend changes that they would like to occur. As a result, the utopian phase can create an imaginative atmosphere in the group, often producing innovative ideas that draw part of their inspiration from earlier statements by other group members. It is in this phase that participants most keenly feel a group dynamic, which may produce a sense of exhilaration at the prospect of a different future.

Participants again select the most important ideas and formulate them as general themes. The utopian themes lead into a discussion, finally, of what is to be done. Examining possible forms of social *action*, this final phase is the most future-oriented, politically relevant component of a workshop. The social action phase thus entails a concrete discussion of means in relation to ends: Are there any examples of the group's utopia in other cultural or historical contexts? Which aspects of utopia would be realistic ends in the short term? And what are the relevant forms of action in the given context of political, economic, and other social institutions?

The social process that has been initiated by a workshop is not meant to end with the workshop itself. Participants may publish their conclusions, raise funds, lobby, and so forth. Furthermore, it is common to reestablish the workshop from time to time, thus creating a *permanent workshop* where the group can examine new ideas as well as reassert their collective interests. Instead of dissipating within existing institutional frameworks, the insights gained can point to new forms of political practice, as evidenced by many instances of grass-roots and community action (Jungk and Müllert, 1981: 43). In sum, workshops on the future represent a forum of reflexivity regarding public issues, providing a social context that enables participants to reconsider social ends and means.

From social practice to research methodology

The application of the workshop technique as part of a scientific methodology raises two issues concerning validity. First of all, while the technique is reminiscent of focus groups and similar methods (Merton and Kendall, 1955; Mishler, 1986), television audiences, unlike communities and organizations, might not have a shared sense of purpose or identity. Most television addresses viewers as a mass of dispersed and heterogeneous individuals. Nevertheless, the existence of lobby organizations such as Action for Children's Television and Viewers for Quality Television bears witness to the existence of cultural publics with conflicting interests. Newcomb and Hirsch (1984) have suggested that such organizations serve to identify "fault lines" (p. 69) or fundamental issues of American society by questioning the representation of these issues on television.[2] It is likely that audiences generally approach television's representation of these fault lines in accordance with a socially specific set of interpretive strategies.

A second objection to a workshop methodology would question the validity of the resulting data. Traditionally, social science has argued that observational and interview studies should be designed so as to minimize the influence of researchers on respondents and of respondents on each other. The implicit assumption is that studies can tap the experiences and opinions of their subjects in a form that is uncontaminated by the research instruments. Much recent work on validity (for example, Kirk and Miller, 1986; Kvale, 1989) has suggested, instead, that any research instrument represents an intervention that reconstructs the social context being examined. As argued by Lindlof and Anderson (1988) with reference to reception analysis, the best that methodologies may hope to do is to specify the *contexts* in which researchers and respondents interact for various *purposes* through particular *roles*.

One limitation of standardized social-scientific methodologies is a tendency to answer the *how* of a study before addressing *what* and *why* (Kvale, 1987; also Lang and Lang, 1985). The methodologies appear to ossify as standard procedures which are then applied to quite different subject matters and purposes of inquiry. Specifically, the predominant experimental and survey methodologies of the communications field are not suited to capture the audience response to possible alternative forms of social communication. In terms of their knowledge interests, studies thus tend to approach respondents as objects of predictive control responding to already existing programming. By contrast, respondents might engage each other as subjects in examining forms of mass communication that do not yet exist, thus performing a critique of current media. In addition to being a means of gathering data, similar to meters, telephone interviews, and diaries, workshops establish a context of reflexivity that is collective and empowered.

Finally, it might be objected that the workshops are merely a variation on focus groups and other interview methods. Three features, however, distinguish the workshop methodology. First, a workshop is structured primarily according to the three phases, each of which develops its own foci, and the workshop leader, like any other participant, is not allowed to refocus the group process on predefined issues. Second, the third phase, emphasizing action, is oriented toward the future, unlike focus groups, which normally address already developed concepts or programs. Third, and perhaps most important, a workshop raises the possibility of *social* action, in the sense that the initiative is not left to programmers or individual citizens but can be taken by the group as a public. Whereas audience workshops alone could not transform American television, workshops on the future address certain television futures that are not normally encountered in the mainstream of research and public debate.

Methodology

The empirical study examined perceptions of American television among viewers of different age groups. One of the most consistent findings of previous survey research is that the amount of television viewing increases with age (Barwise and Ehrenberg, 1988: 14). Different age groups prefer different types of programming according to the ratings (Nielsen, 1988: 11), and the viewing styles of old and young audiences differ, for example, with respect to 'grazing' (Ainslie, 1988). Research is only beginning to understand, however, how television enters into the daily lives of different age groups and family types (Moores, 1993; Silverstone, 1994).

Moreover, changes in the total configuration of media contribute to longterm changes in the social psychology of nations and communities (Lowe, 1982). For example, as the media have become the central locus of politics, major political figures can be seen to change their conduct in response to new media (Seymour-Ure, 1989). While some earlier work has overstated the transition from a print culture to a visual culture (McLuhan, 1964; Ong,1982;

Postman, 1985), historical evidence suggests that transformations of the communications infrastructure in recent decades have resulted in a qualitatively new form of media environment (for an overview, see Jensen, forthcoming). Individuals' exposure to media has intensified at most times and in most locations (Chambers, 1986). Television has blurred the boundaries between the private and public spheres of everyday life (Meyrowitz, 1985). And new media and genres – from the music video (Kinder, 1984) to computer-based media (Greenfield, 1985; Turkle, 1984) – have entered center stage. The new media environment is likely to be understood in different ways by old and young audiences, who may rely on different interpretive repertoires.

The study, conducted in January of 1989, engaged two groups, each with twelve respondents, who met for one workshop session lasting three hours. Workshops on the future sometimes have a larger number of participants and sometimes last for several days. The small group size was chosen to facilitate interaction. Furthermore, respondents without a special organizational commitment could not be expected to participate in longer sessions, despite a small payment. The groups, representing the age segments below thirty-five and above fifty-five respectively, were selected from the greater Los Angeles area by a local market research company to represent a diversity of socio-economic backgrounds. Each actual group comprised an equal number of women and men, most of whom were white. In occupational terms, both groups consisted primarily of clerical and sales personnel, even though other manual as well as managerial occupations were represented. Most in the older group had retired.

Although media habits were not examined in detail, it should be noted that viewers in this area have access to a wide variety of broadcast and cable television channels. Three in the older group and seven in the younger group subscribed to at least one pay cable service, and two younger respondents had basic cable. All respondents except one in the younger group had videocassette recorders. Supplementing broadcast television in various ways, then, these respondents may be relatively selective consumers of television.

The central object of analysis was the list of statements that had been documented on posters in the course of each workshop. These statements may be conceived as discourses through which each group negotiated a conception of the television medium. All the posters were transcribed verbatim, and the transcripts were subjected to discourse analysis. Unlike formal content analysis employing independent coders and decontextualized analytical categories as part of a quantitative design, discourse analysis seeks to establish the meaning of linguistic features in their discursive context, giving priority to measures of contextual meaning over measures of recurrence. The procedure thus captures the processes of critique and brainstorming that occur during a workshop.

The linguistic form of workshop discourses is relatively simple. Most sentences are simple statements (Leech and Svartvik, 1975: 28), evaluating an aspect of programming. This means that, rather than examining linguistic structure in detail, the analysis of workshop discourses could focus on the participants' concrete formulation of their conceptual categories. Three aspects of discourse, accordingly, were singled out for analysis. First, it was established how the groups characterized positive as well as negative features of television. Such characterizations carry *connotations* (Barthes, 1964/1984a: 89–94), or meanings that imply historically- and culturally-specific perspectives on the world. As such, connotations add up to a conception of social reality. Connotations may be implied by single words, statements, or connected discourse.

Second, a *reconceptualization* of the issues sometimes occurs in the course of a workshop, generating new perspectives on a problem and suggesting, as well, the labile nature of media recipients' conceptual categories, their polysemy. Such recontextualizations can be detected by comparing the various adjectival and substantival references to the problem at hand or its solution. Reconceptualizations may thus imply a reconstruction of social reality.

Third, the possible reforms of television suggested by respondents were noted and compared with traditional concepts of *normative communication theory* (McQuail, 1987: chap. 5; Siebert et al., 1956). The discourse analysis thus leads up to a discussion of the political relevance of the results.

Findings: Television futures

The analytical results are reported in two parts. First, the discourse analysis is summarized. It should be emphasized, however, that counts (for example, of how many times a particular negative connotation recurs) are seldom meaningful. The categories of analysis become relevant for the description of workshop discourses in connection with concrete textual examples. The characteristic functions of the three categories are thus summarized, but their explanatory value appears only from specimen analyses. Second, some illustrative analyses of the statements made in each workshop group are offered. These examples show how ordinary viewers may engage in a critique of television.

Discourses on the future

At the most general level of discourse, the connotations of the statements made during the opening, critical phase of the workshops indicate the range of criticisms that participants direct at television. Negative connotations are associated with both the mix of available programs and the industry practices that shape programming. In the group of younger respondents, for example, criticisms ranged from references to the virtual absence of certain program types ("There's not enough foreign films") to assertions about undue influence ("The sponsors determine programming").

Whereas a negative evaluation may be expressed simply in terms of "not enough" or "too much/many," in other cases a negative connotation is implied by the choice of a verb (or substantive, adjective, or adverb) or through an entire statement or assertion. Such connotations can be understood as pragmatic presuppositions (Culler, 1981) or expectations (Leech, 1974), which give away speakers' basic assumptions. Thus, the choice of "determine" in the example above carries the implication that programming should be decided not by economic interests, but with reference to standards of quality, relevance to the audience, or other substantive criteria. Similarly, in the statement, "The networks copy each other," the verb implies that copying tends to limit the overall diversity of programming.

The younger group also offered this very specific structural criticism: "Programs are increasingly made to be put into syndication." In discursive terms, it is the assertion as a whole – that the influence of syndication on programming is intensifying – which assumes that such influence is already a fact, implying that this is not in the best interest of viewers. In political terms, this form of argument begins to indicate the workshop participants' understanding of television as a social structure.

In selecting and summarizing their most important criticisms, the groups made explicit a set of conceptual categories and interrelations which help to explain the specific connotations. (Each participant had three votes in the phase of critique, and again in the utopian phase, which might be cast either individually or en bloc for one statement.) Through the selection process, the participants can be said to reflect upon a deep structure of assumptions and values which had emerged as connotations in the surface structure of discourse. Discussions in the younger group served to articulate, at first, two concepts that summed up the criticisms receiving the most votes, namely, the organization of television as a business and the repetitive structure of programming. The business concept included criticisms to the effect that television is not an "art form," or that there is "little learning television," whereas repetitiveness summarized criticisms of copying and recycling, particularly of news and commercials. The discussion later linked the two concepts, suggesting that the repetitive content structures are the result of business considerations.

The negotiation of concepts came to the fore in a number of reconceptualizations. In the group of older respondents, concepts were gradually developed and reworked in the last workshop phase, when the prospects for change were considered. During this phase, participants normally are asked first to consider changes that are now, or will soon be, possible. The older group engaged in a lengthy discussion with reference to the concept of "the possible," moving from examples of what is technologically possible to arguments about what would be economically possible (and impossible). The discussion was sparked by a reference to three-dimensional television, an existing technology that may not be profitable in its present form. More important, the group held that a greater diversity of programming, including, for example, live transmission of cultural events, was practically possible, but not economically viable. The workshop, while exploring alternative forms of broadcasting, thus equally identified some of the obstacles to reform.

Reconceptualizations could be detected in the critical and utopian phases, as well. Whereas the younger group extended the concept of viewer choice to suggest that "you [can] pick your own commercials based on needs and wants," the older group proposed that a truly interactive form of communication would include "feedback from every viewer to every channel." Considering possible concrete changes, the groups advanced several different interpretations of the notion of technological change, discussing what "development" is and to what degree cultural development may be technology-driven. The reconceptualizations, accordingly, indicate one way in which workshops test the limits of the social imagination.

References to concepts from normative theories of the press and other media were especially apparent in the final phase of the workshops. The central concepts included the specific standards of diversity and fairness by which programming should be evaluated, the legislative and other frameworks enforcing such standards, and the legitimate sources of financing mass media. The older group weighed the pros and cons of government funding of television, suggesting that, while "socialized TV" might pose a danger of government control, a system of public-service television without centralized control is conceivable. Similarly, the younger group considered the possibility of doing away with local cable monopolies by enforcing antitrust laws so as to promote the overall diversity of programming in the local community.

Both groups offered a contribution to normative communication theory during their utopian phase. Whereas normative theories traditionally have focused on the national level of legislation, the development of satellite television and other transnational media has redefined the agenda for media policy. Both workshops suggested that an important criterion of diversity would be for viewers to have access to television from many other countries. (The problem of language differences was solved in a utopian manner by the older group: "Worldwide programming is available on demand in automatic translation.") The argument, of course, implies that viewers do not think of American television as culturally diverse. A different, more diverse television future, from the audience perspective, apparently would require more than an increase in the number of national channels through new technologies.

The older group

The participants in the older group arrived at two main criticisms. First, negative evaluations were repeatedly given of programming featuring "too much violence" or "too much sex." These criticisms opened the workshop, and the participants returned to the issue toward the end of the critique phase, adding "too much profanity" and "too much obscenity" to the list of complaints. This set of criticisms also received the most votes. Afternoon news shows, in particular, were referred to as "too explicit" and "too sensational." Interestingly, however, the group did not return to the issue when considering utopian ideas or changes in television structure. The outburst of criticism, then, may have been an initial effect of the group context – a 'halo effect,' which induces respondents to offer the socially or contextually legitimate answer. At the same time, it is likely that the outburst expressed the respondents' more general attitude about contemporary mores, for which television provides a cultural forum (Newcomb and Hirsch, 1984) without being either the root problem or the solution.

The second main criticism was that, "There's no meaningful input from ordinary viewers to stations, networks, [or] advertisers." A related criticism, which received fewer votes, made the point that, "There's no good measuring mechanism of what is good TV." Thus, part of the reason why television offers objectionable programming might be that, beyond the market economy of ratings, there are no explicit, public standards by which programs are discussed or evaluated and, by implication, no accountability to viewers. The older group returned to this issue at length when considering television reform.

In the utopian phase, the older participants particularly associated positive connotations with references to freedom of choice for the viewer. The most highly rated ideas were summed up in two concepts of an unlimited program choice and unlimited transmission (including the live transmission of cultural events). What this group referred to as a "library" of all programming, comprising not just past and present American programming but the programs of all stations worldwide, would make this unlimited choice possible.

Apart from the concept of "the possible," the older group reconceptualized an interesting notion of "space-time travel television." The very first statement of the utopian phase had referred to three-dimensional television, and this presumably sparked a later sequence of statements that conceive of television as a means of omnipresence. Referring first to the use of television for "observing on the spot any past event," the group later introduced the possibility of observing distant locations and future events, all of which television would communicate in the form of a "complete sense experience." However, it was not until the group began summarizing ideas that the notion of space-time travel television emerged as a way of "going anywhere, any time, by pushing a button." Far-fetched though this idea may be, it identifies a capacity for imagining alternative realities that workshops are able to tap.

Examining strategies for change, the older group considered both technological progress and political solutions from normative communication theory. The possibility of government funding was introduced with the implication that this might increase the diversity and quality of programming by removing television from the logic of the market. Although some participants worried about the possibility of government influence, others held that such a system would be workable, if, for example, funding were provided through grants.

A second type of reform would entail some form of subscription television. Reference initially was made to "subscription-by-event TV," which one participant commented might be the ultimate result of current developments in cable technology. Furthermore, the older group reintroduced the recommendation that there ought to be "systematic procedures of feedback from the audience" about their interests. This would constitute a form of subscription television in which "audience organizations" or "organized viewing clubs sponsoring programs" would represent viewers to programmers. It was also argued that such procedures "must be easy." Television reform, then, was not perceived as a high priority, even though "lobbies" were mentioned as a means of realizing some of the group's utopian ideas. The social issues and contexts represented on television may overshadow the medium.

The younger group

The negative connotations of the younger group's discourses, as noted, implied the general argument that repetitive programming is due to the business organization of television. Furthermore, like the older group, this group directed special criticism at the ratings system. One participant with experience from working in advertising argued that the ratings are not, in a technical sense, an "accurate measure of what people watch." This argument was reconceptualized to the effect that the ratings do not measure "what people like," and when summarizing the critique, the group linked the ratings system to the virtual absence of "learning television." Hence, while the group stopped short of arguing that if the ratings were accurate they would document an interest in "learning television," the implication was that television does not fulfill its potential because its entire organization is premised on the ratings.

Whereas the representation of sex and violence was not a major issue for the younger group, they did refer to "too much violence on TV," to children's programming that is "not appropriate for children," and to commercials that "are designed to influence kids to want things." However, these criticisms emerged as an afterthought during the summary. On the one hand, then, the criticisms were a product of group reflexivity. On the other hand, it appeared that the younger group did not address these criticisms initially because, unlike the older group, they did not hold strong attitudes about contemporary social mores as portrayed on television.

Special attention should be given to similarities and differences between the two groups' specific utopian ideas. The younger group also associated positive connotations with the possibility of unlimited program choice, and they attached special importance to "unbiased news," in the form of either one or several programs. Reference again was made to "universal access to all programming in the world with automatic translator," implying a criticism of the scarcity of programs from other cultures on American television.

Yet, considering the possible mechanisms of unlimited choice, the younger group pointed to a solution that is quite different from the program library. Most votes were given to the statement, "There's 24-hour specialized channels from which you can make your own program." By making any program available at any time, both the specialized channels and the program library might provide for simultaneous diversity, but the different vocabularies imply different conceptions of the television medium. It is interesting that the older respondents cast their television of the future in the form of the quintessential institution of print technology (the library), while the younger group recast television *qua* television, perhaps influenced by their experience since childhood of television as a full-fledged, culturally central medium as well as by current developments toward a continuous flow of specialized channels. Further research is required to examine the historically and culturally specific processes through which the introduction and social construction of various mass media are accomplished.

Other highly rated utopian statements in the younger group referred to different aspects of the technology. While technological development might create "good TV reception regardless of where you live," the television set could also be conceived of as a terminal for various "interactive" services, so that audiences would call up, for example, "any information and instruction on how to learn," or even "pick your own commercials based on needs and wants." This understanding of an interactive potential, again, may be the result of the younger group's greater familiarity with new electronic media. Some other utopian statements, referring to "funding available for independent producers" and to situations where "creative people are in control," apparently originated from a few of the participants who had media-related occupations.

When considering strategies for change, the younger group particularly referred to technological progress, focusing on such services as pay-per-view systems, home shopping, 24-hour specialized channels, and private movie-viewing on VCRs. Indeed, several comments noted that "cable is forcing change in network programming," and that "technological development will ultimately force legislative change." Referring to this last possibility, one participant made a suggestion to "enforce antitrust laws against local [and] city governments" in order to "do away with local monopolies" in cable television, thus presumably providing viewers with more diversity of programming. In view of this technological optimism, it is not surprising that the group considered reform, to be justified by normative communication theory, as a "low priority" or "non-issue."

One participant did argue for the possibility of an economic reform of network television, so that the commercial rates would be decided not by the specific program ratings but by time of day, suggesting that this would be a "practically possible" change. A lengthy interaction ensued, during which several participants challenged this possibility with reference to the current principles of supply and demand applying to commercial time. Ultimately the latter position was accepted as the most basic, inescapable premise also by the advocate for change. By dismissing the suggested minor reform, which would address an important aspect of the group's initial critique, the younger group in effect endorsed the organizational status quo of American television. Reconceptualizations of what is possible may also serve to *contain* the social imagination.

Implications for research

The findings document, first of all, that 'ordinary' media users are capable of sophisticated reflection regarding the ends and means of mass communication. Addressing the kinds of issues that normally confront media professionals – programmers, regulators, and researchers – the workshop participants' discourses represent a critical commentary on the predominant techniques of audience research, which focus on individual responses to current media forms. The capacity to evaluate several alternative forms of mass communication may be an *emergent* feature of *social* processes, including research processes (see further Chapter 10 on the concept of emergence).

The special contribution of workshop data to empirical reception studies is twofold. First, the participants offer specified, exemplified, and substantiated criticisms and alternatives. While general complaints about, for example, lack of variety or commercialism have been documented by survey studies, as well (Bower, 1985), survey research does not establish a reflexive context in which the specific ends and means of reform can be addressed. Second, unlike most other audience methodologies, whether qualitative or quantitative, workshops are oriented toward the future, toward *action* that the group might collectively undertake. The references to utopias and possible reforms suggest audience perspectives on what television might be.

The findings, further, contribute to a theoretical understanding of audiences with reference to their specific *interpretive repertoires*, in two respects. First, though the older and younger respondents are in agreement about certain general ideals regarding a diversity of programming and freedom of choice, they differ in their conception of the technological means (the program library and the continuous flow of specialized channels). This implies that old and young viewers have been socialized to different media environments. The two groups constitute historically specific cultural formations, manifesting themselves in the interpretive repertoires that serve to mediate the consumption, decoding, and impact of television. Second, both groups present themselves as an interpretive formation in the sense of an *ad hoc* social collective with a vested interest in the forms of communication and culture. The workshop groups have the capacity to function as a cultural public, negotiating and articulating a common interest in relation to television.

The connotations and reconceptualizations of the workshop discourses, in particular, serve to identify the specific social construction of television by its audiences. The audience conception of media is likely to affect the social uses and effects of media content in ways that are not well understood. Whereas some earlier survey research has examined the perceived gratifications of different mass media synchronically (Katz et al., 1973), further studies should explore the conception of different media also in a diachronic perspective, as old media establish a division of labor with new media being introduced.

Two aspects of the critique of American television call for further research. First, both groups noted the limited cultural diversity of American television content. Departing from the specific issues articulated in the workshops, survey studies may indicate whether, in view of the potential of new transmission technologies, this is a widespread criticism. Cross-cultural studies, moreover, are of interest in order to establish audience conceptions of the potential of television and other mass media as resources of social and political life in different cultural contexts.

Second, and perhaps most important, more focused studies should explore the nature of the criticism directed at the business aspect of American television and its implications for political reform. Both workshop groups offer a fundamental critique of the television industry that recalls classic positions in normative communication theory, but their suggestions for reform are less fundamental. The younger group, particularly, voices a faith in reform through technological progress which suggests a set of implicit, contradictory conceptions of the social potential of television. Studies that employ a workshop methodology will be relevant for making explicit the several conceptions of media that are held by different age, gender, and socioeconomic groups. Focused interviews, moreover, can serve to elaborate audiences' utopian ideas, while the more specific policy issues of economic or organizational reform lend themselves to survey studies. By employing a multi-method approach, reception studies may begin to address some of the issues of power being raised by audiences' complex experience and multiple uses of mass media.

Finally, the present study has suggested that media reception be analyzed with specific reference to the contexts of social action embedding mass media. The workshop discussions about sex and violence on television, and about possible reforms, imply that audiences focus on television not primarily as an institution or technology, but as a cultural forum commenting on a particular social and historical context. Other reception theory has argued that mass media should be thought of, accordingly, as relatively open discourses and flexible resources that acquire their meaning and pragmatic relevance in contexts of social action (Anderson and Meyer, 1988). It is with reference to these contexts that the historical form of television may be negotiated and reconstructed.

Conclusion

If television represents a cultural forum (Newcomb and Hirsch, 1984), workshops on the future constitute a second-order forum in which audiences come to evaluate the performance of television and other mass media. While differing from other reception methodologies in their definition of the purpose, context, and participant roles of research, workshops produce valid knowledge about the interests of audiences vis-à-vis media. The workshop methodology provides a context in which participants are empowered to reflect upon their ambiguous status as audience-publics, being at once interpretive formations, or media users, and social formations, or publics. In sum, workshops on the future are a contribution to the ongoing theoretical and methodological reconception of audience studies (Jensen and Rosengren, 1990).

One distinctive feature of the workshop methodology is its orientation toward the future. While thus exercising, in Habermas' (1968/1971) terms, a critical knowledge interest, workshops on the future are also in keeping with a central tenet of the social theory that grew out of pragmatism (Joas, 1993). John Dewey, as noted in Chapter 2, contrasted the orientation of empiricism toward the past with pragmatism's future orientation, emphasizing the practical, constructive role of reason in human action (in Rorty, 1966: 210). Workshops on the future evaluate not just what is or has been, but what might be on television.

7

Reception as Flow:
Media Constituents of Social Semiotics

This chapter reexamines a neglected condition of mass media reception, namely, the structured flow of media discourses. Both 'administrative' and 'critical' studies particularly of television have suggested that viewers autonomously select, interpret, and apply programming within their everyday context. Research in the industry has referred to increasingly selective viewers who zip, zap, and graze their way through an expanding TV universe (for example, Ainslie, 1988). Critical cultural studies have interpreted the documentation of oppositional decodings of whatever material is shown as evidence of viewer control over the medium.[1] The present study of television reception as flow in a sample of American households entails a critical assessment of the common notion of a 'new television viewer.'

Having shifted the theoretical emphasis from text to audience, current research may be losing sight analytically of the textual aspect of the reception interface, in effect implying that there is no text in this living-room (Fish, 1979). Like the institutional frameworks of mass communication, however, the discursive structures of media could be conceived as determinations in the first instance (Hall, 1983). If, in methodological terms, meaning flows from the media to the audience and into the wider social context (Chapter 4), this makes media discourses a necessary, constitutive element of empirical designs. Whereas it is especially apparent in the case of radio and television that audiences are confronted not with 'works,' but with sequences of discourse, and with complex discursive relations between segments, newspapers and other print media also offer the experience of a sequence of more or less related segments. In each case, moreover, the segment refers back to a long history of earlier segments as received and processed by audiences. In a sense, the flow never stops.

The empirical study examined both the actual flow segments that were watched in the households and the potential meaning of the discursive relations between segments. Starting from a redevelopment of Williams' (1974) concept of flow, I first report on the 'viewer flows' that households constructed for themselves out of the available programming, asking to what extent viewers can be said to select their flow autonomously. Next, I analyze and interpret the viewer flows with reference to their discursive form and thematic universe. Thus, whereas the study emphasized the media constituent of *flow*, it addressed the context constituents of actual *consumption* and potential *decoding* with reference to a range of *demographic* categories of the audience constituents; the objects of analysis were the videotaped *records* of the viewer flows that were examined, first, through a *coding* of channel changes and, second and primarily, through *discourse analysis*. Finally, I discuss the implications of research on media flows, both as a new, complementary source of data about the reception process and as a contribution to theory development.

From one to three flows of television

Raymond Williams first introduced the concept of flow into communication theory. His definition is worth quoting in full:

> In all developed broadcasting systems the characteristic organization, and therefore the characteristic experience, is one of sequence or flow. This phenomenon, of planned flow, is then perhaps the defining characteristic of broadcasting, simultaneously as a technology and as a cultural form. In all communications systems before broadcasting the essential items were discrete. A book or pamphlet was taken and read as a specific item. A meeting occurred at a particular date and place. A play was performed in a particular theatre at a set hour. The difference in broadcasting is not only that these events, or events resembling them, are available inside the home, by the operation of a switch. It is that the real programme that is offered is a *sequence* or set of alternative sequences of these and other similar events, which are then available in a single dimension and in a single operation. (Williams, 1974: 86–7)

While this classic definition captures a distinctive feature particularly of commercial television, Raymond Williams appears to imply that broadcasting leads, as a matter of course, to a specific audience experience. John Ellis has taken that implication one step further by suggesting that it may be in the nature of television to structure communication in a sequence of very short segments, each about the length of a commercial break (Ellis, 1982: chap. 7).

In order to capture the specificity both of the historical form of American commercial television and of its reception, I propose an analytical distinction between three aspects of TV flow (Figure 7.1). First, a *channel flow* is the sequence of program segments, commercials, and preannouncements that is designed by the individual station to engage as many viewers as possible for as long as possible. The assumption is that an appropriate form and mixture of segments may retain the viewers who are already in the flow, and that it may further recruit new viewers who are grazing the spectrum. It is this strategy which results in the characteristic narrative structure that climaxes, with increasing intensity, before each commercial break, a *bricolage* in which the boundaries of the sequence are blurred.

Second, viewers create their own customized *viewer flow* from the available channels. Whereas viewers are likely to stay with a given channel, carrying over or flowing from one program to the next (Barwise and Ehrenberg, 1988: 34), they are free, in principle, to make any type and number of changes at any point. It is not well-understood how the process of selection comes about, or what kind of experience arises from viewing as flow.

Third, the sum total of possible sequences represents a *super-flow*. Stations must establish a profile, or house style (Ellis, 1982: 219), that is recognizable

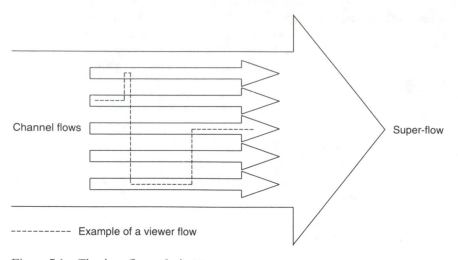

Figure 7.1   *The three flows of television*

within the super-flow of competing stations. Viewers equally must be able to orient themselves in the super-flow in order to make an informed selection. The super-flow of competing channel flows, rather than flow as such, should be seen as the defining characteristic of American commercial television in its present stage of development.[2]

The interrelations between the three flows, while bearing on the relative power of medium and audience, have not been analyzed in previous empirical reception studies.[3] Research in the area follows the familiar tendency for social science to focus on audiences, while humanistic studies focus on texts. The issues relating to the audience selection and use of program sequences have primarily been examined through quantitative measures of audience behavior, such as the ratings (Nielsen, 1989) and the overlap between audiences for different programs (Barwise and Ehrenberg, 1988). Because of their commercial purposes, however, these studies emphasize aggregated measures of the audience for particular segments of the flow, while giving less attention to the combination of segments in individual or household viewing. And because no record is produced, for example on videotape, of actual viewing, it is normally not possible to explore the relationship between viewers' channel selection and the discursive structures of the content. Some recent research has examined the flow of individual viewers across broadcast and other television channels (Heeter and Greenberg, 1988; Pingree et al., 1991), again without examining the discursive structures of the selected programming in any detail. Cultivation studies (Gerbner and Gross, 1976), while offering one relevant, if contested, conception of audience-cum-content analysis, have not approached television as a structured flow.

In the humanistic tradition, a couple of studies have analyzed television flow as a text. Nick Browne (1987), first, has argued that the American networks' historical strategy of aiming for a common denominator that would appeal to as many of the available viewers as possible has resulted in the relative homogeneity of TVs 'super-text' (in the present terminology, super-flow). There is a political economy at work which limits the diversity of the super-flow at any given time, and which helps to explain the placement of different genres in the course of the television day. Browne argues further that this homogeneity is self-perpetuating because, over time, viewers have been socialized through the 'mega-text' of television history to expect particular (super-)texts. The 'mega-text' lives on, then, in the audience's interpretive repertoires.

A second, culturally optimistic perspective on flow has been advanced by Horace Newcomb (1988). Through a thematic reading of a 'strip' (viewer flow) of network programs on a particular evening, he develops the argument that television represents an open forum (Newcomb and Hirsch, 1984) for diverse political and cultural issues and viewpoints. The programs are said to enter into dialogue – with each other and with viewers – about social problems, gender relations, and other issues of public debate. Surprisingly, however, Newcomb's reading does not include the commercials and preannouncements that are constitutive elements of flow; it also does not consider selections made by specific audiences. Instead, the analysis, which is also an appreciation by a fan who normally watches the series in question, focuses on possible combinations of the program segments as such. Television flow, thus, highlights the need for several forms of data about the reception process and for comparative analysis of audience and media discourses.

Methodology

The empirical study, first of all, produced a 'reverse video' – a record of the viewer flow in specific households on a particular night – by asking the respondents to make all channel changes with their VCR running and attached to their main TV set.[4] The videos document what was shown (but not necessarily watched) on the set. The recordings were made on a Wednesday evening (February 1, 1989), an 'average' night of regular programming when the scheduled programming was not disrupted by specials replacing regular shows or by major news events. It was also a night in the middle of the TV season when neither specific program choices nor extensive grazing would more likely be due to new program offers. Respondents were asked to watch some TV between 7 and 9 p.m., but not necessarily for the entire period. The early evening was chosen because this is a time when members of a household are likely to be selecting and viewing programs together as a group. In addition, respondents filled in basic questionnaires about demographics and television use as well as a diary concerning their channel selections and changes. The additional information provided by viewers, for example on motivations for channel changes or disagreements in the viewing group, had few details, but helped to identify programs and in some cases served to explain the combination of programs in the recordings, which were examined as the primary objects of analysis. The local *TV Guide* (January 28–February 3, 1989) documents the availability of network, independent, and public TV stations in the super-flow, as well as additional cable channels, to which a majority of the households in the study had access.

A sample of twelve video households from the Los Angeles metropolitan area was selected by a local market research firm. The aim was to explore a range of household types in terms of household size and socioeconomic status; the actual sample was predominantly white and middle class, but included both young and elderly viewers (in their twenties to sixties) as well as households with/without children and with one/two parents.

Before reporting two sets of findings, I note that while relying on a small sample, the study identified several types and structures of viewer flow. These structures lend themselves to further research on a representative scale, possibly in combination with TV meter data; they also complement previous interview and observation studies on the decoding and social uses of specific texts and genres. Although the design entailed an intervention into daily routines, the households were familiar with the video technology, and they were not required to watch for the entire two-hour period. The recordings document some actual instances of reception as flow that bear on the notion of a new and powerful television viewer.

A power index of television?

The first form of analysis examined the number of channel changes made by the respondents, compared to the content changes resulting from a channel's introduction of a commercial, a preannouncement, or a program segment. The ratio between these two kinds of changes may be interpreted as an index of the relative power of TV and its viewers, in the sense that each change controls which flow segment is subsequently shown on the screen. The capacity to control which texts and genres one is to receive can be defined as a minimal form of cultural self-determination. This is in spite of the fact that the variety of segments in itself may also be part of the attraction for viewers. The basic implication of the 'new television viewer' is that the selection of a *specific* variety of contents is left to the discretion and free choice of viewers.

This first form of analysis accepts, for the sake of the argument, the premise of the industry position, namely, that, increasingly, viewers select the segments they prefer to watch while avoiding not least the commercials. Simultaneously, the analysis prepares the ground for an immanent critique (Bernstein, 1991: 315) of the logic behind the argument. Even if one pursues the industry argument on its own terms, an alternative conclusion suggests itself.[5]

Table 7.1 reports the number of viewer-initiated and channel-initiated changes. The channel-initiated content changes include only changes between commercials, preannouncements, and program segments, *not* between scenes of fictional series, news stories, or music videos, and only simultaneous changes of image and sound. The viewer-initiated channel changes include the initial switching on of the set. Channel changes were made both at the transition between programs and in the middle of a program segment or a commercial break.

Table 7.1 *A power index of television*

Household no.	Viewer-initiated channel changes	Channel-initiated content changes
1	30	71
2	3	77
3	1	48
4	2	88
5	4	49
6	1	87
7	3	110
8	2	34
9	5	48
10	2	64
11	2	54
12	4	92
Mean	4.92	68.50

The ratio of viewer-initiated to channel-initiated changes:

Mean:	1:13.93
High:	1:87.00
Low:	1:2.37

The average ratio of 1:13.93 suggests a relative, but notable degree of control by the medium in these terms, at least in this sample of viewers and given the super-flow at this time of day; the findings call for replication on a representative sample and during other time periods. The highest ratio (1:87) occurred in the viewing of a live sports program on commercial broadcast television. To exemplify how the lowest ratio (1:2.37) came about, an intensive sequence of viewer-initiated channel changes occurred in this household when the credits at the end of news program began to roll, and the household, in making the eighth change, managed to return to the same channel before the news credits had been completed. Even this form of viewer activity, while standing out in the sample as a whole, still does not put the viewer in control.

To anticipate a few counterarguments, I recognize that viewers have been socialized to the super-flow and thus have a sense of how long an ongoing segment will last. The point is that no information with sufficient detail is available, on television or in the listings in print media that list only 'real programs,' so as to make an informed choice of particular segments on a particular channel. In effect, viewers can only make a negative choice, knowing what they are changing *from* (a specific program segment, commercial, or preannouncement), but not what they are changing *to*. Viewers do not in fact control the specific variety of their own flow. Even the conceivable devotees of commercials, watching advertising as either shopping information or a cultural form in its own right, will find it most difficult of all to orient themselves in the flow, since 'their' genre is defined negatively as an unlisted absence within other programming.

Rather than concluding in quantitative terms that, hence, viewers are powerless, or that more frequent channel changes as such would make them more powerful, my purpose has been a preliminary critique of the widespread conception of a 'new television viewer' in industry rhetoric as well as some academic research and public debate. The super-flow establishes particular conditions of reception, which are not eliminated through even a great measure of zapping or, as I go on to argue, an oppositional decoding of particular segments. The next step is to ask which specific range of meanings are available in the viewer flows that audiences construct for themselves from the super-flow? An answer is suggested by a second form of analysis examining two types of discursive structures – intertextuality and super-themes – across the different genres of flow.

Flows, genres, and super-themes

The *genres* which predominate in American television on weekdays between 7 and 9 p.m. present an opportunity for viewers to negotiate the relationship between private and public areas of life, and between everyday life and major social institutions. The three predominant genres are situation comedies, tabloid journalism (for example, *A Current Affair, Entertainment Tonight*), and tabloid science (for example, *Unsolved Mysteries*). In social-structural terms, the genres of this period serve to mediate between the public life of work or school during the day and the private life of evening (Scannell, 1988: 26). On the one hand, situation comedy is a fictional genre which, though focusing on the home, raises social issues pertaining to families and individuals; on the other hand, the tabloid programs present facts about the world that affect families and individuals in fundamental respects. Despite other options, including cable programming, the households themselves also emphasize these three genres in their actual viewer flows. It is interesting to note that some of the subscribers to pay movie channels would only watch part of a movie before selecting another channel, thus apparently treating a pay channel as any other element of the super-flow. Similar findings in a study of a larger sample (Heeter and Greenberg, 1988: 167–76) suggest that, from the viewers' perspective, commercial-free movie and other pay channels may not in fact be conceived as a distinctive alternative to broadcast television, even if this conception is commonly taken to explain, in part, the development of cable television.

Information from the diaries suggests how the specific combination of genres were negotiated in the households between parents and children, and between male and female viewers. The information is in keeping with earlier research finding that male viewers may be especially oriented toward news and other factual programming, whereas female viewers may prefer sitcoms, soaps, and other fictional genres (Hobson, 1980; Morley, 1986), even if some women in the sample indicate a preference for news. Children specifically report liking (or actively disliking) particular sitcoms. The sample includes examples of both news and fiction genres prevailing as well as family compromises involving the selection of first a news program and later a sitcom. Moreover, the negotiation of program selection bears witness to gender and other family roles and conflicts. In one case, a father labels *The A Team* (an action series featuring Vietnam veterans as its main characters) one of the worst programs on television, while his twelve-year-old son labels it one of the best. The series can be said to place gender identities on a cultural agenda, offering an occasion to explore definitions of masculinity. In another case, *Charles in Charge* (a sitcom with a male teenager as the central character) is labeled as one of the best programs by a twelve-year-old boy, and as one of the worst by his fourteen-year-old sister.

The viewer flows, as recorded on videotapes, were analyzed in detail with reference to the category of *super-themes*, defined as specific, highly generalized concepts that serve to establish meaningful relations between the discursive realities of programs and the everyday social realities of viewers. Previous research in the United States, Denmark, and Italy has identified such super-themes as principles structuring the reception of television news as well as the everyday conceptualization of politics (Crigler and Jensen, 1991; Jensen, 1988a; Mancini, 1990). The present study identified a set of super-themes across the different genres of the super-flow. Although the study did not observe or interview viewers apart from the questionnaires and diaries, the actual viewer flows are examined as potential structures of meaning, as constructed by the respondents, and the flow sequences are interpreted with reference to the theoretical categories of discourse and reception analysis. The configuration of super-themes in the present sample of viewer flows is summarized in Figure 7.2, and discussed below.[6]

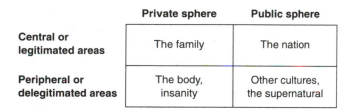

	Private sphere	Public sphere
Central or legitimated areas	The family	The nation
Peripheral or delegitimated areas	The body, insanity	Other cultures, the supernatural

Figure 7.2   *Super-themes of television flow*

Flow as discourse

The super-themes were inferred from a detailed analysis of three categories of television discourse: actors, coherence, and presuppositions or implicit premises. First of all, the verbal and visual representation of *actors* and their actions carry a range of positive and negative connotations (Barthes, 1964/1984a: 89–94). Further, such representations cumulatively imply the appropriate public and private roles of actors. To exemplify, the viewer flow of one household (Household 2) featured *Charles in Charge*, *A Current Affair*, and *Unsolved Mysteries*, in which actors relating to all four super-themes appeared. *A Current Affair* reported, for example, on a doctor's sexual abuse of a patient, a Congress politician allegedly having sex with teenagers, and an update of a story on marriage fraud. Articulating a discursive boundary between the family and a deviant private or sexual life, and employing a terminology of insanity, the reports on these cases establish a contrast with the 'normal' family life of *Charles in Charge*. Similarly, a contrast is established between the nation and supernatural dangers. *Unsolved Mysteries* included coverage of the exploration of Mars, where traces of ancient civilizations may be found. In the reference to "America's romance with Mars," it is significant that "America," not humanity or Earth, engages with other forms of life. Supernatural powers in the form of UFOs also appear briefly in *Charles in Charge* as a threat to family security.

Second, the discursive *coherence* of the flow contributes to developing the super-themes. Coherence is carried not just by the explicit verbal and visual structures of television, but as importantly by the functional relations between shots and verbal segments, which indicate, for example, a causal or temporal relationship or a conclusion (van Dijk, 1977). Crucially, such relations obtain both within and between the three types of flow segment. Exemplifying coherence within a segment, Household 2 selected *Unsolved Mysteries*, which included a classic narrative comparable to folk tales (Todorov, 1968). This was the story of a little girl who, when living with her parents in Austria as a refugee following World War II, was taken to a Christmas party by an American soldier. Now, through the intervention of this program, the two have been reunited in the United States. The story of their lives, then, can be interpreted through categories such as The First Encounter, Separation, Quest, and Reunion.

Most important, coherence is established between segments, not least through the intervention of commercials. In the course of the video from Household 2, several commercials represent other cultures with an implied contrast to the American nation. A soldier wearing a Nazi uniform and speaking with a heavy German accent drives his tank up to a fast-food stand, and, discovering the low prices, he decides to "fill up the tank." The immediately following item advertises a new book with reference to an ominous atmosphere in a Japanese context. And several later commercials featuring a cream cheese depict a band of dancing cucumbers singing a Latino tune and wearing Mexican hats. Another commercial in Household 2's flow is a parody of a United Nations assembly debating heatedly where to have dinner, leading up to the solution: a local hamburger chain.

Finally, *presuppositions* carry the fundamental assumptions of discourse (Culler, 1981; Leech, 1974). Whereas they may be explicit, presuppositions are often the implicit premises of an argument or narrative, constituting the conditions of possibility for interpretation. One commercial for a traditional steak dinner that presents a singing cowboy, while behind him what is evidently a movie set is being dismantled, may mobilize the viewers' interpretive repertoire (Potter and Wetherell, 1987) for the Western genre. At the same time, the ambiguity regarding the status of the myth of the West, and by implication the American nation, suggests the more general point that the super-themes, in articulating a common conception of social reality, can also bear witness to specific contradictions within that conception. This conclusion is substantiated by a further analysis of the configuration of super-themes in the entire sample.

Four super-themes

The family is represented as an institution offering physical and emotional security. Even though some families, including a family unit of orphans (the video of Household 5), differ from the common nuclear form, here also the oldest child manages to set up a home providing for traditional needs and roles. The families of sitcoms are a source of caring also for friends of the house, and in commercials families are assisted by companies, such as a law firm enabling one family to keep their home (Household 10) and a children's cable channel keeping the whole family (viewing) together (Household 11). There are also many portrayals of traditional gender roles, from a husband cooking food out of a can for his children, to a housewife who is said to love her family 25 per cent less after cooking with a margarine of 25 per cent less fat, which is humorous precisely because of a presupposition about her caretaker role (both in Household 5). Even the TV medium itself may serve the family, as in a game show referring to two boys at home watching their father on the program (Household 7) and in the commercial for the cable channel keeping the family together.

The primary threat to the family appears to come from *the body*. The camera feasts on the human body, particularly in tabloid news and commercials. The most explicit sex is seen on MTV (Household 9), but there are comparable visuals reporting on Jamaican resorts, where "hedonism" is "the key word" (Household 1). Lady Di of Great Britain is shown in a swimsuit in another story, which is immediately followed by a cereal commercial whose camera slowly pans up a young woman's presumably naked body as she pulls on her swimsuit (Household 10). The point is, however, that the body represents a narrative boundary between more or less legitimated aspects of private life. If one indulges the body, the result is likely to be immoral or criminal, as suggested by the examples of doctor–patient and politician–teenager sex. Further, bodily drives may lead to insanity, as in a news story of a man murdering the husband of a woman who had promised to then marry the murderer (Household 10), or a father convicted of killing his children (Household 7). The movie *Psycho III*, as selected in part by Household 1, emphatically links the body to insanity.

The body sometimes is present only as an absence. It is peculiar, for example, that a tabloid report on nudism does not show one naked body (Household 2). While this is explained by the regulations and conventions of US television, it bespeaks the limits of television as a cultural forum (Newcomb and Hirsch, 1984). An episode of a sitcom, *Head of the Class*, addresses AIDS and condoms in the context of a date. After consulting a teacher, the boy buys condoms, but sex is never mentioned, and finally the couple agree that they would rather just talk. In silencing a vital, if culturally controversial, aspect of private life, television comes to suggest emotional security as an alternative to sex, both here and in another sitcom, *TV 101* (Household 12), which may encourage teenagers to choose conventional family life.

It is hardly surprising that the *public domain* is depicted less frequently in these genres and at this time of the television day.[7] Still, several segments establish a link between private and public domains, sometimes by suggesting that America is a nation of families. Some car commercials refer to the family as a base for operations into the public domain, for example when a father teaches his son how to sell cars (Household 9), or when another father teaches his daughter how to test a truck before buying one (Household 7), both reiterating traditional gender roles. Moreover, in numerous commercials, viewers will encounter various key American values that cut across private and public domains: cars are associated with nature, animals, and freedom; nature is a value in itself, for which one company is said to be caring, and which a travel agency offers as an "antidote for civilization"; and a bank claims to join freedom and success for its customers in "the freedom to succeed." Whereas money, being the bottom line of public life, may thus remain an implicit reference, it becomes the explicit object of television discourse in game shows, and a PBS play, *A Raisin in the Sun*, portraying the life and troubles of a black family, specifies how money is a condition of public success (Household 8).

The nation apparently is subject to more contradictions than the other super-themes. In particular, the status of the nation is continually undercut by irony and humor, despite the references to "America's" romance with Mars and to an "American original" beer and a genuine coffee from the American West. When one of the characters of the sitcom *Growing Pains* decides to join the Marines, the narrative commutes between two viewpoints, noting his earnest commitment but humorously exaggerating his parents' patriotism (Household 1, 5, and 7). Further, *M*A*S*H* contributes an alternative declaration of independence when the local bar secedes from the union, founding a nation on "life, liberty, and the pursuit of happy hour" (Households 9 and 12). Only once in the sample does one encounter an unambiguous statement on possible national political ideals, and then in the form of a criticism of national policies regarding an international conflict: a teacher announces in *Head of the Class* that the next class will address recent US initiatives in South Africa, "if we can find any" (Household 5), a statement that is not underscored by the laugh track.

If the discourse of the viewer flows implies some current difficulties of defining the American nation in positive terms, the representation of *other cultures* can be seen as a negative definition, projecting what American culture is *not*. In addition to the already noted stereotypes of German, Japanese, and Mexican culture, and of the United Nations, *The Gong Show* (a program featuring amateurish performances that may be stopped by other participants by sounding a gong) opens with a disclaimer to the effect that, "This is not a tribute to Russia," and proceeds to introduce a Gorbachev lookalike and his punk-style companion, who are asked to "go take a seat-ski" (Household 10). Later features in that program include Rocking Rasputin, who is stopped by "almost a Chernobyl gong"; Olga, an "athlete who missed one day of hormones," singing "Those Were the Days" in Russian while Gorbachev does a cossack dance; and Eric Clapenov, who allegedly grew up in Chernobyl, then defected to New Jersey, and now "naps in the microwave." Viewers are asked to stay tuned for the next segment to learn the cause of the Cold War and the "nagging postwar nasal drip." Other, less spectacular images of other cultures include a few news reports, a commercial for a hotel chain presenting itself as a common denominator for many cultures through reference to their music (Household 6), and the tabloid news story on Jamaica's picturesque features (Households 1, 4, and 10).

African-American culture, finally, appears to occupy a border area between the nation and other cultures. The study was conducted during a black-history month, and several news programs addressed the issue of whether blacks living in the United States should be called African-Americans. Furthermore, in the play *A Raisin in the Sun* (Household 8), an African foreign student starts a relationship with the daughter of the black family, which again serves to thematize the question of what is American culture, at the level both of the family and the nation.

It should be added that three of the sample's twelve families selected other genres than the sitcoms, tabloid journalism, and tabloid science informing the super-themes. Nevertheless, these viewers were also likely to be exposed to related themes in the commercials that are frequently identical across program genres. Moreover, the programs that were selected by the other three households – a feature movie (Household 3), a basketball game (Household 6), and a combination of a game show and a theatrical performance (Household 8) – did explore aspects of the four super-themes. The movie *Gaslight* is the story of an insane person, speaking with a foreign accent, who destroys his marriage and threatens his wife's life. The theatrical performance and the game show, as noted, both focus on the theme of money as the bottom line of family as well as public life. The sporting event, while focusing on the body, stays within the legitimated, athletic uses of the body. It is for further empirical studies to examine the presence of super-themes in the actual reception of different flows and genres at various times of the television day.

Intertextual flows

If super-themes are defined as discursive structures primarily of the subject matter or content of television flow, as realized in reception, *intertextuality* can be defined as a more *formal* feature of television discourses and their reception. Deriving from the work of Bakhtin and Volosinov and mediated through the structuralist theories of Julia Kristeva and Roland Barthes (for overview, see Coward and Ellis, 1977; also Greimas and Courtés, 1982: 160), the concept of intertextuality emphasizes that no text is an island: it refers to the complex structure of interrelations that exist between single literary works or media products, "a use of language that calls up a vast reserve of echoes from similar texts, similar phrasings, remarks, situations, characters" (Coward and Ellis, 1977: 51). The point is that discursive processes and structures constitute a textual system that may generate meanings without the intentional participation of sign users, perhaps behind their backs. Hence, intertextuality is not merely or even primarily a stylistic device, for example the use in literature or media of a metaphor, character, or plot line originating from another author. I define intertextuality as the process in which elements of discourse communicate specific meanings to audiences by implicit reference to other, familiar discourses, themes, genres, or media, which may also be present in or implied by the context of reception.

Intertextuality is perhaps an especially prominent feature of mass communication, because the media feed on each other as part of the simultaneously economic and cultural dynamic that shapes the contemporary integrated media environments. Moreover, the prevalence of intertextuality raises difficult issues for media effects studies: whatever impact one text can be said to have, is thus reinforced by intertextuality. The impact of intertextual media is more than the sum of the impacts of individual media. Notwithstanding campaign studies (Rogers and Storey, 1987), the general, structured recycling of cultural themes and political issues through the mass media remains a pivotal, but underresearched aspect of the history and impact of mass communication (but see Bennett and Woollacott, 1987; Pearson and Uricchio, 1991).

It is useful to distinguish analytically between two aspects, namely, structural and thematic intertextuality. While *structural* intertextuality has not traditionally been emphasized in literary and humanistic studies, it contributes crucially to the configuration of media texts as part of an institutionalized communicative purpose which goes beyond socalled 'primary,' 'secondary,' and 'tertiary' texts (see Chapter 4). Concretely, the program segments of a channel flow are strung together by preannouncements, and during commercial breaks commercials and other announcements are edited as one integrated message. The discursive boundaries between program segments and commercials are blurred further when, for example, in the present sample a sports announcer reads the list of sponsors for the program (Household 6). Another form of structural intertextuality is achieved in advertising for other media, such as the many commercials in the sample for new film releases. The repetition over time of a commercial message, either in the same or a different medium or genre, similarly serves to prestructure audience attention. In sum, structural intertextuality is a major aspect of most mass communication, comprising campaigns within product marketing and politics, advertising in one medium for another medium, the representation of media use *in* media, and the repetition of themes and issues across media and genres of fact as well as fiction.

The other aspect is the classic literary or *thematic* intertextuality, incorporating discursive elements from one text, genre, or medium into other texts, such as the myths of Oedipus, Faust, or Genesis. Three varieties could be identified in the present sample. First, a number of commercials adopt an entire format from other genres, particularly game shows, sitcoms, and news. An additional example is a series of car commercials with faithful reconstructions of famous Norman Rockwell drawings, representing quintessentially American themes and values, with a commentary spoken by the artist's granddaughter (Household 2).

Second, programs and commercials may include a character or narrative element from other texts. Discussing whether there are Martians in the kitchen, one character in *Charles in Charge* suggests that they should "nip it in the bud," and a second character responds: "This Bud's for you!", the Budweiser slogan, drawing a great response from the laugh track (Household 2). Incidentally, some viewers may have associated this remark with the then recent Super Bowl of American football on television, which featured a much publicized series of commercials that depicted two opposing 'teams' of Bud and Bud Light cans competing for the championship. The concept of 'super bowl' is also used by a network referring to its programs as "the Super Bowl" and "World Series" of television comedy (Households 2, 4, and 11). Moreover, characters from TV series frequently appear in other genres, for example, when a character from *Growing Pains*, during a commercial break of this program, appears as 'Columbo' in a preannouncement of the latter series (Household 1, 5, and 7), or when sports stars recommend equipment (Household 6).

Finally, intertextuality may serve to defamiliarize a representation of social reality to the viewer, as in poetic uses of language (Jakobson, 1960/1981). In some cases, this is an intentional technique, for instance, when the characters of a commercial argue with the voice-over about the product (Household 7). Elsewhere, defamiliarization is an incidental consequence of the flow structure when the 'arrest' of a 'suspect' in *M*A*S*H* is immediately followed by a preannouncement for the tabloid documentary *Cops* showing a suspect being arrested (Household 12). Thus, the flow may indeed communicate the point that the television representation is only one version of social reality. Like the super-themes, such intertextuality may become a resource for viewers to establish the coherence and relevance of television flow for their own lives. Nevertheless, both the super-themes and the intertextual structures of flow constitute specific conditions of sense-making that prefigure the audience decodings and social uses of television.

Conclusion

This study has examined some of the structural factors affecting the scope of television reception. The three flows of American television, arising from a specific social organization of the medium, set particular conditions for the participation of audiences in the communicative process. Whereas the power index furnishes a preliminary, immanent critique of the notion of a 'new, powerful viewer,' my main argument has been that the discursive structures of television flow, particularly the range of super-themes and the network of intertextuality, serve to prestructure the meaning potential of television and hence the political and cultural agenda that viewers encounter. After a decade of research documenting the relative autonomy of audiences, there is a need to explore also the structural limits of autonomy, including the ways in which media agendas may override marginal or emergent aspects of audience agendas. Reception studies that continue to focus on individuals' decoding of single texts and on their microsocial uses of media in the immediate context, so as to neglect the embedding of reception in discursive contexts and macrosocial structures beyond individual control, run the risk of becoming theoretically incoherent and politically irrelevant.

The category of super-themes represents a contribution to communication theory and theory of science, as well (Chapters 9 and 10). In preliminary terms, it is interesting to note that the two dimensions of Figure 7.1 are comparable to the metaphorical and metonymic axes of semiosis (Jakobson, 1960/1981). While the channel flows correspond to the metonymic or combination axis building discursive sequences, the viewer's channel changes correspond to movements on the metaphorical or selection axis. The super-themes can be said to mediate between the two axes, thus establishing meaningful relations between diverse flow segments, while at the same time linking the discursive sequences of television to the flow of everyday reality. Super-themes can be understood as overdetermining metaphors which become points of access to several metonymic sequences.

The conclusions of the present chapter also lend themselves to further empirical studies, both on reception as a flow *internally* in the electronic media and on the *external* or intertextual flow of audiences between different media and within media environments. It will be of special interest to explore different audiences' experience of television flow, at different times of the television day, in interview and observational studies. The 'reverse video,' especially if combined with a meter system and applied to a larger sample, can produce new insight into viewers' interaction with television. It may also be combined with the video observational techniques which, while rediscovered in the 1980s (Svennevig, 1986), go back to the work of Bechtel et al. (1972). Audience perceptions of, for example, intertextual relations between segments lend themselves to survey and experimental research. In a comparative perspective, the currently changing structure of flows in European television call for more in-depth studies (see Jensen et al., 1994). The quality of 'public service' that is offered by national and transnational television institutions to viewers should be evaluated not just at the level of channel flows, but equally at the level of the super-flow, and with reference to actual viewer flows.

8

Discourses of Research: Analytical Constituents of Social Semiotics

The procedures for collecting and analyzing data remain one of the least developed aspects of the new reception studies, despite the recent growth of reference works on qualitative research (Denzin and Lincoln, 1994; Jensen and Jankowski, 1991; Miles and Huberman, 1994). If reception analysis is to justify its role as a form of inquiry that is complementary to other types of audience research, having independent explanatory value, then explicit criteria and principles of analysis must be developed. To simplify the argument, I call below for a 'statistics' or systematic methodology of qualitative reception studies (Jensen, 1991a), suggesting that linguistic discourse analysis is the primary candidate for this task. In the wider semiotic perspective, discourse analysis relies on a specific sign system, different from, but equal to, that of statistical analysis. This chapter examines the specific requirements of systematic qualitative reception studies, while Chapter 9 returns to the general complementarity of quantitative and qualitative research.

By way of introduction, the first section briefly discusses the recent, widespread call for 'ethnographic' methods to replace other, qualitative as well as quantitative approaches to data collection. Proposing a methodological pluralism, I refer in the second section to historical studies of reception as a case in point substantiating the argument that a creative combination of different forms of evidence is a necessary research strategy and, indeed, is sometimes the only possible source of new insights into the social conditions of reception. The 'how' of science depends on the 'what' and the 'why' (Kvale, 1987), the knowledge interests and anticipated uses of findings. In the third section, I return to the 'how' of different research procedures, exploring the analytical constituent of *linguistic discourse analysis* and its relevance for qualitative studies of the context, audience, and media constituents of social semiotics. Qualitative research may be conceived as a set of communicative practices, working *through* verbal language and other signs to understand more *about* the signs of social semiosis.

Reception analysis and, not versus, ethnographic research

The issue underlying the research debate about ethnographic approaches is which aspects of the social and cultural context of reception must be included, and which may be excluded, in empirical work, assuming that no empirical study could be all-inclusive. Janice Radway (1988) early on pinpointed two positions on this issue. On the one hand, she suggested, reception studies may be said to have reached a dead end because they tend to reify their domain of analysis:

> Audiences [...] are set in relation to a single set of isolated texts which qualify already as categorically distinct objects. No matter how extensive the effort to dissolve the boundaries of the textual object or the audience, most recent studies of reception, including my own, continue to begin with the 'factual' existence of a particular kind of text which is understood to be received by some set of individuals. Such studies perpetuate, then, the notion of a circuit neatly bounded and therefore identifiable, locatable, and open to observation. (Radway, 1988: 363)

On the other hand, Radway proposed, as a less reifying alternative, the use of classic ethnographic fieldwork about all the social and cultural practices of an entire community, including, but not privileging, media use. This alternative adds to both the scale and complexity of the empirical enterprise:

> [...] I have begun to think about the possibilities of a collaborative project that would begin within the already defined boundaries of a politically constituted municipality and attempt to map there the complex, *collective* production of 'popular culture' across the terrain of everyday life. [...] To make this even more concrete, I should say that what I have in mind is a project that would take as its object of study the range of practices engaged in by individuals within a single heterogeneous community as they elaborate their own form of popular culture through the realms of leisure and then articulate those practices to others engaged in during their working lives. [...] My proposed project, then, is grounded in a more traditional form of ethnographic fieldwork – that is, in a fairly lengthy stay within a community. This would be undertaken now not by a single scholar but rather by a team whose members would fan out across a range of sites. (Radway, 1988: 368–9)

In *Desperately Seeking the Audience* (1991), Ien Ang took the argument one step further by suggesting that an ethnographic methodology represents a radically different epistemology than both qualitative reception studies and more traditional, quantitative forms of audience research. Neither 'projects' in Radway's wide sense nor 'cumulative studies' as understood within most research traditions will satisfy the requirements of this epistemology, since, to Ang, the scientific act of categorization is in itself an act of violence committed against the public and the everyday:

> From this [ethnographic] perspective, 'television audience' is a nonsensical category, for there is only the dispersed, indefinitely proliferating chain of situations in which television audiencehood is practised and experienced – together making up the diffuse and fragmentary social world of actual audiences. (Ang, 1991: 164)

Instead, she argues, one should "take this dirty reality seriously" (p. 167) and "develop another kind of knowledge on [the] ruins [of ratings and other institutional research]" (p. 160). The ethnographic alternative entails particularization, "a form of interpretive knowing that purports to increase our sensitivity to the particular details of the ways in which actual people deal with television in their everyday lives" (p. 165). In a political perspective, Ang further suggests, ethnographic knowing in particular can enrich public debate about, for example, the future of public-service broadcasting by "securing more flexible conditions in which a plurality of qualities can find their expression. The further political task would then be the construction of institutional arrangements that can meet these conditions" (p. 169).

It is far from clear, however, that the ethnographic perspective warrants the dichotomization into methods that are both theoretically reflexive and politically correct, and those that are neither of these things. Whereas Ang's (1991) meta-analysis of audience research offers new insight into the history and politics of communication research, the soft interpretation of her argument – that "the ironic thrust of ethnography fundamentally goes against the fixities of the institutional point of view" (p. 166), that is, that science serves to question and, to a degree, defamiliarize reality – only makes ethnography one dialect of science. The strong interpretation of the argument – that categorization and conceptualization inevitably misrepresent the multiple realities of audiences in the interest of prediction, control, and power – in effect corners research in the untenable position of epistemological doodling (Chapter 1). Indeed, the argument is not taken to that last, logical conclusion by Ang, but is only implied through the dichotomization.

Against Ang's (1991) articulation of ethnographic research, I suggest that current audience studies are less in need of the deconstruction of abstract, generalized others in opposing research traditions than the construction of consistent, if fallible, positions that may be argued for and against with reference to both theoretical and empirical arguments. Television ratings, while sometimes reified as final answers in search of good questions, do provide good answers to certain questions.

Against Radway's (1988) replacement of reception studies by ethnographic projects, I suggest that the two modes of inquiry provide different answers to different questions. If, in theoretical terms, meaning flows from social contexts and agents to the media (Chapter 4), this should be seen as the fundamental condition not just of ethnographic studies, but of reception analysis, as well. What distinguishes the two traditions is the focus of their empirical methodologies, which tend to emphasize either a specific medium or a particular audience group. Reception methodologies have probed the experience and use of specific media and genres by several audiences with reference to their different contexts, whereas ethnographic methodologies have begun to explore how specific audiences engage several different media and genres as part of their particular context.[1] This complementarity suggests the more general point that empirical research needs to consider multiple discourses with a bearing on media reception, while assessing their explanatory value with explicit reference to the methodological constituents of research (Figure 4.5).

The case of historical reception studies

History offers a standard for assessing the state of contemporary research: To what extent will our colleagues of the future be able to rely on our work to gain a better understanding of mass media reception in their past than we will ever publish about our past and, perhaps, our present? Historical studies of reception, while identifying new forms of evidence to fill gaps in our know-ledge of the past, may also suggest new research procedures in a contemporary perspective. Reception studies represent, in fact, a test case of the explanatory value of communication research: unlike other aspects of the communication process that may be examined through traditional historical sources such as legislative documents, the records of media organizations, and some (admit-tedly imperfect) archives of media contents, *reception does not exist for the historical record*, unless it is reconstructed through the intervention of research. Whereas ratings and readership figures presumably will survive, the social and cultural aspects of mass media reception are literally disappearing before our eyes and ears.

Media reception in the present

History may be read as a set of discourses that are articulated increasingly through the mass media, and rearticulated in part by their audiences. In order to tap this discursive process, empirical reception studies can draw on several research traditions from historical research proper, notably 'life history' and 'oral history.' The motivation underlying oral history is that crucial aspects of social life are not documented in the most readily available, written sources, but need to be complemented and corrected by oral evidence (for overview, see Thompson, 1978). Similarly, life history assumes that individual biographies represent a relevant level of analysis, since the dynamic of macro- and micro-processes is played out in the lives of concrete social agents (Bertaux, 1981). To capture not least the perspective of everyday life, the historian may have to become a fieldworker. Oral history may, further, provide a perspective on his-tory 'from below,' from the unofficial, unrecorded viewpoint of the disempowered, as in labor history (Terkel, 1974). Moreover, various ethno-graphic methods can produce what Geertz (1973) has called a "thick description" also of media in everyday life, combining observation, interview-ing, diaries, family photographs, and other evidence. Finally, as suggested by Fiske's (1987) notions of horizontal and, especially, vertical intertextuality (Chapter 4), movie reviews, letters to the editor, and other media discourses *about* media participate in the circulation of meaning in society (Gripsrud, 1994).

It is hardly an exaggeration to say that, in the ideal-typical contemporary audience study, a particular methodology tends to assume the status of a fetish, becoming an answer in search of a question. The lesson concerning the value of combining several forms of evidence can be learnt from early work in the field of communications. In his classic study of the public response to Orson Welles' radio production of *War of the Worlds*, Hadley Cantril (1940) showed the value of including unstructured conversations and other sources of information in order to arrive at an overall interpretation of the event. Equally, as part of the Mass Observation studies in Great Britain during the 1930s and 1940s, cinema audiences were examined. While the information on audiences cannot be related directly to the content of specific films, the source materials, as made available by Richards and Sheridan (1987), comprising observation protocols and questionnaire responses, contain rich evidence for the historical study of media use during a period of economic crisis and war.

More recently, the British Film Institute in 1988 organized a large-scale documentation of one day in the life of British television, including both program schedules, viewer responses, and commentary from media professionals. The materials were collected in a book edited by Sean Day-Lewis (1989) and reflect, among many other things, on the changing role of television in Britain during a period witnessing deregulation and the growth of transnational satellite channels. Comparable evidence, though without the special focus on media, has been produced in similar participatory diary studies, for example in Denmark (Olsen and Skougaard, 1993). One can only hope that this wealth of discourses about everyday life will later become the basis of focused case studies in historical reception analysis.

Media reception in the past

Whereas the quantity and type of source materials that are available concerning the audiences of any given period in media history are limited, the methodological imagination may compensate, to a degree, for the absence of historical or social-scientific facts by examining other discourses that have traditionally been the domain of humanistic scholarship. Historians refer habitually to literary works to support their interpretation of past societies and cultures. Since literature and other high cultural forms often carry a perspective from the top of the social hierarchy, communication researchers must also look to the discourses of popular culture.

In her study of the introduction of TV into American homes, Spigel (1992) examined the representation of television in magazines of the period. The premise of the study was that new media are introduced to the general public through old media, so that the analysis of magazine discourses would suggest the cultural agenda on which early American TV was placed. The findings show, among other things, that television was constructed as a new cultural resource which could either unite or divide the family at a time when a general restructuring of family and gender roles was in progress. It is interesting to note that, both in purely quantitative terms and in their mode of address, advertisements for TV sets were addressed especially to women. Whereas it would be an exaggeration to claim that television thus became a medium under female control, the advertising strategy was a way of accommodating television within the daily routine of women working in the home (and increasingly outside the home) (see further Gray, 1987; Modleski, 1984). A similar finding is offered in Moores' (1988) study of the introduction of radio into Great Britain, based on an oral history methodology. His analysis suggests that, after initially being conceived as a technical toy for the father, radio gradually became a routine activity to be subordinated to, or at least integrated with, the mother's other chores in the home.

Another study of the introduction of British radio has emphasized how the temporal structures of the medium and of the everyday were assimilated.

Examining the daily flow of programming, Scannell (1988) concluded that early radio contributed to a new experience of time. Not only did British radio of the 1930s establish a regular daily rhythm in its programming, but the specific content of programs at various times of day may have served as a new form of boundary rituals mediating between the private sphere of the home and the public sphere of work and school. The study goes on to suggest that the temporal structures of the media and the everyday should also be conferred with superordinate temporal structures, for example recurring national political and cultural events, as represented in the media. Historical time, as experienced by the audience-public, is structured in part by the temporal arrangement of national events in the mass media. The methodological implication is that program schedules, along with national statistics of time use, present important sources of evidence regarding reception.

A last example shows that, by examining in depth a few audience members about whom much evidence is available, one may throw light on some fundamental conditions of reception that would apply to the audience at large. Seymour-Ure (1989), in an ingenious study design, examined how the interaction of prime ministers with television has changed over time. Focusing on prime ministers from Great Britain, Australia, and Canada, and conferring the age of each prime minister with the age of the medium in each national context, the analysis concludes that politicians are gradually socialized to use new media such as television, in part through their own media use. Seymour-Ure concludes that the politician's degree of success depends, in large measure, on an ability to articulate his/her message within the characteristic form of TV at a given historical juncture. In this respect, it is correct to speak of a certain segment of the prime ministers as 'TV politicians,' and it may be justified to think of the audience as belonging to different 'TV generations,' to the extent that they have been subject to a specific construction of politics and society through television (Chapter 6). While both politicians and their voters, then, are socialized to television, the difference remains that, for all practical purposes, only the politicians become actors *on* television, in addition to being recipients *of* television.

Media reception in the future

Perhaps the most important task for reception analysis lies in the future. Like other social science, mass communication research tends to focus on modern and contemporary issues, to the exclusion of historical developments or the understanding of the present as a specific moment in social and cultural history. Reception studies, by contrast, may become both retrospective and prospective by asking what could be done to facilitate historical reception studies in the future.

This implies a reformulation of the research agenda for qualitative empirical reception analysis. Much of the effort in this domain over the last decade and a half has been focused on theoretical and methodological research that would serve to consolidate, legitimate, and integrate reception analysis in the general enterprise of communication studies. I conclude that this task has now been accomplished, insofar as interpretive modes of inquiry are now said in a standard chronicle of the field to constitute a 'meaning paradigm' currently challenging traditional positions (Lowery and DeFleur, 1988: 455–9) (even if no studies from the new paradigm are as yet considered fit for inclusion among the other 'milestones' of the field). Having established the independent explanatory value of qualitative research, current studies have begun to apply the tools of reception analysis to specific problematics, such as the audience response to politically and culturally controversial issues – ethnicity, violence, nuclear power – as disseminated by the mass media (for example, Corner et al., 1990; Jensen, 1991d; Jhally and Lewis, 1992; Schlesinger et al., 1992).

One purpose of 'applied' reception studies should be to produce source materials for future research. An example of such a project has been outlined by Russ Neuman under the heading of "parallel content analysis" (Neuman, 1989). The basic idea is to conduct a parallel and continuous registration over time, first, of the content of a whole range of mass media and, second, of the 'content' of the audience reception and uses of media. The premise is that both the thematic focus of media items and their formal articulation may, to a degree, be traced in the foci and rearticulations of the audience response. If conducted on a grand scale, the project might document some long lines of the interaction between mass media and the audience-public, including processes of agenda-setting (McCombs and Shaw, 1972) and cultivation (Gerbner and Gross, 1976). Neuman's (1989) further assumption is that several different content and audience studies will be able to draw on the same data base, which may also facilitate collaborative and comparative studies across disciplinary and, perhaps, national-cultural boundaries.

Two caveats concerning the design should be indicated. First, data sets always carry a theoretical framework, explicitly or implicitly, which specifies the significance of the individual items and their interrelations. This limits the value of a grand data base for a theoretically diverse field. Nevertheless, the development of the data base presumably could give rise to principled, interdisciplinary discussions about theory and methods, and it is likely that a common ground could be found, not for all, but for a substantial number of studies. Second, and more important in this context, it is decisive, as also suggested in Neuman's (1989) proposal, that qualitative data forms be included to enable future audience research to address various contextual and discursive aspects of media use. When the proposal was discussed and critiqued in a 'Research workshop on time series measurement in communication effects research' at the 1991 meeting of the International Communication Association, all interventions were made with reference to the concepts and standards of quantitative survey methodology. Still, the construction of a common resource for qualitative and quantitative audience studies would provide a welcome opportunity to explore basic theoretical and methodological issues facing the field as a whole.

Another proposal, while growing out of a different perspective in critical theory and cultural studies, identifies a similar resource for research and for public debate. Green (1991) outlines the idea of general-purpose, multi-media data bases that would include qualitative data on the audience reception, experience, and social uses of media along with audience surveys as well as a more traditional form of media archives. There are, of course, many ethical and methodological problems associated with archiving, access, anonymity, and copyright in communication history (Schudson, 1991), and the problems multiply in the case of multi-media-cum-audience data bases, not least since qualitative studies produce especially sensitive data, such as interviews, diaries, and video observations. In principle, however, the accumulation of such data bases is of interest not just for historical research on the relationship between media and audiences, but also for contemporary public debate on what and whom the media are for – meta-communication on the social ends and means of mass communication. Reception should be documented, in part, to empower audiences vis-à-vis media. Basing his proposal on approaches developed in oral history, community studies, and museums, Green suggests that one may

> develop historical projects on media in relation to social change and the specific transformation of neighbourhoods and communities. Such a project, in addition to representing audience interests and concerns, could create a fund of knowledge that would be made available to the community as a whole through various print and electronic media forms. The project would constitute a cultural resource facilitating meta-communication on media past and present, ideally feeding back into the media in the form of discussions, repeat screenings, and other formats. (1991: 230–1)

The economic cost of any of these resources will be high, the methodological difficulties considerable, and the political conflicts over inclusion of and access to data intense. But, unless we as a field admit audiences to history, little will be heard from them in the future. It is indeed striking that only a very limited portion of mass communication, and an even smaller portion of the audience response, are preserved for the historical record through research and museums. The various forms of high culture and criticism still reign supreme in the conception of culture that is being passed on to present and future generations. Some redressing of this historical bias seems overdue in the name of both cultural diversity and scientific impartiality. Time may question current cultural standards and rewrite the history of contemporary popular culture. It is one of the responsibilities of mass communication research to produce the discourses that would make a rewriting of history possible.

Discourse analysis: Semiotics beyond statistics

The 'how' of qualitative research

Since language is constitutive of most types of social action, it is also the main medium for gaining access to the lifeworlds of other people, the world-views of other cultures, and the changing forms of consciousness in historical perspective. In a court of law, the presentation of evidence and the pronouncement of verdicts are performatives or speech acts (Austin, 1962) that may mean the difference between life and death. In social science, the wording of survey questionnaires on living conditions affects the conclusions drawn, perhaps with major implications for social policy. Language is a resource for the social construction of reality (Berger and Luckmann, 1966). Through language, reality becomes social.

While departing from linguistics and from examples of interview analysis, this section outlines a communicative, semiotic conception of research practice generally. In the case of qualitative methodologies, it is especially clear that the discourses of research are the product of verbal communication with sources past and present. Also in quantitative forms of research, however, communication is a condition of the knowledge produced. Survey and experimental studies, in addition to relying extensively on questions and instructions, treat their data as signs of the respondents' more or less explicit opinions and more or less intentional performances, and of their cognitive states at varying levels of consciousness. The typology in Figure 8.1 summarizes the three main qualitative approaches to data collection and analysis with reference to their characteristic uses of language.[2]

Interviewing   Language is constitutive of qualitative interview studies, serving two different purposes in the research process. On the one hand, verbal language is the basic *tool* of interviewing, being a form of interpersonal communication. Through language, interviewer and respondent negotiate an understanding of the subject matter in question, each performing preliminary interpretations of responses and offering commentary as well as additional questions. On the other hand, the interaction as a whole, in the form of tapes and transcripts, subsequently becomes the *object* of further textual analysis and interpretation.[3]

Observation   Although communication with informants is normally an integrated element of observation studies, either during observation sessions or as separate interviews, frequently the interviews are not documented or analyzed

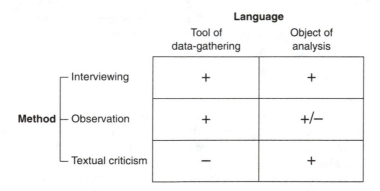

Figure 8.1   *The role of language in qualitative research*

in any detail. In such cases, language tends to become a tool of gathering supplementary information, but not an object of analysis in its own right. At the
same time, as suggested by the double notation in Figure 8.1(+/–), language
may enter into observational analyses in several other respects. For one thing,
the notes taken during and after observational sessions bear witness to the
vocabularies and concepts of the population under investigation, as reconstructed in discourse by the researcher, and the researcher's own debriefing
account of the observation may take the form of a narrative. For another
thing, since questions and comments are essential means of intervening in a
social context, the researcher's communicative behavior represents a measure
of his/her participation as well as an object of analysis. The more actively the
researcher relies on language in the research context, the higher the degree of
participation. In anthropological fieldwork, of course, one of the researcher's
first tasks has been learning the local language as a key to both understanding
and survival. However, also in organizational studies of bureaucracies in the
home culture, for example, a major source of information is the language of
meetings, memoranda, and letters.

Textual criticism   Finally, textual criticism is defined here as the variety of historical, literary, and linguistic forms of analysis that are applied to records,
source documents, visual representations, and texts in the widest sense. While
written accounts are used less frequently as tools of data-gathering in social
science, in part because of their bias in favor of more educated groups, they
remain important objects of analysis, for instance for cross-reference with
other types of evidence. The language of records, from legislation and business
correspondence to newspapers, suggests, for example, how political and cultural rights have been conceived in different social and historical contexts.
Moreover, the analysis of linguistic minutiae in fact can have major implications for the interpretation of history. One example was the publication in 1984
of what was alleged to be the diaries of Adolf Hitler. An important means of
assessing their genuineness (or falsity, as it was established) was the analysis of
language: vocabulary, sentence structure, as well as handwriting. Similarly,
when with regular intervals the discovery of a 'new' drama by Shakespeare is
announced, the tools of stylistics are introduced together with computer-aided
word counts. Language, in sum, is key to constructing, communicating, and
challenging particular versions of past and present.

From communicative practice to data analysis

Because interviewing is a communicative practice, language enters into both
the planning of interviews and the training of interviewers. According to
Gorden (1969), interviewing involves three levels of planning: strategy, tactics,
and techniques. *Strategy* addresses the general setting and the organization of
the interview as such. Considering the 'what' and 'why' of the study, the
researcher seeks to create a context of communication that is appropriate in
terms of the time available, the psychological environment, the assumed roles
of interviewer and respondent(s) including their degree of formality, the

relevance of note-taking (language use, again), and other practical matters. The selection and sequencing of questions, next, is a matter of *tactics*. In order to probe and focus particular issues, it is important that the interviewer be familiar not just with 'the issues,' but also with the conventions of turn-taking in ordinary conversation (Coulthard and Montgomery, 1981). Finally, *techniques* are the specific linguistic or extra-linguistic means of carrying out strategy and tactics, including body language. The choice of vocabulary and, crucially, the use of silence for eliciting more information, far from being merely matters of empathy or intuition, are both techniques that can be learnt. Especially in qualitative interviewing, where the scope for variation of tactics and techniques is greater than in surveys, interviewers must be aware of their options as language workers.

Depth interviewing is an extremely efficient generator of language, so that ultimately qualitative researchers find themselves facing a mass of data requiring some form of categorization and interpretation. In a first step, computer programs are efficient tools, also in qualitative research, for organizing and cross-referencing data in terms of their vocabulary, particular structures of argument, or through codes added in the analytical process (Fielding and Lee, 1991; Pfaffenberger, 1988). The computer may thus replace personalized paper-and-pencil notations with systems that are more manageable, further allowing for data-sharing with other researchers. When studying linguistic structures in social context, however, it takes an interpretive subject to establish potential meanings with reference to several levels of discourse at once.

By way of introducing discourse-analytical procedures, I refer to the four classic levels of language study (Figure 8.2). While linguistics is itself a specialized discipline that may contribute to more, genuinely interdisciplinary group projects, linguistics does offer a number of analytical procedures that may be applied by scholars across the communications field. At each level, certain features of interview discourses can be taken as *linguistic danger signals* calling for detailed analysis, interpretation, and, perhaps, re-interviewing.

The *grammatical* form of a respondent's sentences may raise issues concerning his/her self-image. If, for instance, no explicit reference is made to the agentive force behind events affecting a respondent, is s/he expressing a sense of impotence, a lack of knowledge, or some other self-conception? Often such impersonal accounts take the form of a passive grammatical construction ("It

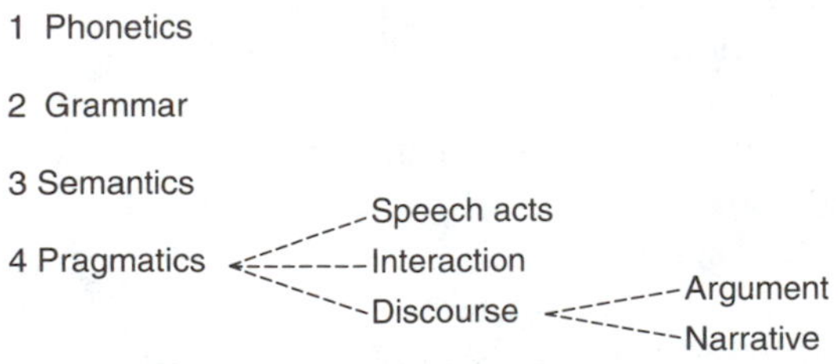

1 Phonetics

2 Grammar

3 Semantics

4 Pragmatics
  - Speech acts
  - Interaction
  - Discourse
    - Argument
    - Narrative

Figure 8.2   *Four levels of linguistic analysis*

was decided that . . ." – by whom, one wonders), or they are suggested by the use of pronouns (as in the English 'one,' the German 'man,' the French 'on') (Fowler et al., 1979; Jensen, 1987a; Mortensen, 1977).[4]

The *semantic* analysis of meaning also can identify a particular conceptual organization of, and orientation toward, social reality. A complete listing of the terms associated by a respondent with individuals or institutions discussed in an interview is a simple but powerful first step of a semantic analysis. The connotations (Barthes, 1957/1973) of nouns as well as verbs serve to situate each of these social agents along various evaluative scales. Beyond such classic distinctions as "terrorist" versus "freedom fighter," semantic analysis can establish the presence of conceptual networks in the respondents' discourses that carry a message about themselves.

Even the *phonetic* level can be relevant for interview studies. Whereas learning a foreign language, most of us know, involves difficulties of identifying and reproducing alien sounds, a specific language, as perceived from within another language, culture, and historical context, also lends a particular texture to the world. This is equally true of the subcodes of 'one' language, its dialects and sociolects, including the presumed standard. Working with tapes and transcripts of interviews that the researcher commands as a secondary language is a helpful, defamiliarizing exercise, sensitizing both the practice of interviewing and the analysis to the mediating role of language.

The most important analytical level for communication research broadly speaking is *pragmatics*, the study of language use in social context (Halliday, 1978; Leech, 1983; van Dijk, 1985). While the study of language, beginning with classical philology, had traditionally been preoccupied with form, linguistics over the last few decades has focused increasingly on the social uses of language in everyday contexts, from family conversation and classroom interaction to patient–therapist interviews.

Pragmatics: Language as communication

Speech acts   The fundamental constituents of discourse are the utterances or statements, referred to as speech acts (Austin, 1962; Searle, 1969), that can be thought of literally as minimal instances of linguistic action. As discussed in Chapter 4, language does not simply or even primarily work as a descriptive representation; it performs a variety of everyday actions. In empirical research, a respondent's evaluative statements and the arguments, exemplifications, and later modifications supporting them are particularly relevant because they articulate a specific rationality. Whereas the typologies of language as action are still being worked out, speech-act theory has offered one of the most important contributions to interdisciplinary theory of science, bridging a gap between humanistic and social-scientific conceptions of communication as language and as social action.

Interaction   The interaction between interviewer and respondent(s) is an inherently communicative process. Both sides introduce and develop particular themes while closing off other aspects of the discursive universe. In negotiating a form of common understanding, the participants can be seen to build semantic networks that are indicative of their worldviews. Also observational studies establish complex forms of interaction that lend themselves to linguistic analysis as developed in studies of everyday conversation and classroom interaction (for example, Antaki, 1988). The interactive dimension, moreover, is of special interest for the planning and execution of qualitative research. Linguistic analysis of an interview transcript can suggest how conceptual distinctions and interrelations are worked out during the interaction. Such an analysis may assess the extent to which studies fulfill the promise of qualitative researchers to 'ground' their theoretical categories in the respondents' lifeworlds (Glaser and Strauss, 1967). Conducted by another researcher, this evaluation of interviewer performance addresses the intersubjectivity of qualitative findings. Thus, discourse analysis, in complementing traditional measures of reliability and validity in the administration and coding of interviews, may reopen the field for discussion of the criteria of scientific knowledge. The understanding of empirical research as communicative interaction may also support the planning of specific designs and the training of interviewers and field-workers.

Discourse   It is at the level of discourse that the different linguistic categories come together to constitute a coherent structure, a text with a more or less unified message to be interpreted. Both respondents and historical records will tell stories and develop arguments in forms that draw on literary and rhetorical genres. Whereas certain aspects of coherence are due to formal features of discourse (Halliday and Hasan, 1976), other aspects arise from the functional interrelations between the speech acts and interactive turns of a specific discourse. Functional interrelations must normally be interpreted with reference both to the discursive context and to the context of use (see van Dijk, 1977, 1991). While Chapters 5–7 have presented concrete analyses of research data as discourses, below I discuss two major types of discourse. Since humans seem to be constantly telling stories or arguing about something, whether in formal scientific discourse, conversation, or public debate, any typology of discourse is of necessity complex. Bruner (1986) has suggested a general distinction between two modes of experience and discourse: the paradigmatic or argumentative mode and the narrative mode.

Argumentation   As noted in Chapter 5, argumentation appears to draw on a relatively fixed repertoire of strategies combining premises and conclusions, assertions and substantiations, one characteristic form being the combination of generalizations with supporting exemplifications and other forms of evidence. Moreover, each step may be founded on presuppositions (Leech, 1974) or implicit premises (Culler, 1981) that are taken for granted and not otherwise elaborated. Tracing each of these elements in a sample text suggests how particular premises and ideas underlying and structuring an argument can be identified.

In Chapter 5, one of the quotations from the study of American television news reception concerned a story about an airplane that had technical problems before landing. The respondent found himself paying special attention to those visuals:

> [...] with that particular story you look, I was looking at the airplane to see if there was any explosion. It turns out that there weren't. Everything, everyone was, was prepared. I was a little bit curious, interested or curious to find out that it was actually broadcast that way. It could have been a near fatal catastrophe, and it was just, it would have been broadcast on national TV. That would, that caught my attention.

Whereas adverbial constructions, conjunctions, and various forms of emphasis may signal the generalizations of a statement, here it is the repetition of semantically related terms that serves to identify the most general level of response. Having mentioned that he was focusing on the plane landing, the respondent notes twice that these visuals made him "curious," and that they "caught my attention," the last statement serving as a summary of the response. Noting the possibility of an explosion, the respondent further substantiates his interest with reference to the danger of a "catastrophe," which might then have been broadcast.

Although the importance of visual drama in television news comes out both in this and other interviews, the striking feature of this particular response is the assumed reality of news visuals. The respondent's point is that if the landing had resulted in a catastrophe, "it would have been broadcast on national TV." The implied premise, then, is that the story was aired *before* it was known whether it would result in a catastrophe. The expression "that way" in the preceding sentence sums up the assumption that this was live coverage, which ostensibly it was not. The 'mistake' suggests the fascination of visual mass media, the see-it-here-and-now experience, raising a number of issues concerning the impact of visual communication on audience perceptions of reality (see Chapter 10).

Narrative   Current research refers to respondents' discourses as narratives (Mishler, 1986). Humans also tell stories to make a point, and in doing so they draw on a variety of oral as well as literate forms. A general aim particularly of structuralist theories of narrative has been to arrive at a 'grammar' of multiple concrete stories (Culler, 1975; Eagleton, 1983), by analogy to the grammatical distinction between surface structure (concrete sentences) and deep structure (Chomsky, 1965). Among the most intensively studied forms has been the folk or fairy tale, being a highly standardized genre with a variety of social uses in many cultures. The background to contemporary studies is the work of Vladimir Propp on traditional Russian folk tales. Any of these tales, Propp concluded, draws on a fixed repertoire of roles, which appear in a particular sequence and interact according to specific conventions. In later research, notably by A.J. Greimas (Greimas, 1966; Greimas and Courtés, 1982), the approach was systematized, and has been applied to different genres, including romantic fiction, advertising, and other forms of popular culture.

Probably the most widely applied structuralist model of narrative is Greimas's *actant model*. The model makes a fundamental distinction between the actors and actants of narratives: *actors* are the characters of particular narratives, whereas *actants* are the deep-structural elements or positions of the narrative matrix. To exemplify, a Subject position (actant) in a folk tale might be occupied by a prince (actor), setting forth on his quest for the Object, represented by the princess or the holy grail. Along the way the prince encounters Opponents as well as Helpers, from witches to dragons. Ultimately the prince is victorious and becomes the Recipient of the princess and half the kingdom from a Donor such as the old king. Importantly, there is no one-to-one relationship between actants and actors, so that several characters can occupy the same actant position, and the narrative identities of one character may be split and distributed upon several actants. The prince, for example, may be his own best Helper and worst Opponent. The model, comprising six agencies and five interrelations, is presented in Figure 8.3.

Like other theoretical schemata, the actant model poses a danger of reductionism. Having been developed to account for delimited narrative segments of formulaic genres, it may be especially appropriate for the analysis of other standardized genres in mass communication. For research employing interviewing, observation, or records, however, narrative models also have heuristic value by identifying several fundamental categories of discursive universes. Moreover, the specific configuration of these categories may bear witness to shifting points of view at different stages of a narrative or to conflicting interests from the perspective of different agents, and even to the conflicting interests of one agent. The distribution of major themes and issues onto different discursive positions and narrative sequences, thus, allows for an understanding of the dynamic, processual nature of meaning as it is emerges in research discourses. The actant model, for one, is helpful in uncovering certain implicit aspects of self-reports in interviews, the 'Story of Me.' For example, internal conflicts regarding a personal or professional choice may manifest themselves as the simultaneous presence of the respondent in several actant positions at once. In organizational studies, equally, interviews in different sections and levels of a hierarchy may produce very different narratives of what is the common quest or project. Conflicts of interest and unresolved tensions can revolve around several different axes: the axis of desire (the Subject–Object relationship, concerning the definition of the very purpose of

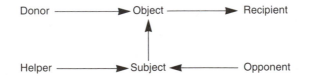

Figure 8.3   *The actant model (Greimas, 1966: 180)*

a project); the axis of conflict (Helper–Subject–Opponent relations, including the definition of friend and foe and of their relative strength); and the axis of communication (Donor–Object–Recipient relations, involving questions of who will be the ultimate beneficiaries of a project).

Conclusion

In a stimulating, provocative article, Meaghan Morris (1990) has suggested that research within the cultural studies tradition, prominent also in qualitative reception studies, tends toward banality. Her point is that, because many analyses stay too close to the discourse of everyday life and common sense, they lack both social contextualization and reflective distance and, therefore, exaggerate the complexity and profundity of their data showing, for example, public resistance to a dominant social order. The challenge, accordingly, is to develop more comprehensive and systematic forms of analysis to probe the common sense of everyday interaction, as well as of particular research traditions, as part of a meta-discourse of scientific semiosis. Verbal language offers an analytical common denominator in which to substantiate or transcend what may appear banal.

This chapter has argued for a pluralism of both methodological designs and concrete analytical methods, not merely in the case of historical reception studies, but within an overall strategy of complementarity. My premise has been that different research traditions tap different aspects of the process of communication. Each analytical constituent is a semiotic vehicle addressing the media, audience, and context constituents of mass communication from a position in theoretical discourse. While there is thus no way around signs, different signs document different aspects of reality. Peircean semiotics enables both a first-order theory of communication and a second-order theory of science, elaborated in Part III.

PART III
THEORY OF SCIENCE: SECOND-ORDER SEMIOTICS

9

The Epistemology of Communication: Abduction and the Logic of Qualitative Research

Two types of complementarity

Apartheid[1]

The distinctions between natural-scientific and humanistic conceptions of science which still divide the communications field are commonly summed up in conceptual pairs at the epistemological, theoretical, and methodological levels of analysis. Figure 9.1 collects the dichotomies accumulated in several different traditions and periods of research.

By way of introduction, I emphasize that my brief account follows the history of the dichotomies as received, rather than the practice of science in actual laboratories and libraries. Few concrete studies may conform to one or the other ideal type, instead combining different modes of hypothesizing and inferencing. Nevertheless, the conceptual pairs continue to inform scientific

Epistemology	
Subject	Object
Intention	Cause
History	Nature
Theory of science	
Ereigniswissenschaft	*Gesetzeswissenschaft*
Idiographic	Nomothetic
Geisteswissenchaften	*Naturwissenschaften*
Verstehen	*Erklären*
Meaning	Information
Internal	External
Methodology	
Occurrence	Recurrence
Experience	Experiment
Exegesis	Measurement
Process	Product

Figure 9.1   *Two paradigms of science*

self-conceptions, and they still serve as premises of interdisciplinary debate after a century of social-scientific research. In the present context, the juxtaposition leads into the discussion of a possible third paradigm, a theory of science that may accommodate the understanding of scientific semiosis as a form of social action.

The founding conceptual pair remains that of *subject* and *object*. Whereas objects can be defined in formal, relational terms as objects *of* the subject's cognition, many objects of human cognition are in fact other subjects and *their* cognition of us, as suggested by Mead's (1934) momentous concept of the significant other. The issue for social and communication theory is how, specifically, people engage each other as subjects or objects in everyday life, how the coordination of social action is achieved, and how subjects' motivated actions accumulate as objective social structures: How do *intentions* become *causes*? Such questions have been addressed from the perspective of *history*, defining society as a sequence of unique events, or from the perspective of *nature*, defining society as a complex, but law-abiding entity – second nature.

The epistemological distinctions are implied by the disciplinary theories of science that predominate in different areas of empirical inquiry. While sciences associated with either column can be said to establish facts of human experience, facts are of at least two kinds. A basic distinction was formulated by the Neo-Kantian, Windelband, between the study of singular events (*Ereigniswissenschaft*) and the study of laws (*Gesetzeswissenschaft*). To these types of fact, further, there correspond two scientific attitudes, namely, the *idiographic* approach seeking what once was, and the *nomothetic* approach establishing what always is, or in the terms of Windelband's colleague, Rickert, the individualizing and the generalizing method. The distinction was reemphasized by Wilhelm Dilthey, not as two ways of addressing the same reality, but as two categories of reality calling for two forms of science, that is, *Geisteswissenschaften* (on 'spirit') and *Naturwissenschaften* (on 'nature'). Spirit is to be understood (*verstehen*); nature is to be explained (*erklären*). These notions can be retraced in contemporary communication research, specifically in models of what is being communicated, either as *meaning*, being an indivisible phenomenon linked to a particular context, to be interpreted from an *internal* perspective, or as *information*, being a technical construct that may be mastered, manipulated, and transmitted from an *external* perspective. The two models have been labeled by Carey (1989), drawing on John Dewey, communication as ritual and as transmission.

The methodological implications of the two paradigms are expressed in the last set of conceptual pairs. If one can precisely delimit meaning, as it is communicated by message segments, then quantification of meaning and hence the measurement of its *recurrence* becomes possible. Furthermore, *measurement* makes possible an *experiment* manipulating the parts of the message in order to establish the relative impact of part meanings. Conversely, if meaning cannot be understood outside of the message in its entirety or the context as a whole, then one can only note the *occurrence* of meaning. The *experience* of meaning, accordingly, would be autonomous and unique, arising from a process of exegesis by, as the case may be, audiences or researchers. Most generally, communication has been approached as the *process* serving to constitute meaning, or as the final set of *products* of meaning.

Imperialism[2]

Although it is now common to denounce scientific apartheid, it is not clear how to avoid the opposite extreme of scientific imperialism. To suggest the difficulties, I note one of the most elaborate arguments for convergence, made by Karl Erik Rosengren in a series of articles during the last decade. In his contribution to the stock-taking 'Ferment in the Field' issue of the *Journal of Communication* (1983), 'Communication research: One paradigm or four?' (published in a longer version in Rosengren, 1985), he concluded that there really is, and should be, only one paradigm. Rosengren's point of departure is a typology of scientific approaches, borrowed from the sociology of organization, that comprises two dimensions, namely, the distinction between objective and subjective orientations, and a distinction between sociologies of regulation and sociologies of radical change. A crossing of the dimensions produces a fourfold typology consisting of the Radical Humanist, the Radical Structuralist, the Interpretive, and the Functionalist paradigms. The main point of the article is that it will take Functionalism to provide scientific answers, even if the other, 'dissident' paradigms are good at raising troublesome questions. "The paradox is that; *Those who can give the answers did not ask the questions; and those who asked the questions cannot provide the answers*" (Rosengren, 1985: 240).

In terms of the two master paradigms above, then, a science of the object, to be measured as it recurs under identical circumstances, is placed firmly in control by Rosengren (1985). In the end, the article does away with the regulation/radical change dimension as a relevant criterion altogether, advocating instead a particular conception of objectivism against an untenable subjectivism:

> The regulation/radical change dimension in particular does not build upon basically different ontological and/or epistemological assumptions. This dimension is more politically than scientifically valid, mistaking hopes, wishes, and fears for basic assumptions about actually-existing traits of society. The subjectivist dimension, on the other hand, builds more directly upon basic differences in ontology and epistemology. A truly subjective perspective, however, is very difficult to combine with any kind of serious scientific activity: The more extreme variants of existentialism and phenomenology have flourished mainly in literature and non-academic philosophy. (p. 261)

Rosengren, thus, does not leave much scope for different ways of researching "actually-existing traits of society." And, while he does conceive of the subjectivist–objectivist dimension as a continuum, he is unwilling to grant broadly idiographic forms of understanding the status of science, requiring that they accept the epistemological premises of another paradigm:

> Several of the basic assumptions of the paradigms can be formulated as empirically-answerable questions about conditions in actually existing societies, and the fact that some of these questions or hypotheses have their origin in one research tradition and their answer in another should not prevent the community of communication scholars from addressing them seriously and open-mindedly. (p. 261)

Two central questions are being begged here, both how an issue may be addressed empirically, and what is an open scientific mind. The begging of questions multiplies when Rosengren goes on to indicate the obstacles to convergence around a consensual approach:

> The main hindrance to such movement probably is the interest which leading representatives of rival schools have vested in demonstrating to themselves, to their followers, and to their opponents that somehow they are radically different. In the long run, however, such claims cannot hold their own against empirical evidence. (pp. 261–2)

The unargued, uncompromising premise is that soft questions come in many forms, hard answers only in one form, and, hence, that any dissidence concerning the privileged status of hard empirical answers is a sign of less than scientific motives in a less than open mind.

Recently, Rosengren (forthcoming) has specified his requirements concerning empirical evidence by distinguishing between substantive theories and formal models. Having articulated a theory in rich verbal language, he suggests, scientists need to state it in logical, mathematical, or statistical terms, and perhaps graphic models, in order to subject it to empirical tests. Referring to examples from uses-and-gratifications studies and research on life styles, Rosengren argues that these traditions became successful, from the perspective of the Functionalist paradigm, precisely when they began to rely on formal models facilitating the study of representative samples of specific populations in unambiguous circumstances with reference to strategic variables. By contrast, he argues, qualitative reception studies will remain promising pilots until they enter the formal fold.

While practically all of Rosengren's examples of formal models are statistical models as applied within quantitative survey research, his ten-year reassessment of the 1983 article, appearing in the 'Future of the Field' issue of the *Journal of Communication* (1993), mentions the importance of logic for the development of formalized qualitative models, and he cites Charles Ragin's (1987) work in this area approvingly. One problematic assumption of Ragin (1987), however, is that, in a comparison of various types of social events in different cultural or historical circumstances, there will be no loss of important information if in each case the researcher notes the presence or absence of particular factors that might serve to explain the event. It is not clear, for instance, how one might approach the decisive contextual interrelations between factors, or how one may determine the level of social organization at which the factor is operative, and it is significant that the examples given are of 'objective,' macrosocial units, whereas issues regarding the participants' perspective on events are left out entirely.

This understanding of what qualitative researchers ought to do, but are still not doing, helps to explain the title of Rosengren's (1993) article, 'From field to frog ponds.' The implication is that the field is not growing toward one paradigm, but toward fragmentation characterized by the sort of mutual tolerance that implies indifference. I conclude that Rosengren (1993), along with a substantial portion of the field, in practice insists on staying in his own frog pond by refusing to explore the explanatory value of alternative conceptions of science, "seriously and open-mindedly." While logical positivism may be a dead horse not worth flogging, the upshot is crypto-positivism, still kicking and dominant at annual conferences and in major journals, which retains the three key features of a positivistic theory of science (Hammersley, 1989: 17): the conception of science as the identification of universal laws or, in a weaker version, regularities that are independent of contexts; the grounding of knowledge about these regularities in elementary sensations; and, most important, the requirement that all knowledge rely on the same methodological principles. In sum, the ideal of formal models represents the questionable methodological premise that the entire social universe is also written in the signs of mathematics and thus may be studied with a grounding in elementary, quantifiable data, ultimately revealing regularities across all contexts of inquiry and action.

Unification in the last instance

Difference and emergence

If the aim of crypto-positivism is a unified science in the first instance, that is, at the level of elementary data and methodological principles, social semiotics proposes unification in the last instance, in a community of inquiry that allows for multiple scientific signs. And, whereas semiotics may not satisfy Rosengren and others' notion of formal models, Peircean semiotics points toward a richer, more liberal logic of inquiry.

This development is possible in spite of the fact that Peirce himself was decidedly ambivalent concerning the standards of interdisciplinary science. On the one hand, he emphasized that major scientific breakthroughs occurred through the application of methods from one science in the domain of another:

> The scientific specialists – pendulum swingers and the like – are doing a great and useful work; each one very little, but altogether something vast. But the higher places in science in the coming years are for those who succeed in adapting the methods of one science to the investigation of another. That is what the greatest progress of the passing generation has consisted in. Darwin adapted to biology the methods of Malthus and the economists. (quoted in Fisch, 1986b: xxxvi)

On the other hand, Peirce noted the importance of formalizing and quantifying analytical procedures, that "a science first begins to be exact when it is quantitatively treated" (Peirce, 1986: 276). Simultaneously, as noted in Chapter 2, he distanced himself from the positivism of Comte, particularly the principle of verification, that "it must not suppose anything you are not able directly to observe" (Peirce, 1955: 268). And elsewhere Peirce develops the argument that multiple phenomena, including metaphysics, lend themselves to scientific investigation (CP 6.2–3).

I conclude that Peirce's semiotics lends itself to the development of a differentiated theory of science. Before turning to its sources in Peirce's logic, I note two general implications of a semiotic theory of science. First, the concept of *difference* applies to scientific semiosis: it is through a configuration of signs in relations of difference, reconstructed as interpretants, that we gain insight into a particular set of objects in reality. Signs represent the basic condition of science. Second, it is only by conferring normally distinct categories of signs that we are able to address interdisciplinary issues of meaning and impact, in terms of discursive, interpretive, and social differences. The resulting set of concepts and analytical procedures is *emergent* in relation to those of various disciplinary research traditions. In semiotic terms, the theory of science thus shifts the emphasis up one level in the hierarchy of interpretants or discourses (Figure 4.4). An example may clarify the implications for empirical research.

Can machines think?

The computer has set a new agenda for public as well as scientific debates about the nature of the human mind. While an article originally published in 1950 by Alan Turing, 'Computing machinery and intelligence,' posed the question of how indeed one may be able to distinguish between responses from humans and machines (Turing, 1950/1981), one of the most widely debated versions of this socalled 'Turing test' is John Searle's (1981) Chinese-room thought experiment. The experiment places a native speaker of English, with no knowledge of Chinese, in a locked room and furnishes that person with two batches of Chinese writing along with a set of rules in English for correlating the two batches. Then a third batch of Chinese writing is introduced into the room with a set of instructions on

> how to give back certain Chinese symbols with certain sorts of shapes in response to certain sorts of shapes given me in the third batch. Unknown to me, the people who are giving me all of these symbols call the first batch a 'script,' they call the second batch a 'story,' and they call the third batch 'questions.' Furthermore, they call the symbols I give them back in response to the third batch 'answers to questions,' and the set of rules in English that they gave me, they call the 'program.' (Searle, 1981: 355)

The experiment further stipulates, first, that the person also be given stories in English and questions in English about those stories to be answered, and, second, that s/he becomes so good at following the instructions concerning the Chinese symbols that her/his answers in Chinese appear indistinguishable from those of native Chinese speakers, just as her/his answers in English appear indistinguishable from those of other native English speakers, since the person is in fact a native English speaker. The point is that from the perspective of somebody outside the locked room, the person in the room produces equally good answers to the Chinese questions and the English questions. In the Chinese case, unlike the English case, the person works like a computer.[3]

The rest of Searle's article is an attempt to refute the argument of some artificial intelligence research that the programmed computer, and the person in the Chinese room, can be said to understand the stories, and that the program thus explains human understanding. His counterarguments include, for example, that "there is no principled way to distinguish the motivation for saying the Chinese subsystem understands from saying that the stomach understands" (Searle, 1981: 360–1). In the present context, it is of special interest to note the underlying premise, namely, that intentionality is a separate realm of existence, a unique feature of humans. Responding to why a computer program is not a sufficient condition of understanding, Searle says:

> Because the formal symbol manipulations by themselves don't have any intentionality; they are quite meaningless; they aren't even *symbol* manipulations, since the symbols don't symbolize anything. In the linguistic jargon, they have only a syntax but no semantics. Such intentionality as computers appear to have is solely in the minds of those who program them and those who use them, those who send in the input and those who interpret the output. (1981: 368)

Perhaps the most surprising aspect of the argument, as encountered also in other scientific and public debate, is its vehemence, which is apparently designed to rescue the human mind from contamination by its association with matter and machine. Intentionality may be the last stronghold of the Logos tradition. I propose an alternative, pragmatist response to the computer challenge comprising two elements. In defensive terms, I suggest that we evaluate the cognition and communication of computers with reference to what Haugeland (1985) has called the 'poor-substitute strategy,' rather than the 'hollow-shell strategy.' The poor-substitute strategy concludes that, most likely, computers will never be that advanced, contextual, or 'human,' but, nevertheless, computers should be evaluated *a posteriori*, according to how well they in fact simulate humans. This would also be the scientific approach, in almost any conception of science. (The hollow-shell strategy would hold, as an ontological *a priori*, that machines do not 'really' understand because they lack that special human something – consciousness or intentionality.) In offensive terms, moreover, the rise of the computer is an occasion for reassessing classic issues of what is a human being and a machine, mind and matter, as witnessed in current cognitive science. The computer gives rise to a cultural Rorschach test (Turkle, 1984).

In the perspective of social semiotics, the computer example suggests that the signs produced by a computer must also be evaluated by the *difference* they make. Computer discourses are a configuration of discursive differences that bear witness, among other things, to the nature of the sender or addresser of communication. The computer user's understanding of the communicative context and her/his interaction with the computer, further, consists in interpretive and social differences: the conclusion that one is in fact interacting with another human being is a potential, if unlikely, difference that may follow from the interaction. Finally, interpretive and social differences are *emergent* in relation to the categories of discursive difference: the categories of interpretation and action do not follow from the elements and structures of discourse, even if most computer users will find it easy to infer the nature of their computer from its discourse.

The ability to make inferences with reference to a particular, complex context may be what distinguishes human intelligence. Critical studies of artificial intelligence commonly conclude that the context knowledge required to simulate human cognition and action is both so vast and so fuzzy that the odds against the entire enterprise are overwhelming (Dreyfus, 1979). The most difficult form of inference for computers to perform, and a central form in qualitative studies of communication, is what Peirce called 'abduction.'

Deduction, induction, and abduction

The relationship between the three main forms of logical inference can be explained with reference to the interrelations between the three constituents of the Peircean sign (Figure 9.2).[4] Deduction articulates the relation between a sign (or *representamen*) and its interpretant. For example, a mathematical equation, itself a complex sign, is solved in the form of another sign, provided that one knows the status of both signs as well as the procedures of transformation from one category to another. It is the definition of the signs as such, not their link to any object in reality, that enables us to deduce the solution. Induction, next, confers the sign and the object, or rather many objects, thus establishing certain common features in these objects, with reference to a context of other objects. This arguably remains the central form of inference in contemporary communication research, from ratings to recall studies.

Abduction, relating an interpretant and an object, may be defined as a redescription or a recontextualization (Chapter 3) of the object. Because the object appears, or is inscribed by someone, in a particular context, its status in our understanding may change. A famous example of abduction would be

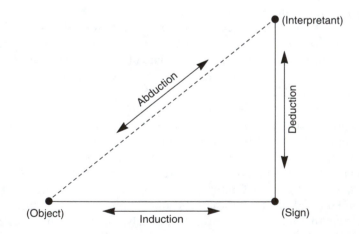

Figure 9.2   *Three forms of logical inference*

Darwin's recontextualization of humans as animals, being the (preliminary) conclusion of a long process of evolution and natural selection. This recontextualization became possible in a particular context, namely, a historical period when the natural sciences had developed a variety of advanced methods and when, equally important, a pervasive secularization of society was in progress, enabling the articulation and gradual acceptance of a new model of world history.[5]

While deduction and induction are the more familiar forms of logic, abduction is original to Peirce and follows, in part, from his triadic conception of reality. The key article relied on a simple example to explain the three principles of inference. In fact, the same elements – referred to by Peirce as a "rule," a "case," and a "result" – enter into all three syllogisms, but in a different sequence, as either premises or conclusions of the argument:

DEDUCTION
Rule. All the beans from this bag are white.
Case. These beans are from this bag.
Result. These beans are white.

INDUCTION
Case. These beans are from this bag.
Result. These beans are white.
Rule. All the beans from this bag are white.

[ABDUCTION]
Rule. All the beans from this bag are white.
Result. These beans are white.
Case. These beans are from this bag.
(Peirce, 1986: 325–6)[6]

The examples should be taken as prototypes indicating three principles of inference, not final conclusions in concrete instances. In the induction, one certainly needs to know how many beans have been examined, and how many beans the bag contains, before estimating the probability of the conclusion. Similarly, in the abduction, one needs to know what other bags, beans, and other items occur in that context, before making a conclusion and perhaps acting on it. The last point may be especially important since abduction is the form of inference that detectives can rely on to solve crimes. Peirce himself told a story of how he once inferred, through abduction, who had stolen several valuables from his cabin on a ship (Sebeok and Umiker-Sebeok, 1983), and he drew other examples freely from both science and everyday life:

I once landed at a seaport in a Turkish province; and, as I was walking up to the house which I was to visit, I met a man upon horseback, surrounded by four horsemen holding a canopy over his head. As the governor of the province was the only personage I could think of who would be so greatly honored, I inferred that this was he. This was an [abduction]. Fossils are found; say, remains like those of fishes, but far in the interior of the country. To explain the phenomenon, we suppose the sea once washed over this land. This is another [abduction]. Numberless documents and monuments refer to a conqueror called Napoleon Bonaparte. Though we have not seen the man, yet we cannot explain what we have seen, namely, all these documents and monuments, without supposing that he really existed. [Abduction] again. (Peirce, 1986: 326)[7]

The farreaching implication of Peirce's concept of abduction, and generally of logic understood as semiotic, is that a distinction must be made between formal logic and other warranted forms of inference that characterize scientific practice. The last section of this chapter notes that, historically, much scientific research may depend less on logical argument than on rhetorical forms, hypothetical rules of inference, and contextual evidence. In the present, systematic terms, specific methodologies may be understood as combinations of the three canonical forms of inference in which one is dominant (as in the Peircean sign including aspects of the index, the icon, as well as the symbol, even while one is dominant; see Johansen, 1993: 95). Whereas formal sciences, such as logic and mathematics, are sometimes held to be deductive, and empirical sciences inductive, the Peircean framework suggests another difference in orientation between the ideal-typical paradigms of natural sciences and arts. On the one hand, natural-scientific practice can be conceived as the inductive matching of empirical objects to descriptive categories, signs, being in the extreme version a form of atomistic extrospection without a constitutive human interpretant. On the other hand, the practice of arts and humanities can be conceived as the deductive differentiation of signs into interpretants as a source of deeper insight, being in the extreme version a form of associative introspection without, in a nominalist variety, any object. While I return briefly to more orthodox conceptions, for example of hypothetico-deductive methodology, it is possible to characterize qualitative empirical research in terms of a dominant principle of abduction.

One of Peirce's important points in the 1878 article was, in fact, that abduction is a distinctive form of logical inference which cannot be reduced to either deduction or induction. Abduction is neither inferior nor superior, but simply a different form of understanding with independent explanatory value for specific purposes of research:

[Abductions] are sometimes regarded as provisional resorts, which in the progress of science are to be replaced by inductions. But this is a false view of the subject. [Abductive] reasoning infers very frequently a fact not capable of direct observation. It is an [abduction] that Napoleon Bonaparte once existed. How is that [abduction] ever to be replaced by an induction? It may be said that from the premise that such facts as we have observed are as they would be if Napoleon existed, we are to infer by induction that *all* facts that are hereafter to be observed will be of the same character. There is no doubt that every [abductive] inference may be distorted into the appearance of an induction in this way. But the essence of an induction is that it infers from one set of facts another similar set of facts, whereas [abduction] infers from facts of one kind to facts of another. (Peirce, 1986: 336)

Abduction in practice: Three examples from reception studies

The act of reading

Janice Radway's (1984) study of female romance readers was an early, exemplary case of empirical reception analysis. Addressing an overlooked genre in an overlooked print medium, the study contextualizes romance reading with reference to the history of the genre, the system of production and distribution, as well as the social and cultural processes in which romance reading is embedded. The findings were produced through a combination of textual criticism, historical research, and an ethnographic approach comprising interviewing and observation in a community of readers that had formed around a particular bookstore.

The research process served, step by step, to articulate the readers' conception of romance reading. At one stage, informants were asked to rank their three most important motives for romance reading. In forty-two returned questionnaires, regarding "Which of the following best describes why you read romances," the responses were in absolute figures:

a.	To escape my daily problems	13
b.	To learn about faraway places and times	19
c.	For simple relaxation	33
d.	Because I wish I had a romance like the heroine's	5
e.	Because reading is just for me; it's my time	28
f.	Because I like to read about the strong, virile heroes	4
g.	Because reading is at least better than other forms of escape	5
h.	Because romantic stories are never sad or depressing	10

(Radway, 1984: 61)

Radway concludes, not unexpectedly, that romances provide an experience beyond the ordinary everyday. More particularly, however, "it creates a time or space within which a woman can be entirely on her own, preoccupied with her personal needs, desires, and pleasure" (p. 61). Radway specifies the procedure leading up to the conclusion:

> It is important to point out here that the responses to the second questionnaire are different in important ways from the answers I received from the women in the face-to-face interviews and in the first survey. At the time of my initial visit in June 1980, our conversations about their reasons for romance reading were dominated by the words 'escape' and 'education.' [...] Both answers *c* and *e* on the second form were given initially in the course of the interviews by two unusually articulate readers who elaborated more fully than most of the women on the meaning of the word 'escape.' They considered these two answers synonymous with it, but they also seemed to prefer the alternate responses because they did not so clearly imply a desire to avoid duties and responsibilities in the 'real' world. Although most of the other women settled for the word 'escape' on the first questionnaire, they also liked their sister readers' terms better. Once these were introduced in the group interviews, the other women agreed that romance reading functions best as relaxation and as a time for self-indulgence. (pp. 61–2)

Importantly, the research process was not separated into a pilot phase clarifying terms and a survey phase establishing the distribution of terms in the responses. Instead, each step above must be seen as a contribution simultaneously to theoretical and empirical analysis of what is romance reading. Furthermore, this recursive process in which informants reformulate and recontextualize concepts from their perspective, produces new insights not just for the researcher, but equally for the informants as they verbalize conceptions for the first time. Although such a process is sometimes associated with the grounded-theory approach of Glaser and Strauss (1967), it is in fact characteristic more generally of qualitative empirical research, being constituted by a sequence of contextualized inferences. By contrast to a survey-cum-pilot approach proposing to test a fully operationalized hypothesis in terms of probability, qualitative research is premised on the dialectical process of theoretical and empirical work in what is, in principle, an infinite scientific semiosis. By contrast to the implication of grounded theory that no theoretical prejudice guide that very first field trip, social semiotics suggests that any scientific study has a set of first premises – a knowledge interest and a context of inquiry – to be recognized and engaged reflectively in meta-theoretical discourse.

Radway's (1984) study documented, among other things, the informants' sophisticated interpretive ability, their learning of social and emotional skills from romances, and the ambiguity of their discursive strategies when measured against their social condition. I take one of the pivotal findings to be the understanding of romance reading as a specific social act, as recapitulated by Radway:

> In summary, when the act of romance reading is viewed as it is by the readers themselves, from within a belief system that accepts as given the institutions of heterosexuality and monogamous marriage, it can be conceived as an activity of mild protest and longing for reform necessitated by those institutions' failure to satisfy the emotional needs of women. Reading therefore functions for them as an act of recognition and contestation whereby that failure is first admitted and then partially reversed. Hence, the Smithton readers' claim that romance reading is a 'declaration of independence' and a way to say to others, 'This is my time, my space. Now leave me alone.' (Radway, 1984: 213)

This conclusion may be explicated in the form of an abduction:

> Romance reading is a declaration of independence.
> All uses of texts by readers to claim their own time are declarations of independence.
> Conclusion: Romance reading is a use of texts by readers for claiming their own time.

Whereas the first premise presents a puzzling fact from the empirical universe of romance readers (puzzling to the extent that romances represent women in dependent roles which might be accepted by readers), the second premise introduces the specific conception of texts as resources in everyday life.

Further, the second premise sums up the research process that helped to gradually articulate various conceptions of romances, and it may thus build on several earlier abductions concerning the act of reading. Put systematically, the first premise is a problem statement referring to empirical data, the second premise is the emergent outcome of the analysis of data in context, and the conclusion is a preliminary theoretical conception of romance reading as a social practice.

The formalized abduction, though leaving out several analytical steps and conceptual nuances, captures a characteristic form of reasoning in qualitative research. The second example illustrates how a relatively 'macro-'abduction such as this, may relate to 'micro-'abductions in the course of the research process.

The social uses of television

James Lull's early study of television viewing and family communication also broke new ground for qualitative audience studies, methodologically and substantively. Contrasting the mostly individual uses of media focused by uses-and-gratifications research with the social uses of television in the home context, Lull proposed an ethnographic approach to the processes of communication around television: "The ethnography of mass communication is meant to be a sustained, microscopic, inductive examination of the natural interactional communications which connect human beings to the mass media and to each other" (p. 200). The resulting typology of the social uses of television is especially instructive regarding the qualitative research process.

The typology identified two primary uses of television: *structural* and relational. On the one hand, television serves the structural purpose of creating a general environment of background noise, being a companion and a source of entertainment for those doing chores in the home. Equally, television serves to regulate activities by punctuating everyday time and the patterns of talk. On the other hand, television has a variety of *relational* uses within practical routines, of which television viewing becomes a constitutive part. Lull (1980) singled out four subcategories of relational uses: the use of television content to facilitate communication about other aspects of viewers' lives; 'watching television' as an occasion for affiliation or, conversely, avoiding contact during viewing; using television to learn about other people, places, and problems; and, finally, referring to television as a resource for demonstrating one's competence, for instance as a 'good parent' or knowledgeable person. Each category, demonstrating the embedding of television in everyday practices, provides new insight into the interchange between interpersonal and mass communication. In terms of other theories of everyday life (Chapter 3), television thus contributes to the continuous structuration of time and space (structural uses) and of interpersonal relations (relational uses).

The typology grew out of research in more than 200 families over a period of three years, each family being observed for two to seven days. The resulting data included observational notes, a debriefing summary, audiotape recordings of the interviews held with each family member at the conclusion of the observational period, and transcripts of the recordings. Lull (1980) notes that a preliminary review of the data identified themes to be examined in further, comparative analysis, and he indicates how the various items were reexamined and reconfigured as the research process developed explanatory theory:

> In this way the researcher can arrange and rearrange the 'bits' of data until the proper internal consistency is found within each topic. These data help the ethnographer of mass communication demonstrate the internal validity of areas which are to be developed theoretically. (1980: 200)

The process can be understood as a sequence of abductions, leading the researcher from concrete and complex empirical examples to abstract and simple theory. One example comes from a family in which the husband and wife were observed to rarely touch:

> The man was a hard-working laborer who nearly always fell asleep when he watched television at night. He dozed as he sat in a recliner rocking chair with his shoes off. He snored loudly with his mouth open. His wife, who had been sitting on the floor in the same room, pushed herself along the floor until she was close to his chair. She leaned back until her head rested against his bare feet and smiled as she created this rare moment of 'intimacy.' (Lull, 1980: 203)

In Lull's words, this illustrates television viewing as being "rare moments of physical contact in front of the television screen, an intimacy which need not be accompanied by conversation" (p. 203). Within the typology, this is a relational use, namely, affiliation in the family during viewing. In abductive terms, television viewing gives rise to intimacy as a general context and atmosphere of home life:

> Viewing television together is an occasion for physical interaction between spouses.
> All instances of intimacy are occasions for physical interaction between spouses.
> Conclusion: Viewing television together is an instance of intimacy.

In another example of relational uses, namely, viewers' assertion of their own competence in reference to television, "a housewife who majored in French in college repeatedly corrected the poor pronunciation of French words uttered by an American actor who attempted to masquerade as a Frenchman" (Lull, 1980: 205–6). Again, an abduction suggests the point:

> Viewing television is an occasion for viewers to demonstrate their abilities in comparison with television characters.
> All viewers' demonstrations of their special competences to other household members are occasions to demonstrate their abilities in comparison with television characters.
> Conclusion: Viewing television is an occasion for viewers to demonstrate their special competences to other household members.

Next, each of these conclusions enters as a first premise into a following stage of abduction that serves to specify the uses as *relational*. For example:

Viewing television together is an occasion for intimacy.
All forms of relating socially are occasions for intimacy.
Conclusion: Viewing television together is a form of relating socially.

Finally, at the most general level of the typology, the conclusions regarding relational and structural uses become first premises in an abduction concerning the social uses of television *generally* in everyday contexts. For example:

Viewing television together is a form of relating socially.
All structuration of everyday contexts is a form of relating socially.
Conclusion: Viewing television together is an instance of the structuration of everyday contexts.

In sum, while each abduction leads to a higher level of abstraction, the researcher has recourse at any point to the concrete, contextualized cases constituting a sequence of inferences. What is commonly understood, in Lull's (1980: 200) words, as a way to "demonstrate the internal validity of areas which are to be developed theoretically" can be specified, then, as recursive abduction.

Super-themes of news reception

Part of my empirical research has explored how viewers' decoding of specific television news stories conditions their use of the information as a resource in other social contexts (Jensen, 1988a). The findings suggest a revision of the frameworks of cognitive psychology as applied in studies of how audiences arrive at a coherent understanding of media discourses (for example, Graber, 1984; Höijer, 1990; Livingstone, 1990). Not least in studies of news, the assumption has been that the audience's processing of news stories proceeds according to highly standardized schemata (for an overview, see van Dijk, 1988). One limitation of the approach is a preference for formal analysis, emphasizing the common structure of otherwise quite different news reports and, by implication, the common structure of their reception (for a critique, see Crigler and Jensen, 1991). Less attention is given to particular content themes or to the interpretive constructs that audiences derive from stories in their particular context of reception. An important aspect of audiences' interpretive constructs is what I refer to as super-themes.

The study of Danish viewers' reception of television news had respondents retell the main points of each story in a particular program (for details of the design, see Jensen, 1988a). Not only did the analysis establish the familiar variation between different socioeconomic groups in terms of their recall and comprehension of information, but there were also major differences between 'the journalists' story,' as defined by professional standards of selection and composition, and 'the viewers' story,' as it appeared in the interviews.

Specifically, a number of the respondents relied on certain highly generalized concepts in order to construct any coherence at all in several stories. These super-themes apparently served as a common denominator for the universe of television news and the respondents' universe of everyday experience. Although some respondents accounted in detail for story information addressing a particular political agenda, for others the super-themes were their only interface with the information and agendas.

In one international story, the journalistic theme was 'an exchange of hostages' between the two sides of the civil war (1985) in El Salvador, one of the hostages being the president's daughter. This last aspect, illustrated with visual details in the first half of the story, led some respondents to introduce the theme of 'a family reunion' as a framework for understanding the event. Other respondents, however, suggested that the story showed how, if people are placed high up in a social hierarchy (a president's daughter), they will be taken care of and rescued. One super-theme, then, was class difference or social privilege that may account for many events in both everyday reality and media representations. The abduction serving to identify this super-theme may be reconstructed as follows:

The rescue of the president's daughter is an enactment of class difference.
All rescues of privileged persons by social authorities are enactments of class difference.
Conclusion: The president's daughter is a privileged person being rescued by social authorities.

Another, national story reported government plans of moving part of the coin production at the Royal Mint of Denmark to (then West) Germany. The journalistic themes included conceptions of the Royal Mint either as a private enterprise that should move production to the most profitable location or as a public institution with a special responsibility, for example for the level of employment in Denmark. (Interestingly, few respondents commented on the symbolism of producing the national currency in another country.) Instead of weighing the two conceptions of the Mint, some respondents focused exclusively on the Mint as a source of jobs for its employees, in part with reference to one employee who was interviewed in the story. While the formalized abduction is self-evident, it brings out a political-conceptual insistence on defining the Mint as just another production facility where coins happen to be made:

The Royal Mint is a source of jobs.
All production facilities in Denmark are sources of jobs.
Conclusion: The Royal Mint is a production facility in Denmark.

Super-themes are simultaneously very general and very concrete categories of understanding, simultaneously a strength and a weakness of reception. They are general, or flexible, to the extent that they accommodate a variety of perspectives on, domains of, and propositions about social reality; they are specific to the extent that they relate to details of the news event, as represented in visuals or commentary, and perhaps to viewers' concrete life experiences. Super-themes are a strength in that they allow viewers to make personally relevant sense of news, but a weakness in that they do not empower viewers to act on that sense in political contexts. The theoretical implication is that super-themes are articulated in a complex process of inference, interpretation, or semiosis that matches categories of everyday experience (as derived partly from mass media) with the categories of media discourses. Class difference, for one, may account for many events in media as well as in everyday life.

In conclusion, the research process articulating the super-themes was comparable to the one traced in Lull (1980) above. Even if no comprehensive typology of super-themes was produced, other research, for example in the United States (Crigler and Jensen, 1991) and in Italy (Mancini, 1990), has suggested that a typology may be forthcoming. At this point, one may summarize the nature of super-themes through an abduction:

Viewers' categories of news are generalized categories of social reality.
All forms of everyday experience are generalized categories of social reality.
Conclusion: Viewers' categories of news are forms of everyday experience.

Abduction and the logic of qualitative research

Peirce, Holmes, and Eco

Peirce did take different positions concerning the status of abduction compared to other forms of scientific analysis: "[...] my opinions, I confess, have wavered" (CP 5.146). Earlier in the same text, Peirce had argued that abduction is the source of all new scientific ideas:

> All the ideas of science come to it by the way of Abduction. Abduction consists in studying facts and devising a theory to explain them. Its only justification is that if we are ever to understand things at all, it must be in that way. (CP 5.145)

Moreover, Peirce compared scientific abduction with human perception and reasoning as such, and suggested that abduction may be the evolutionary missing link between perception and reasoning. Thus, abduction is

> of the general nature of Instinct, resembling the instincts of animals in its so far surpassing the general powers of our reason and for its directing us as if we were in possession of facts that are entirely beyond the reach of our senses. (CP 5.173)

Indeed, the examples from reception studies suggest that the researcher's abduction primarily serves to explicate the abduction already performed by a respondent. This helps to explain why some abductions appear so close to common sense, yet produce new insight.

However, in another article of the series containing the beanbag example, Peirce (1986: 276) had emphasized that true science must rely on induction and quantitative methods. Accordingly, abduction could be seen to constitute a first surprising observation, a pilot study, and the development of theory from which predictions are deduced that must be tested through induction. In this vein, Robert K. Merton (1968: 158) referred to Peirce's notion of abduction as a precursor of what he himself called an "anomalous datum" in social science.

Over time, Peirce apparently ruled against the independent explanatory value of abduction. Schillemans (1992) concludes that Peirce held this position at least after 1891. Hence, abduction could be considered a first step in scientific investigation, so that "abduction is situated in the domain of the plausible, the possible, the hypothetical" (Schillemans, 1992: 265). Given Peirce's historical context, this development is hardly surprising. His conception of research methodology was derived from the natural sciences and from the discipline of philosophy which was being institutionalized and legitimated as science. In hindsight, I propose an alternative conclusion that reads the late position of Peirce against the grain.

What Peirce named abduction informs an undercurrent in modern science whose history I told, in part, as the very brief history of signs in Chapter 2. Ginzburg (1989) has identified a comparable "evidential paradigm" in which the analyst identifies key aspects of the phenomenon under investigation with reference to marginal elements that may be outside conscious control, both in the analysts and in their objects of analysis. This method is practiced, for instance, in Freud's interpretation of symptoms, in Sherlock Holmes' investigation of clues, and in the art historian Giovanni Morelli's attention to minute pictorial details revealing the artist behind a painting. In each case, an abductive inference produces an insight that could not have been arrived at by other forms of analysis, and it may, further, be assessed with reference to its practical consequences. The general method is familiar, not just from theory development across many scientific fields, but specifically from humanistic scholarship on language, culture, and history. In-depth analysis of human discourse can be understood as the recursive probing of those individual elements that may become a point of access to the universe that is carried by the entire discourse. A single word or pictorial sign may be conceived as a black hole, funneling the analyst into that universe.

While I emphasize below the need to clarify the procedures of abduction in empirical research as well as its specific domain of relevance, Umberto Eco (1984) has offered a preliminary typology comprising overcoded, undercoded, and creative abduction. Overcoded abduction, first, is a basic form of comprehension that appears to work semi-automatically. "When someone utters /man/, I must first assume that this utterance is the token of a type of English word" (Eco, 1984: 41). No complex inference is needed to first establish the fact that people may speak different languages, even if this knowledge might not be self-evident in other historical and cultural circumstances. Second, in performing an undercoded abduction, the interpreter must choose between several possible alternatives. In Eco's (1984: 42) words, "when one utters /this is a man/, we have to decide whether one says that this is a rational animal, a mortal creature, or a good example of virility, and so on." Third, creative abduction occurs when the rule of interpretation has to be invented for the specific purpose. For example, Darwin's interpretation of humans as the latest animal of evolution was a creative abduction. In each case, however, abduction is "the search for a system of rules which endow the sign with meaning" (Schillemans, 1992: 266).

If abduction can be understood as theory development at varying levels of analysis, Eco's typology identifies several different forms of integration between theory and empirical research.[8] Creative abduction, first of all, refers to the inferences that bring about socalled 'scientific breakthroughs,' what Kuhn (1970) called "revolutionary science," with general implications for the theoretical, methodological, and perhaps epistemological levels of research. Such breakthroughs presumably occur in any scientific field, regardless of its subject matter, previous conceptual frameworks, and qualitative or quantitative approaches. More important perhaps, undercoded abductions constitute both the hypotheses that are tested by quantitative methodologies and the sets of interpretations that qualitative methodologies generate. The examples from reception studies have suggested that a sequence of undercoded abductions, in a specific contextual configuration, is characteristic of qualitative empirical research. The normal science (Kuhn, 1970) of qualitative communication research may be the work of abduction.

Logic, rhetoric, and semiotics

The disenchantment with mathematical and other formalized modes of analysis in social and cultural studies has produced a renewed interest in rhetoric. In addition to the classical sources, research has drawn on the contemporary, socalled "New Rhetoric" (Perelman, 1979) and on analytical philosophy from the ordinary-language tradition about the structure of informal argument (Toulmin, 1958). Whereas the history of ideas has long witnessed a tension between logic and rhetoric, recent studies have addressed two different aspects of this tension. One body of research has documented that scientific practice conforms neither to logic textbooks nor to the ideal-typical methodologies said to constitute different disciplines. This research includes both concrete studies of how scientists work (Brannigan, 1981; Gilbert and Mulkay, 1984; Latour, 1987) and general arguments concerning science as a form of social action (Giere, 1988; Hacking, 1983, 1992). An early study by Mary Hesse (1963) summed up the point that conceptual and rhetorical analogies, far from being alien to the research process, are in fact indispensable elements in the logics of scientific research.

The second body of research ranges from rhetorical analyses of particular scientific genres and arguments (Bazerman, 1988; Gross, 1990) to stylistic, linguistic research on scientific writing as a form of communication (Barton and Ivanic, 1991; Brodkey, 1987; Enos and Brown, 1993; Nash, 1990; Nelson et al., 1987; Simons, 1989). Some of the most notable contributions come from anthropology and ethnographic research, reemphasizing the point that scientific knowledge is a cultural construction (Clifford and Marcus, 1986; Clough, 1992; Marcus and Fischer, 1986; Van Maanen, 1988). The contributions in

Clifford and Marcus (1986) especially have reopened discussions about the status of scientific discourse in light of its rhetorical, even poetic, forms of expression as well as its political uses.

The dark side of the return to rhetoric, admittedly, is the implicit (and sometimes explicit, as in Clough, 1992) argument that scientific discourse equals the rhetorical exercise of social power – that science is rhetoric in the everyday, pejorative sense. While science is enabled by, and may be examined as, discursive forms, it is also a social practice that lends itself to reflexivity and reform. Second-order semiotics may thus highlight the interdependence of logical and rhetorical forms, which are not universal, transhistorical keys to the structure of reality, or "pure syntax" (Greimas and Courtés, 1982: 311), but social resources in a context of action. Science relies, to sum up, on sign categories that are specific to various domains of reality; on disciplinary forms of analysis that produce different rhetorical configurations, models, and other semiotic vehicles in the course of the research process; and on particular forms of logical inference and interpretation that are rooted in scientific and cultural traditions.

The semiotic interest in the different signs of science also prepares the ground for a renewed discussion of classic issues in the theory of science. Abduction can be defined formally as consisting of a first premise that is particular and factual, a second premise that is general and hypothetical, and a conclusion that is particular and hypothetical. Concretely, the second premise introduces a new conception which subsequently in the conclusion serves as a recontextualization of the puzzling fact in the first premise. The Peircean triad helps to explain this inference as a way of grasping the object through a more developed sign, the interpretant, in an interpretive process that is recursive and in principle infinite (Figure 9.2). Furthermore, the triadic structure may clarify what is ambiguously known in social sciences as 'generalization' (Figure 9.3). Theoretical generalization consists in abduction, that is, it produces a vertical sequence of interpretants, departing from a particular sign-and-object pair and generating a more developed understanding at a higher level of abstraction. As applied to several empirical cases in context, this procedure has emerged as a distinctive feature of the qualitative research process. Empirical generalization, conversely, referring to an inference from the examination of a representative sample (what might more appropriately be called extrapolation), is based on the repeated matching of similar signs to similar objects from the perspective of a similar interpretant, building a horizontal row of triads at the same level of abstraction.[9]

The bulk of mass communication research still relies, in principle, on a hypothetico-deductive methodology generating predictions that researchers seek to falsify in empirical tests at a specified level of significance. In practice, it is an open question to what extent concrete studies, combining deduction with a significant element of inductive and other procedures, live up to the prototypical standards outlined by Popper (1972) across the different sciences. Meta-theoretical research on the epistemologies that characterize different traditions of communication research remains rare (but see Anderson and

Meyer, 1988).[10] Second-order semiotics provides a framework in which to reconsider the explanatory value and complementarity of deduction, induction, and abduction.[11]

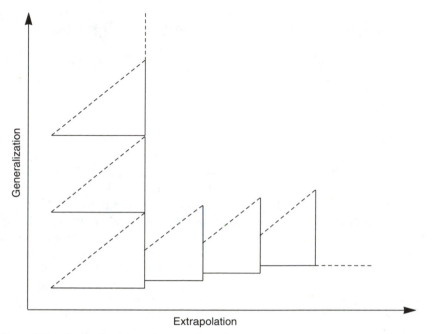

Figure 9.3   *Generalization and extrapolation*

10

The Ontology of Communication: Another Guess at the Riddle

In a manuscript entitled 'A Guess at the Riddle,' Peirce had outlined a book about ontology, based in his categories of Firstness, Secondness, and Thirdness, which his editors preface as "perhaps Peirce's greatest and most original contribution to speculative philosophy" (Peirce, 1992: 245). Ontology, defined as the study of the necessary conditions and forms of existence, is commonly taken to be an obsolete philosophical discipline with little practical relevance, certainly for modern sciences.[1] Not least within interdisciplinary fields, however, the different, inescapable ontological premises of the contributing disciplines suggest conceptual interfaces with a potential for theory development. Ontological premises represent both enabling conditions of inquiry and the eventual, ideal agreement of the community of inquirers (Hancock, 1972: 298). This chapter considers the implications of Peircean semiotics for a general theory of communication in light of recent research on cognitive and semiotic networks. Being another guess at the riddle, the essay addresses the ontological conditions of semiotic action and meaningful society.

Remembering bodies

In Wim Wenders' feature movie *Paris, Texas* (1984), the protagonist, Travis, who recently has reappeared out of nowhere in the Mojave desert, suffering from amnesia, is asked by Walt, his brother, whether he remembers how to drive a car. Travis's response is: "My body remembers."

Addressing memory as a link between meaning and action, the first section summarizes two models of how memory may be constituted in different material domains, namely, in the neurophysiological basis of human communication and in its discursive articulation. With reference to the super-themes of media reception, developed in Chapters 7 and 9, I examine the models as specifications of Peirce's concept of interpretants. In the middle section, I briefly reconsider the entire structure of signs, objects, and interpretants, suggesting how interdisciplinary studies of cognition and communication point beyond Peirce's formal conception of sign types. Finally, I discuss a typology of the signs of audiovisual communication which, in addition to being key ingredients of the contemporary media environment, raise theoretical issues for both first-order and second-order semiotics.

Two models of semiosis

Connectionism

One of the distinctive features of super-themes is their apparent embeddedness in networks that comprise a variety of concepts, images, and propositions. The presence of one such element of meaning, accordingly, may call up or actualize other meanings, depending on the specific context in which potential meanings are encountered and on their perceived relevance for action. The contextual embedding of meaning is implied by the understanding that "the body remembers." One further implication is that meaning is articulated by human agents who are always both mind and body, as suggested by Giddens' notion of practical consciousness (Chapter 3). Social semiotics thus arrives at classic issues concerning the relationship between consciousness and action.

Connectionism, being an important recent development in the field of cognitive science and psychology, has reconceived the interrelation between, in the terminology of that field, mental representation and behavior (for an overview, see Eysenck and Keane, 1990: chap. 7).[2] While cognitive science has succeeded in reopening the black box that behaviorism had sealed by employing the computer both as a theoretical metaphor and as a methodological tool, the cognitive approach has encountered at least two difficulties. First, in assuming that human cognition works through symbolic and rule-governed representation, a major part of cognitive science has presupposed a spatial and essentialist concept of meaning, namely, that mental contents reside in symbols that can be identified, delimited, and manipulated by explicit rules. Accordingly, symbolic theories quickly become very complicated, entailing almost scholastic mazes of interrelated symbols and levels of manipulation and, perhaps, an infinite regress regarding human agency, even in the attempt to characterize an arguably simple activity such as driving a car.

The second weakness has been the unclear basis of symbolic structures in the biological structures of the brain, which had been downplayed or avoided altogether in cognitive theories. While reflecting the persistent split between the academic cultures studying mind and matter respectively (Snow, 1964), part of the interest of cognitive science is that it might develop concepts bridging the split. Quite apart from much empirical evidence concerning the localization of different cognitive processes in the brain, few communication researchers would deny the interrelation between different phenomenal aspects of consciousness.

The distinctive feature of connectionist models is that they do not rely on symbolic units of meaning, but represent a given phenomenon through a system of differences, thus articulating meaning in terms of *relations*. The relations enter into configurations which, taken in their entirety, constitute a meaningful pattern. Such configurations or networks can be operationalized in computer programs with reference to the connection strengths obtaining between the individual nodes. Without drawing on a complex set of symbols and rules of manipulation, these simple structures may then generate several

complex patterns of cognition and behavior, as documented by computer simulations. Moreover, because of the structural homology of these nodal
relations with the neurons of the biological brain, connectionism may help to
identify some of the specific links between advanced cognitive operations and
their neurophysiological substratum (Rumelhart et al., 1986). In sum, connectionism suggests that meaning is *distributed*, not merely at the sociological
and psychological but equally at the biological level.

Consider the example of two networks presented in Figure 10.1. Whereas
the distinction between local (one concept, one representing unit) and distributed (one concept, many representing nodes) representation can be a
matter of degree, it is the principle of networking or distribution that is of
interest for theories of communication and reception. As commented by
Eysenck and Keane, both networks A and B are examples of a

> three-layered connectionist network. Bottom layer contains units representing par-
> ticular graphemes in particular positions within a word. Middle layer contains units
> recognising complete words. Top layer contains units representing semantic features
> of the meaning of the word. Network (A) uses local representations of words in the
> middle layer. Network (B) has a middle layer using a more distributed representa-
> tion. Each unit in the middle layer of network (B) can be activated by the graphemic

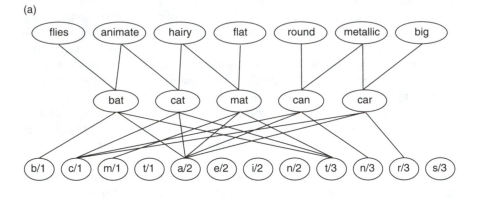

Figure 10.1   *Example of a connectionist network (Rumelhart et al., 1986: 98)*

representation of any one of a whole set of words. The unit then provides input to every semantic feature occurring in the meaning of any words that activate it. Only those word sets containing the word *cat* are shown in network (B). Notice that the only semantic features receiving input from all these word sets are the semantic features of *cat*. (1990: 243)

Networks may generate increasingly complex meaningful units – either concepts, propositions, or other forms of representation – and the possible meanings are constrained only by the available nodes and the specific relations that the system comprises. A high degree of flexibility and adaptability to new contexts is ensured by the modularity and relational structure of the system. Moreover, by contrast to an essentialist conception, the relational conception of meaning within connectionism even promises to do away with the distinction between form and content: the system does not *have* a meaning; its relational structure *is* that meaning. This argument has been taken one step further in a different context by Richard Rorty (1991a: 123), who suggests that humans do not *have*, but *are* mental states.

Certainly, as Eysenck and Keane remind us, "The sixty-four million dollar question, which we have been ignoring until now, is 'What is the relationship between distributed representations and symbolic representations?'" (1990: 243). The assumption is that the two are different, but necessary modes of semiosis, just as the semantic level of analysis that they share is complementary to the physiological level of analysis. The nature of their complementarity may be clarified with reference to the pragmatic level of sign use. In fact, a comparable, relational conception of meaning has been developed from the perspective of semiotics. Connectionist and semiotic perspectives on the social uses of signs together help to explain how super-themes arise.

Semiotics

It is a classic assumption of semiotics, most famously developed by Jakobson (1960/1981), that a given structure of signs is a configuration of the two axes of selection and combination. Selections from several vertical metaphoric or paradigmatic axes are combined along a horizontal metonymic or syntagmatic axis, accumulating a meaningful whole. Whereas Jakobson had originally highlighted the definition of poetic language as a projection of the principle of equivalence from the axis of selection onto the axis of combination, claiming that there is no distinct poetic language but only a poetic use of verbal language, his argument has general implications for the study of audiovisual communication. In Chapter 7, I suggested that the super-flow of television can be thought of as a set of parallel, horizontal axes of combination (channel flows), while the channel changes by which audiences construct their viewer flows are movements along the vertical axis of selection. Super-themes might then be conceived as junctures between these axes that viewers construct in the process of reception. More generally, a super-theme can be thought of as an overdetermining metaphor mediating between several metonymic sequences, including not only the discourses of television flow, but equally the viewer's frames of everyday understanding. If super-themes thus are condensed structures of meaning that make up points of access to several sequences of argument or narrative, they point toward a Peircean definition of individual signs as rudimentary propositions, which, in turn, are rudimentary argumentations or narratives (see Eco, 1984: 43).

Peircean semiotics suggests a more differentiated model of metaphor and metonymy. Umberto Eco, in particular, has taken the notion of unlimited semiosis to suggest that a metaphor is always the end result of metonymic structuration. As summarized by Innis (1985: 247), Eco's position is that "metaphor, by reason of its being embedded in a global semantic field, one of the key notions of his semiotic theory, is actually based on a subjacent chain of metonymies." Semiosis, far from following tidy linear axes, may take place through networks.

Eco's point can be clarified with reference to his notion of 'encyclopedia.' In rejecting Hjelmslev's attempt to isolate the minimal units not only of linguistic forms, but also of their contents – his attempt "to analyze the entities that enter the unrestricted inventories purely into entities that enter the restricted inventories" (in Eco, 1984: 47) – Eco makes the transition from an essentialist to a relational understanding of language. Hjelmslev's 'restricted inventories' are also referred to as 'dictionaries.' The structure of dictionaries is a hierarchy assigning all entities of the world to categories, such as animate or inanimate, sensitive or insensitive, and so forth. However, because any entity belongs to several categories, normally at different levels of the hierarchy, Eco points out, entities must be defined by their position within an entire system of differences without positive elements, or essences. As a result, "[t]he dictionary is dissolved into a potentially unordered and unrestricted galaxy of pieces of world knowledge. The dictionary thus becomes an encyclopedia, because it was in fact *a disguised encyclopedia*" (Eco, 1984: 68). By contrast, an encyclopedia is defined with reference to the actual or contextual selections that are made within the total system of meaningful differences. Again, the encyclopedia does not have a content of meaning; its relational structure *is* that meaning.

In linguistic terms, the encyclopedia implies a pragmatic conception of meaning, whereas the dictionary implies a semantic conception of meaning. Within an encyclopedia, neither the sense nor the reference of a sign is a stable entity that can be imported wholesale into a context of use. Instead, meaning is decided by the uses to which signs are put and, more generally, by the forms of human interaction in which they are embedded. A more farreaching implication of relational semiotics and connectionism is the challenge to the traditional distinction between scheme and content in human thinking, that is, the distinction between general categories and specific instances or events. (I return in Chapter 11 to a critical examination of Richard Rorty's postmodernist inflection of this argument, namely, that reality is what is continually enacted by human beings, not a universal scheme of things.)

Eco specifies some implications of relational semiotics in an analysis of metaphor elsewhere in his writings (Eco, 1985). His aim is to show that "each metaphor can be traced back to a subjacent chain of metonymic connections which constitute the framework of the code and upon which is based the constitution of any semantic field, whether partial or (in theory) global" (Eco, 1985: 251). Examining textual examples from James Joyce's *Finnegans Wake*, Eco suggests that this extremely complex literary work is "an excellent model of a Global Semantic System" (p. 251), thus offering a touchstone of any apparatus of semiotic analysis. He identifies in that work a "vast and articulate network of metonymies that have been wrapped in silence or revealed in another part of the work" (p. 251). While, for example, the pun "meandertale" might be explained as a metaphorical compound of 'meander' and 'Neanderthal,' the term hints at a much more complex network in which every term becomes the point of departure for new associative sequences that link up with other such sequences. Figure 10.2 indicates the network of terms, in English and in German (*Tal*), that relate the two central lexemes.

Eco is careful to warn readers that the sign which is Figure 10.2 "impoverishes the associations in terms of both number and dimension: a bidimensional graph cannot reproduce the game of interconnections produced when lexemes are brought into contact with their respective sememes" (1985: 258). And, I would emphasize, each unit in the figure should be thought of as a node within relations of difference, not as a positive essence of meaning. The nodes that are identified by a term in the figure thus enter into relations with other nodes to form the specific configuration generating the pun "meandertale." At different physiological or psychological levels of analysis, the pun may be described in terms of connection strengths and parallel distributed cognitions.

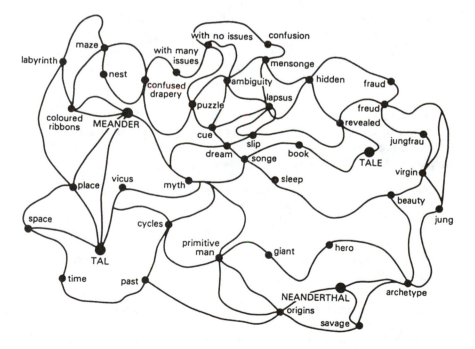

Figure 10.2   *Example of a semiotic network (Eco, 1985: 259)*

Equally, the semiotic modeling of the pun is an analytical construct arresting and depicting a moment in the process of semiosis. The primary meaning of the figure is carried not by the verbal expressions, but by its nonpropositional content, the lines of relation. Its meaning *is* that configuration of relations.

In summary, the semiotic and connectionist models may explain how super-themes enable audiences to relate many very specific mass-mediated items of information to a few very general contextual frames of interpretation. Being integrated yet flexible forms of understanding, super-themes can accommodate new events and ideas within a structure that is generated and revised as part of a particular historical, social, and cultural setting. By transcending the sort of hierarchical models that have predominated in cognitive approaches to mass media reception (Bordwell, 1985; van Dijk, 1988), network models offer a more complicated, but also more valid representation of the conditions of semiosis in actual social practices.

1+, 2+, 3+

Semiotic and cognitive networks may be conceived, next, as domain-specific ontological models of semiosis, demonstrating the internal structure of inter-pretants in human communication. They thus complement the formal ontology that is implied by Peirce's principles of Firstness, Secondness, and Thirdness. A terminological distinction has traditionally been made in philo-sophy between, on the one hand, general or formal ontology and, on the other hand, the regional or material ontologies that account for the conditions of existence in different reality domains, for instance the manifestation of mean-ing in the human brain, respectively in the human mind.[3] Whereas Peirce's second-order semiotics helps to clarify central aspects of formal ontology, I want to argue that his regional ontologies, implicit in the typologies of signs, are restricted by what is largely a deductive, taxonomic approach to theory development.

Applying a Peircean framework to biology, Salthe (1985) has made a simple but powerful argument, namely, that humans only come into contact with reality through qualities, to be conceived as signs, that are the result of "con-templative interaction between us and the things":

> Reflection informs us that these qualities can be analyzed into combinations of more general qualities. Consider as an example how many different odors and scents there can be; and consider, too, that *the biological organism cannot have a sep-arate detector for each.* (Salthe, 1985: 5; emphasis added)

Just as a map might be as large and complex as the territory represented, humans might in principle rely on an infinitely differentiated repertoire of sense qualities. But we do not. The precondition of human perception as we know it is the existence of a specific range of signs that can be interpreted as evidence of particular objects in reality.

Evidence from twentieth-century philosophy as well as different scientific fields also suggests that signs are the inescapable conditions of knowledge.

While Wittgenstein's (1958) engagement with natural language can be seen as an attempt to understand our condition of being in the world by embracing the most common human signs, Heidegger's verbal neologisms represent a major alternative approach proposing to break on through to the other side of signs in order to grasp reality in a more profound sense. More specifically, Gestalt psychology has produced evidence that images are interpreted as one meaningful whole. In the classic examples with two likely interpretations, one may fasten on one or the other, but only on one at a time (Arnheim, 1974). In mathematics and philosophy, the attempt to explicate an entire terminological system in the terms of that system itself tends to create paradoxes, famous instances being Bertrand Russell's paradox and Kurt Gödel's incompleteness theorem (see Hofstadter, 1979: 3–28). They can be understood as variations on the socalled 'liar paradox,' or 'Epimenides' paradox':

> Epimenides was a Cretan who made one immortal statement: 'All Cretans are liars.' A sharper version of the statement is simply 'I am lying'; or, 'This statement is false.' (Hofstadter, 1979: 17)

The point in each case is that there is no place of observation or inquiry outside semiosis, no way of addressing or justifying a sign system except through another sign system. For Peircean pragmatism, this does not entail skepticism or nominalism to the effect that signs are all that we know, but only the insight that signs are the media through which we come to know what we can justify saying we know.[4]

Firstness

The first aspect of Peircean formal ontology is what he referred to as Firstness, represented in the basic triad by the sign. The internal structure of the Peircean sign (or *representamen*) may be conceived with reference to the semiotic square that was developed in European semiology by A.J. Greimas (Greimas and Courtés, 1982: 308–11). The square, depicted in Figure 10.3, comprises four interrelated nodes, namely, two primitive terms, A and non-A, and the terms contradicting each of these, A and non-A. A, accordingly, is defined in relation to the meaningful terms that it calls up by way of contrast, first, a contradicting term that in turn implies the contrary of A, or non-A, and, second, a contradiction of non-A that again implies A. In the Greimasean model, the diagonal arrows represent relations of contradiction, while the vertical arrows represent relations of complementarity or implication. It is through this entire configuration of relations that one may grasp the apparently simple contrary relation between what is A and what is not A, as suggested by the horizontal, dotted line. Positive meaning, thus, is the outcome of a semiosis of negation and implication.

The sign represents the category of Firstness, immediacy, or feeling in Peirce's formal ontology. However, when categorizing each type of sign according to its relations to different objects, interpretants, and to itself and other signs, Peirce begins to make the transition from formal to material ontology. His various typologies, comprising ten or as much as sixty-six types of signs,

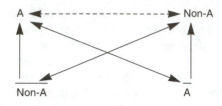

Figure 10.3   *Firstness: The semiotic square (Greimas and Courtés, 1982: 308–11)*

amount to deductions from the rudimentary description of the three primary categories and their possible interrelations, supported by introspective examples. Below I explore an alternative, dialectical approach of theorizing and empirical analysis with reference to the signs of visual communication. Nevertheless, the semiotic square can be taken as a minimal structure of meaning conditioning human cognition and action. Without distinguishable signs, there can be no interpreted interaction. Signs thus are 1+ in number. Each sign, moreover, is open to coupling with other minimal structures, both in the form of signs of increasing complexity and in the interface with interpretants (which are signs in the domain of Thirdness). In sum, the semiotic square identifies the *sine qua non* of meaningful social relations.

Secondness

Objects, being manifestations of Secondness, are 2+ in number: both everyday perception and scientific research suggest that phenomena of radically different kinds exist in reality. The examples are legion, as witnessed by the two conflicting master paradigms identified in Chapter 9. Much contemporary debate concerning social-scientific methodologies may be traced back to the question of whether all objects of science can be reduced to common elementary units and thus might be studied with reference to a common denominator. I take the implication of Peircean semiotics to be that, *mutatis mutandis*, different signs manifest different objects, as apprehended through specific interpretants. In terms of the different forms of causality noted in Chapter 3 (Figure 3.3), one could say that a given phenomenon may be understood, depending on its reality domain, as the outcome of either deterministic, indeterministic, stochastic, or generative principles.

　　Salthe (1985) refers to Peirce's ontology as a differentiation model that assumes distinct, if interrelated, levels of existence. This model, Salthe suggests, may be traced back to Hesiod, and in modern times to German idealism, but received its full articulation in Peirce's writings:

> The world is initially vague, relatively unformed and creative. As it differentiates, it becomes more and more fixed into precise trajectories, gradually supplanting creative possibilities with inflexible routines and realized 'adaptations,' adding to this realized world more and more details of fixed, even machinelike, structure so as to continually restrict the possibilities for creative activity to increasingly more limited spheres of activity. (Salthe, 1985: 144)

A major issue, not least for studies of culture and society, is what scope this

"creative activity" has in different human practices, that is, the issue of determination (Chapter 4). While Salthe interprets the chain of being as a control
hierarchy, in which the lower levels are overdetermined by the higher levels, he
also recognizes the relative autonomy of each level, what he calls "the non-
transitivity of effects across levels" (1985: 115). In the present terms, several
aspects of the communicative process, from neurophysiological processing to
higher-level semiotic networking, qualify as determining factors of mass media
reception.

Peirce's cosmology – premised on his beliefs in the continuity of all mind
and matter (synechism), in absolute chance (tychism), and in a universe pro-
pelled by evolutionary love (agapism) – might tempt some to conclude that the
epistemological chain of interpretants (Figure 2.2) which gradually differentiates understanding would be matched by an ontological chain gradually
differentiating the world through quantum leaps from one level of objects to
another. An alternative model, which, rather, poses ontological differentiation
as an issue for further empirical research, is presented in Figure 10.4. If
Firstness comes in squares, Secondness may be conceived as columns.

The vertical epistemological axes refer to the process of scientific semiosis,
emphasizing that research on different reality domains will draw on categori-
ally different methodological tools and, perhaps, different theoretical
frameworks. The insights from different domains may, however, be unified in

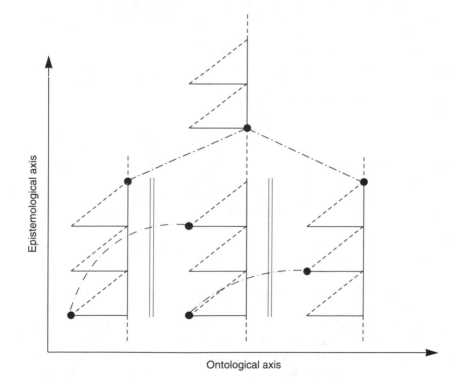

Figure 10.4   *Secondness: Domains of existence and inquiry*

the last instance (Chapter 9) through meta-discourse within the theory of science, as visualized in the topmost triad incorporating several interpretants.

The horizontal ontological axis suggests that processes in one domain can become initiating conditions or boundary conditions for processes in another domain (Salthe, 1985: 67–113; see also Bunge, 1980). In a phylogenetic perspective, particular physiological structures are general enabling conditions for the articulatory capacities of humans. In an ontogenetic perspective, individuals' specific articulatory capacities are further enabling conditions of their communication as part of a social context. The model represents a contrast to "the view that these emergents were in fact immanent in even the simplest systems, thereby depriving them of their special quality of surprising uniqueness and, by implication, of their connotation of being the products of creativity" (Salthe, 1985: 101). While new features and capacities, emerging from lower-level processes and being checked by higher-level boundary conditions, appear stable in an evolutionary perspective, it remains an empirical question for communication research how particular productive and receptive capacities may be realized under different historical circumstances. In this perspective on the nature–nurture thematic, different social contexts may also be considered as high-level enabling and bounding conditions of semiosis.

Thirdness

The understanding that semiosis is multiply determined, but only in the first instance, has also been advanced by recent cognitive theories of meaning and mental models, notably Mark Johnson's (1987) work on "the bodily basis of meaning, imagination, and reason." His central argument is that many discursive forms, both figurative language and common metaphors, are explained by the existence of "embodied image schemata." The term implies not only that understanding is imaginative, but also that mind is literally embodied. Hence, categories of, for example, scale, sequence, and relative position (up/down, inside/outside) in relation to the human body can be seen to underlie most forms of cognition and communication, including creative uses of language. Compared to Chomsky's (1965) formal model of how verbal language is generated from a deep structure, Johnson's (1987) framework outlines another, literal deep structure of bodily meaning, which simultaneously allows for contextual, cultural, as well as individual variations in the uses of language and other signs.

The embodied image schemata may be conceived as instances of Peirce's Energetic Interpretant, but remain to be specified with reference to particular media genres and their reception within specific interpretive repertoires prevailing in a historical and social context. While the biological matrices of meaning thus hint at certain natural boundaries of human consciousness, one current problem for cognitive science is how to approach the more complex aspects of culture and communication, which appear to probe those very boundaries, without extrapolating unduly from perceptual and cognitive procedures identified in a laboratory setting. Network models of reception, drawing on cognitive science and semiotics, may help to bridge the theoretical and methodological gap between experimental cognitive science (Eysenck and Keane, 1990) and the application of its categories in textual analyses of, for example, the film medium (Bordwell, 1985; Branigan, 1992).

Interpretants, manifesting Thirdness, are 3+ in number. While a contemporary notion of networks is not, to my knowledge, found in Peirce's writings, his suggestion that all complex systems can be examined as multiples of three is compatible with the network models of meaning, which in turn imply the notion of unlimited semiosis. Joining the binary, but open structure of one semiotic square to another, one arrives at a new configuration of meaning units that lend themselves to infinite combination. In this perspective, Peirce's definition of the interpretant as "a more developed sign" was a radical understatement.

Excursus: How not to do things with signs

Interdisciplinary research resembles both general philosophy and disciplinary theory development, in that it walks a fine line between common sense and analogies pressed too far.[5] An instructive example of the difficulties is found in René Thom's distinctive approach to semiotics (see Thom, 1985). Being a mathematician, Thom draws his analogies primarily from the field of geometry, and more generally topology, outlining spatial categories which are then treated as the matrix for all other categories – physical, biological, and semantic. Certain transformations of these categories and structuring principles are referred to as 'catastrophes,' from which specific forms of existence and symbolic meaning are said to originate. The ambition is to solve the riddle of existence by showing that "when we analyze symbolism into its elementary mechanisms, we do not find any which do not figure either in inanimate matter, or in the humblest forms of life" (Thom, 1985: 275).

Whereas Thom's argument recalls Peirce's description of the laws of nature as the habits of the universe, and while the catastrophes might be interpreted in pragmatist terms as *Ur*-differences, Thom fails to clarify the origins of his theory in different material ontologies and analytical traditions. On the one hand, he relies on Peirce's triad of icons, indices, and symbols to exemplify increasingly complex forms of representation. On the other hand, he describes these forms of representation in terms of Saussure's dyad of signifier and signified. Furthermore, he pursues a dyadic conception of mind and matter, referring to signs as "a plastic receiver system" (Thom, 1985: 277) that is exemplified by the genetic structure of DNA molecules. Organic life and human mind thus reside as signifieds in material signifiers. Thom concludes that,

> borne along by the universal flux, the signified generates the signifier in an uninterrupted burgeoning ramification. But the signifier regenerates the signified each time that we interpret the sign. And as is shown by the example of biological forms, for the signifier (the descendant) to become the signified (the parent) again, the time-lapse of a generation is sufficient. (1985: 278)

Crucially, it is not explained how the interpreting agency (the 'we' of "we interpret the sign") differs in the case of DNA structures, organic life, and human mind.

It is instructive to retrace the layers of analogy that produce ambiguity. While the form of all catastrophes is said to be deduced from topology, their common function in different domains is that of "control systems," so that "symbolic activity is, in its origin, linked in an essential manner to biological control systems: or more exactly, as said by older thinkers who were not afraid of words, to biological finality (finalité: ultimate purpose)" (Thom, 1985: 283). This line of argument recalls both current systems theory and classic communication theory since Lasswell (1948/1966). "In man, as in animals, symbolic activity originates in the need for regulation, homeostasis in the living organism and similarly, stability in the social body" (Thom, 1985: 283). What distinguishes humans is that their semiosis does not originate exclusively from what Thom calls "major biological regimes," such as food and sexuality: "Only these fundamental 'catastrophes' of biological finality have the power to generate the symbol in animals. This no longer holds true in man [...]" (p. 283). In man, Thom suggests, "symbolic activity, if it is to be effective, rests necessarily on a mental simulation of the catastrophe to avoid (or to provoke)," so that, in summary, "the possibility of simulation of the psychism, originally developing only on the catastropes of biological regulation, has ended by extension to all phenomena of the macroscopic world" (p. 287).

The ambiguity arises not so much from the analogy between different control systems, which, as a heuristic, abductive device is constitutive of most theory development, as from the richly suggestive common denominator of catastrophes that collapses the different control systems and domains. The term 'catastrophes' refers, on the one hand, to death and conception as transitions between existence and non-existence and, on the other hand, to the transition between meaning and non-meaning, as projected into a topological space of representation. Catastrophes thus come to serve as a mythical boundary, an abstract, all-embracing solution to *horror vacui* in different domains of reality, which explains very little in each domain.

Thom simultaneously supports his general, topological notion of meaning with an extremely concrete, commonsensical characterization of what is a sign. "It must not be forgotten that above all signs are forms in space-time, and that consequently their spatio-temporal localization is one of the first factors to consider" (Thom, 1985: 284). Moreover, whereas "[m]an is freed from the enthrallment of things by giving them names," and while "the ego has been able to constitute itself in a permanent manner by taking as support the representation of the true body in space," a third distinctive feature of humans is their capacity to make "the global representation of the geometry of space" (pp. 288–9). This capacity suggests the conclusion that, since "[t]wo things occupying simultaneously two disjoint domains could not be identical," or in other words, "since the identity of a thing has its principle in its spatial localization, *all ontology, all semantics necessarily depends on a study of space – geometric or topological*" (p. 289).

René Thom does not clarify why, at this level of generality, space should be given priority over time or material forms and relations, even though he refers to these other dimensions of ontology in his conclusion:

> As soon as it makes an egg, a living organism initiates the project of colonizing space and time and it is subjected to the 'here and now.' The essential function of the human intellect, to simulate the laws and structures of the external world, is hardly more than the extension or the making clear of this primitive design. Perhaps it is not absurd to see in the most elaborate acts of human psychism, for example, in mathematical discovery, a direct extension of this mechanism of symbolic creation. (Thom, 1985: 290)

Perhaps not. But this form of analysis does not advance interdisciplinary theory development about that classic issue. The upshot is that Thom sometimes refers to the physical space in which discursive signs appear, at other times to the mental simulation of space in which interpreted meanings reside, both of which are subsumed under a specific, disciplinary conception of space within topology. His theory thus bears witness to a speculative, ontological imperialism that is as restrictive as the Logos imperialism of semiology (Chapter 1) and the epistemological imperialism of crypto-positivism (Chapter 9). Thom's theory, in summary, is neither conceptually nor empirically untenable, rather it is ambiguous, uninformative, redundant. Ambiguity breeds epistemological doodling and antirealistic ecstasy.

Visual communication: Toward a typology of signs

Two semiotic systems

Recent cognitive science has suggested that different signs give rise to radically different forms of mental representation, as outlined in Figure 10.5. On the one hand, external representations, or signs, may be divided into two main classes, namely, linguistic and pictorial or diagrammatic signs. On the other hand, internal or mental representations may be either distributed networks, as described above, or sets of symbols. Among symbolic representations, some are propositional, others analogical. While there is no one-to-one fit between external linguistic and mental propositional representations, or between external pictorial and mental analogical representation, and while aspects of the figure such as the continuum from symbolic to distributed representation (Rumelhart et al., 1986) are disputed, experimental evidence supports the existence of two main registers of semiosis (for an overview, see Eysenck and Keane, 1990: chap. 7; Messaris, 1993). "Analogical representations are nondiscrete, can represent things implicitly, have loose rules of combination and are concrete in the sense that they are tied to a particular sense modality. Propositional representations are discrete, explicit, are combined according to rules, and are abstract" (Eysenck and Keane, 1990: 206). Not least for the study of visual communication, which in the form of film, television, and computer media is central to contemporary media environments, research on mental representation raises critical issues.

Allan Paivio (1986) has proposed, further, that human cognition occurs in

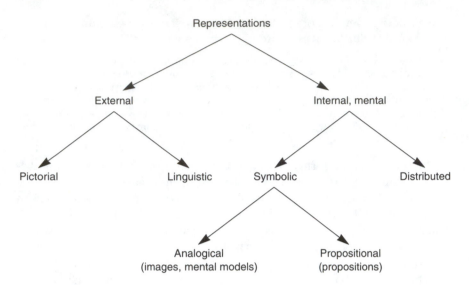

Figure 10.5   *External and internal forms of representation (Eysenck and Keane, 1990: 202). Reprinted by permission of Lawrence Erlbaum Associates Ltd., Hove, UK.*

two independent, if interconnected, systems of coding. The basic argument is that the verbal and nonverbal systems are specialized in receiving, processing, and retrieving respectively verbal and nonverbal types of stimuli, and that the nonverbal system processes spatial and synchronous information, while the verbal system is oriented toward sequential processing. Moreover, each system is divided into subsystems corresponding to the different forms of sensori-motor input (visual, auditory, haptic, gustatory, olfactory), whereas the verbal system has no representations for taste and smell. Finally, Paivio hypothesizes that each system has basic representational units, namely, logogens (the verbal system) and imagens (the nonverbal system), which are interconected by referential links.

The hypothesis has produced much experimental research as well as intense debate with reference to the emphasis on visual images that tends to neglect auditory and other sense modalities. It is also far from clear how, given that different forms of representation are integrated in human phenomenal consciousness, the two systems may interact. On balance, however, the empirical evidence supports the dual-coding theory:

> Allan Paivio has maintained, in his dual-coding theory, that there are two distinct symbolic systems; a verbal, linguistically based system and a nonverbal, image-based system. There is considerable evidence from a variety of task domains for the view that the two systems are separate (e.g. memory and interference studies). Other research, on mental rotation and mental scanning, has concentrated more on the exact nature of images rather than on distinguishing between image and linguistic codes. This research has provided evidence which supports the view that visual images have special, analogue properties. (Eysenck and Keane, 1990: 219–20)

For studies of communication and culture, it is of special interest to ask how the two systems relate to each other in actual sign use, and which one may be dominant in specific contexts. The issue is connected to a major distinction in cognitive science, the one between bottom-up and top-down processing. On the one hand, perception processes may be data-driven, or bottom-up, in the sense that inferences and other mental operations stay close to the original sense stimuli in their analogical form. On the other hand, processing may be structured by more general expectations or hypotheses concerning events or objects, hypotheses which will often be developed through sequential reasoning and may be articulated in propositional form. The distinction, of course, is a variation on the traditional dispute between rationalism and empiricism, holding that either the procedures of the rational subject or the structures of the empirical object may account for perception in the final instance.

A common conclusion in textbooks on cognitive science is that, *mutatis mutandis*, bottom-up processing is the rule. By contrast, "the influence of [...] top-down processes is generally only substantial when stimuli are presented very briefly or in a degraded form" (Eysenck and Keane, 1990: 88). It is likely, however, that this conclusion is due, in part, to the kinds of issues and methodologies which inform experimental psychology. Even though empirical designs vary, the prototypical study is still conducted under controlled circumstances in a laboratory setting with reference to simple or readily specifiable stimulus materials, which limits its explanatory value regarding everyday cognition of complex social phenomena in context (Eysenck and Keane, 1990: 461, 499ff.). Presumably, like a brief exposure to a simple object, a longer exposure to a complex object may entail top-down processing, for instance in the reception of integrated visual and verbal communication. An example suggests how important aspects of visual reception bear witness to top-down processing, and the example leads into a research agenda concerning visual and verbal signs.

Undertakers

In the study of super-themes in television news reception (Jensen, 1988a), a remarkable case of 'misunderstanding' occurred. A brief news story reported that, following criticism of Danish undertakers' exploitation of grieving relatives, the undertakers' organization had agreed to clarify and improve their business practices. Yet, for one respondent, this was the story of a funeral service for a taxi driver who had recently been murdered in the vicinity of Copenhagen.

Certain elements of the news discourse help to explain the 'aberrant' decoding. While the spoken commentary notes the criticisms, the undertakers' response, and the likely consequences of their altered practices, the visuals initially present a hearse leaving an undertaker's establishment and arriving at a church, where the coffin is carried from the vehicle into the chapel by several men, one of whom wears a uniform not unlike that of some Copenhagen taxi drivers. This visual sequence is followed by several shots of coffins and urns with price tags attached.

The respondent, in retelling the story, refers to the taxi driver being taken to the funeral service. While she remembers being confused by the last few shots of "ceramics," it should be emphasized that she repeatedly maintains, against the interviewer's aid, that the program did offer coverage of the funeral. In fact, several other respondents refer to a funeral service for the taxi driver taking place on the day of the broadcast, criticizing the fact that this event, highly publicized especially in the tabloid press, was not covered by television news. In the eyes of one respondent, however, the program did cover the event.

The case could be easily explained with reference to either the respondent's age (in her seventies) or a distracted mode of watching television (Ellis, 1982) which may entirely neglect the verbal information of news. Arguably, this was an elderly, hard-of-hearing viewer who was barely able to catch the journalist's news as she immersed herself in the visuals. Still, the respondent reproduced the main journalistic point of several other stories with reference to their visual and verbal constituents. Alternatively, her funeral decoding can be explained by an overdetermining frame or schema which allows the respondent to tap the meaning of a specific, ongoing, (to her) major event in order to make sense of another, minor event.

Toward a typology of signs

The wider theoretical implication of the funeral decoding, while being a spurious case, is that certain underresearched interpretive constructs mediate between bottom-up, analogical processes and top-down, propositional processes of audiovisual reception, as substantiated by reception studies of super-themes and similar interpretive repertoires. Whereas the analogical visuals of hearses and coffins could be considered enabling conditions of the interpretation, also the general, propositional schema of a 'funeral' and the respondent's specific context knowledge of the taxi driver constitute necessary conditions of the actual interpretation. The interpretive constructs may be conceived as networks, interpretants, or Thirdness. They are not driven exclusively bottom-up by raw data or, in Peircean terms, by an unmediated object (Secondness); nor are they driven entirely top-down by an explicit procedure as laid out in discrete signs (Firstness). Audiovisual communication thus provides a test case for further research on how different types of signs interact in particular communicative practices.

Whereas visual mass communication – from print advertising and film to television and computer media – has been researched from various perspectives, communication theory has only been partially successful in accounting for its visual specificity, or for the possible links between texts and visuals (Barthes, 1964/1984b). Similarly, music represents something of a blind spot in communication research, certainly from a reception perspective (but see Gorbman, 1987; Lull, 1986). Traditionally, spoken and written communication has been studied comprehensively in the humanities by rhetoric, philology, linguistics, and literary criticism, leaving the analysis of images to specialized studies in art history and, more recently, film theory. Social-scientific communication research, in its turn, may have found it particularly difficult to account for visual communication processes, since the analytical categories of its content analysis and survey methodologies are better suited to capture the discrete, digital elements of alphabetic communication than visual, analogical signs. As concluded in a standard textbook on communications, "the systematic analysis of audiovisual languages is still at an early stage" (McQuail, 1987: 202).

Whether visual communication in fact relies on 'languages' is an issue dividing research into two main camps. On the one hand, for at least two decades the mainstream of disciplines ranging from film studies (Metz, 1974; Wollen, 1972), to art history (Arnheim, 1974), and semiotics (Eco, 1976) has assumed that visual communication involves a complex process of encoding and decoding, analogous to verbal communication. The position is supported by historical studies documenting major changes in the forms of representation (Gombrich, 1960; Hauser, 1951; Lowe, 1982) and by theories emphasizing the mediating role of gender and other social-psychological characteristics in reception (Lauretis, 1984; Metz, 1982). So far, however, visual studies have not produced a comprehensive typology of the codes specific to different historical contexts, audience groups, and genres of communication.

On the other hand, the recent turn to cognitive science suggests that certain basic aspects of visual reception are not governed by historically or socially specific codes. Nevertheless, cognitivism shares the tendency of the historicist, constructivist camp to conceive of human cognition in general terms of *representation*, rather than as a constitutive element of interest-driven *action* in a specific social context. For example, David Bordwell's important rearticulation of film theory still implies a conception of going to the movies as an activity of problem-solving, with little reference to its motivation and context (Bordwell, 1985, 1989). Research on computers and cognition further suggests that programs anticipating the user's actions are better candidates for artificial-intelligence systems than programs conceived as representations (Winograd and Flores, 1986).

The current focus on studies of visual communication, while pointing to the growing social significance of audiovisual media in the total media environment, also emphasizes the need for research to reconsider definitions of the fundamental constituents and processes of mass communication, its materially and discursively specific signs. The evidence from the several traditions of visual communication research suggests that further studies are not served by either the linguistic model or Peirce's formal taxonomies of possible signs. Instead, there is a call for interdisciplinary theory development that is informed by a range of empirical approaches, from experimental studies of perceptual capacities to historical research on the changing social forms and uses of communicative capacities. It may be possible to arrive at a semiotic typology that is premised on an ontology of distributed relational realism, as suggested by the network models and the domain-specific reconception of Firstness, Secondness, and Thirdness above. Meaning is real, emergent, and taking effect in and through several interrelated domains of existence; meaning is performative, being a constitutive element of social action. Meaning makes a difference in practice.

11

The Politics of Communication: How to Make a Difference

Political questions address less what is or has been than what may be in the future. One general implication of pragmatism, as noted in Chapter 2, is that the validity of knowledge is decided in a social community with reference to some purpose of future action. This final chapter presents a pragmatist perspective on the classic conception of the mass media as a public sphere, a Fourth Estate, a cultural forum, or an institution-to-think-with (Chapter 4), which has been developed in distinctive ways by recent work associated with pragmatism. I offer a critical analysis of the very different contemporary inflections of the tradition by Richard Rorty and Jürgen Habermas.

Richard Rorty, having deconstructed professional philosophy, invokes John Dewey to support his own alternative position of "postmodernist bourgeois liberalism" (Rorty, 1991a: 197) in both philosophy and politics. I suggest that Rorty is an eclectic guide to the pragmatist tradition and that, ironically, his policy for culture and communication has little relevance for any social practice. Habermas, whose direct references to pragmatism are surprisingly few (Joas, 1993: 9, 90), offers a modernist, normative theory of social communication, combining historical evidence concerning the public sphere with a performative typology of language use. I argue that Habermas's maximalist conception of communication rights, with reference to an ideal communication situation, fails to relate the community of inquiry to the historical and cultural context that it addresses. In conclusion, I consider a minimalist conception of the politics of communication. The key issue may not be how to ensure the right to engage in dialogue, but how to develop the procedures for *ending* dialogue and transforming it into other social action.

Postmodernist pragmatism: Rorty

Mirrors of philosophy

In 1979, Richard Rorty published *Philosophy and the Mirror of Nature*, which made him infamous to much of professional philosophy, and famous in several other fields of research. The volume presents a sustained attack on the self-conception of contemporary philosophy as a profession that might still address the foundational issue of how reality is mirrored in human knowledge, thus providing the basis for specialized sciences and social enterprise.[1] This prototypical understanding of philosophy, Rorty argues, was originated by

Descartes and redeveloped especially by Locke in a form which has since per-
petuated, subtly but decisively, the basic dualisms of the Logos tradition
(Chapter 1) in both philosophy and social practice. Nevertheless, Rorty's pragmatist postmodernism remains a mirror image of that tradition, turned upside
down, as he recontextualizes philosophy as politics, and ultimately as poetics.

A case in point is Rorty's collapsing of reasons and causes into one category,
what he calls non-reductive physicalism. The aim is to do away with the
dualisms of mind and matter, intentionality and causality, by making an ontological distinction *not* between the inner, mental state of humans and the
outer, physical state of the world, but between the individual human and all
other constituents of reality:

> In this model, the distinction between Self and World has been replaced with the
> distinction between an individual human being (describable in both mental and
> physical terms) and the rest of the universe. The former is delimited by the contours
> of the body, and the task of explaining the relations between events occurring within
> that boundary and all other events is a matter of postulating, or observing, entities
> within these contours: inner causes of the human being's behavior. These causes
> include both micro-structural and macro-structural, and both mental and physical,
> items: among them are hormones, positrons, neural synapses, beliefs, desires,
> moods, diseases, and multiple personalities. (Rorty, 1991a: 121)

However, while it may be fruitful to theorize mental states as something that
the person *is*, rather than *has* (Chapter 10), distinctions are necessary for
domain-specific analytical purposes. Indeed, Rorty's line of argument is in
conflict with the bottom line of pragmatism, the pragmatic maxim. The consequences that might conceivably result from distinguishing between reasons
and causes in either science or social interaction are momentous, at least in the
Western communities of inquiry and vocabularies that Rorty considers the
legitimate bases of knowledge and action.

Realizing that this "quasi-Skinnerian level of abstraction" (Rorty, 1991a:
109) is problematic (even as he gives priority to an idiographic conception of
'causality'), Rorty specifies that he wants to shift the emphasis from the *nature*
of different objects in reality to the specific *purpose* of inquiry about them.
This implies a further shift toward nominalism and applied philosophy, "from
a methodologico-ontological key into an ethico-political key. For now one is
debating what purposes are worth bothering to fulfill, which are more worth-
while than others, rather than which purposes the nature of humanity or of
reality obliges us to have" (p. 110). Rorty's position, then, follows from the
premise that philosophy be subordinated to social standards, honoring "the
priority of democracy to philosophy" (p. 175). The modest role of philosophy,
accordingly, is to contribute to 'the conversation of mankind,' which is Rorty's
characterization of infinite semiosis in a human community.

Rorty (1979) had specified the purpose of conversation as edification, so
that philosophy would enable people to appreciate, justify, and modify their
always contingent understanding of the world through dialogue. Importantly,
stories should be told without reference to 'a first philosophy' premised on
essences, systems, or foundational principles. His recent writings (Rorty,

1991a) have radicalized that position to suggest that philosophy should merely enable humans to tell ever more, and more diverse stories about the process of creating a better world for themselves. Rorty's agenda, in sum, is to decenter the subject of philosophy from the mirror of nature to the multiple mirrors of a postmodern culture, from justifying an epistemology of correspondence to persuading others of the coherence of political liberalism. His turn to post-modernism is emphatic, to the degree that he denounces "the tone of urgency" in, for example, Jacques Derrida's writings, because "there is not an urgent task called 'deconstructing metaphysics' which needs to be performed before we can get to work on the rest of culture" (Rorty, 1991b: 104–5).

If philosophy today can simply move ahead as a political practice, one cru-cial issue is who may participate in the community of philosophical inquiry. It is a special understanding of the pragmatist concept of community which enables Rorty to make his transition from philosophy to politics.

Political vs philosophical communities

While Rorty's heroes in the history of philosophy count several controversial fig-ures who had questioned the foundational mission of the discipline – Wittgenstein, Heidegger, and in current philosophy Donald Davidson – his pri-mary reference is John Dewey's pragmatism.[2] Dewey had called for a redefinition of philosophy, not as the dignified and solid basis of human enterprise, but as a preliminary, if necessary, activity that could support the more important business of politics and everyday life being carried on. Following Dewey, Rorty sees "pragmatism not as grounding, but as clearing the ground for, democratic poli-tics," and favors "the idea of a community which strives after both intersubjective agreement and novelty – a democratic, progressive, pluralist community of the sort of which Dewey dreamt" (1991a: 13). Whereas I return to his questionable appropriation of Dewey's ideas, Rorty suggests that such communities may be both the ends and the means of science, philosophy, and politics:

> Is the sort of community which is exemplified by groups of scientific inquirers and by democratic political institutions a means to an end, or is the formation of such communities the only goal we need? Dewey thought that it was the only goal we needed, and I think he was right. (1991a: 43)

When several communities interacting rely on different vocabularies, con-flict over either ends or means is the most likely result. There will be difficulties of both recognizing another vocabulary and accepting its implicit values and perspectives. In Rorty's argument, however, differences in both respects "can get resolved by hashing things out" (1991a: 218). Putting the argument to a severe test, Rorty has repeatedly considered the issue of universal human rights, suggesting that humans must, above all else, avoid cruelty. The only fea-ture that we initially "share with all other humans is the same thing we share with all other animals – the ability to feel pain" (Rorty, 1989: 177). However,

> human beings who have been socialized – socialized in any language, any culture – do share a capacity which other animals lack. They can all be given a special kind of pain: They can all be humiliated by the forcible tearing down of the particular

structures of language and belief in which they were socialized (or which they pride themselves on having formed for themselves). (Rorty, 1989: 177)

At this point of his argument, Rorty commonly refocuses attention on those structures of language and belief that he is unwilling to compromise, rather than the possible consensus of several social or cultural formations. His recent position is summed up as 'anti-anti-ethnocentrism,' implying that whereas ethnocentrism is an inescapable outcome of socialization and acculturation, one should not accept the relativism entailed by anti-ethnocentrism, but should instead reemphasize certain ideals, notably representative democracy, privacy rights, and procedural justice. These ideals "may be local and culture-bound, and nevertheless be the best hope of the species" (Rorty, 1991a: 208). Challenges to the ideals are met with polemic: "We have become so open-minded that our brains have fallen out" (p. 203). If, on the other hand, an increasing number of humans accept these ideals as conditions of access to community, moral progress may be achieved:

> The view I am offering says that there is such a thing as moral progress, and that this progress is indeed in the direction of greater human solidarity. But that solidarity is not thought of as recognition of a core self, the human essence, in all human beings. Rather, it is thought of as the ability to see more and more traditional differences (of tribe, religion, race, customs, and the like) as unimportant when compared with similarities with respect to pain and humiliation – the ability to think of people wildly different from ourselves as included in the range of 'us.' (Rorty, 1989: 192)

The point is that, while one may agree with many of Rorty's concrete ideals, his configuration of ethical ideals and political institutions carries an agenda silencing – "forcibly tearing down" – certain other vocabularies of language and belief. Rorty appears to trade in a Bad First Philosophy for a Good First Politics, which must be accepted unconditionally as a premise of all community, whether local, national, or international. To Rorty, all enemies of liberal democracy are mad as far as "we heirs of the Enlightenment" are concerned: "They are crazy because the limits of sanity are set by what *we* can take seriously" (1991a: 187–8). In social practice, however, such limits are made negotiable, as historians, psychoanalysts, anthropologists, and political scientists will testify. In sum, the absolutization of contingent limits amounts to both an untenable restriction of the (liberal) political process and a fundamentalism premised on force rather than dialogue in international politics and intercultural communication. Presumably, what 'we' cannot take seriously must be neutralized. Characteristically, Rorty never dwells on the resolution of conflicts in practice, but only predicts the theory, namely, "if we take care of political freedom, truth and goodness will take care of themselves" (1989: 84).

A remarkable blind spot in Rorty's political philosophy – the entire domain of economic activity – arises from another absolute distinction that is made between the private and public social realms. Being a liberal, Rorty wants as little government as possible, and as much personal freedom and individual enterprise as possible. His argument entails, first, a small public sector and a large private sector, and, more significantly, an absolute split between the two. Referring to the liberal citizen as an ironist, someone having radical and con- tinuous doubts about any final vocabulary, Rorty proposes that "the ironist's final vocabulary can be and should be split into a large private and a small public sector, sectors which have no particular relation to one another" (1989: 100). While the public sector of politics will work according to a few liberal principles ("duty to others," p. 120), the private sector, emphasizing humans' existential choices ("duty to self," p. 120), should be the object of continuous deliberation through irony. A political philosophy which thus collapses per- sonal choices made by individual agents (referring to what Giddens [1984] calls 'existential contradictions') and economic decisions made by corporations or even government agencies (involving Giddens' 'structural contradictions') into one category of private enterprise has little relevance for the understanding of either modern society during the last two centuries or possible future social reform of the Deweyan variety. It is a political philosophy which, far from con- siderng the practical consequences of action as appropriate economic and political criteria, trusts in formal equality and abstracted irony.

Postmodernism as cannibalism

If postmodernism feeds on an exhausted philosophical tradition (Chapter 1), the resulting problems return with a vengeance in Rorty's postmodernist prag- matism. For one thing, his central arguments would appear incompatible both with the general pragmatic maxim and with Dewey's application of pragma- tism in interpreting and reforming modern American society. Dewey's works were perhaps especially vulnerable to cannibalism. As suggested in Chapter 2, his theoretical sophistication was not on a par with either Peirce or James, and his analyses in the manner of nineteenth-century philosophy prove open to Rorty's recontextualizing readings, in part, because of their conceptual vague- ness. Rorty's stated aim, of course, is to read more and better stories into the philosophical tradition, regardless of the original context and internal consis- tency of the discursive fragments.

    For another thing, Rorty increasingly renounces on the special (in the sense of different, not higher or better) status of philosophical discourse, also in a contemporary perspective. If philosophy is no longer a specific cultural prac- tice, governed by fallible, but constitutive procedures, then there is no limit to the recontextualizations that may be performed in the name of story-telling. The main example of recontextualization in Rorty's writings is the work of the contemporary philosopher Donald Davidson, who has explicitly questioned Rorty's appropriation of his ideas concerning the correspondence and coher- ence concepts of truth, or realism and nominalism. Rorty acknowledges that "Davidson cannot be held responsible for the interpretation I am putting on his views, nor for the further views I extrapolate from his" (1989: 10). Yet, the interpretations and extrapolations are used in the public domain for telling what may be better stories for all. One response has come from another con- temporary philosopher, Daniel Dennett, who proposed introducing a "Rorty Factor," specified as 0.742, to indicate the extent to which Rorty misstates the case of other philosophers. Dennett (1982) finds that he himself agrees with Rorty's non-essentialist representationalism to the extent of 74.2 per cent. Another response in Rorty's own terms would be to suggest that he is crazy, gone beyond the limits that "we heirs of the Enlightenment" (Rorty, 1991a: 187) find practical. Rorty may not be one of 'us.'

Richard Rorty, then, qualifies as a postmodernist pragmatist, deconstructing the conceptual repertoire of modern philosophy and shifting its professional, institutional task into the domain of political action. Yet, his political turn does not entail any apparent change in philosophical practice, comprising publication, conferencing, and other academic activities within communities disagreeing about theory. At the end of deconstruction, it is doubtful what consequences Rorty's neopragmatism could have for political practice, even if advanced by a significant community of philosophers and adopted by a substantial public, and even if supported through the genres of journalism, literature, and poetry that he has characterized as more important sources of modernity and moral progress than philosophy (Rorty, 1989: 192). Postmodernist pragmatism, in sum, makes a discursive difference, perhaps an interpretive difference, but no social difference.

Modernist pragmatism: Habermas

Communities and interests

What unites Rorty and Habermas under a heading of pragmatism is a narrative advocating "as much domination-free communication as possible to take place. Such a narrative would clarify the conditions in which the idea of truth as correspondence to reality might gradually be replaced by the idea of truth as what comes to be believed in the course of free and open encounters" (Rorty, 1989: 68). What divides them is their understanding of how the narrative may be justified in ethical and political terms in relation to a specific historical and social context. In an essay comparing the positions of Habermas and Lyotard in the debate on postmodernity, Rorty has suggested that "the trouble with Habermas is not so much that he provides a metanarrative of emancipation as that he feels the need to legitimize, that he is not content to let the narratives which hold our culture together do their stuff" (1991b: 167). Habermas's concern with legitimation is explained, to an extent, by his understanding of knowledge as socially interested.

In the terminology of pragmatism, the three different knowledge-constitutive interests (Chapter 6) – the technical interest of the empirical-analytic, especially natural sciences; the contemplative interest of the historical-hermeneutic sciences; and the critical or emancipatory interest of the social sciences – imply specific predispositions to act. Sciences anticipate and enable particular forms of institutionalized social action while closing off others. The concept of knowledge interests thus contributes two specifications of Peircean scientific communities with reference to their embedding in society. First, Chapter 9 discussed how the analytical procedures of various sciences bear witness to different social purposes of research. Second, these knowledge interests bear witness to the organization of scientific practices in the wider historical context, the scientific division of labor. Social science is a product of the modern age and its regulative, bureaucratic requirements.

The critical knowledge interest of modern social science (what Habermas calls the 'sciences of social action') has particular relevance for social semiotics. Like pragmatism, this interest focuses on the future as a field of potential developments. According to Habermas (1968/1971), social science, like natural science, may produce lawlike knowledge, but with the important modification that the regularities of social reality can be changed by social science as part of what Giddens (1984) has later called a 'double hermeneutic':

> The systematic *sciences of social action*, that is economics, sociology, and political science, have the goal, as do the empirical-analytic sciences, of producing nomological knowledge. A critical social science, however, will not remain satisfied with this. It is concerned with going beyond this goal to determine when theoretical statements grasp invariant regularities of social action as such and when they express ideologically frozen relations of dependence that can in principle be transformed. To the extent that this is the case, the *critique of ideology*, as well, moreover, as *psychoanalysis*, take into account that information about lawlike connections sets off a process of reflection in the consciousness of those whom the laws are about. Thus the level of unreflected unconsciousness, which is one of the initial conditions of such laws, can be transformed. (Habermas, 1968/1971: 310)

Critical social science, accordingly, can suggest what might be, recontextualizing society to its participants and hence enabling further social action.

Foundations of philosophy and politics

While Habermas thus helps to contextualize and historicize Peircean scientific communities, his conception of the way to social change for the wider community, perhaps surprisingly, remains rooted in a dualism regarding the human subject and a foundationalism regarding the ideal conditions of social communication. The dualism is apparent, for example, in his early work on the theory of science (Habermas, 1968/1971), which included a critique of Peircean pragmatism. Highlighting Peirce's scientistic aspect, Habermas here claims that Peirce reifies the object of inquiry and neglects the constitutive role of a socially situated subjectivity in all science. By contrast, Habermas proposes to reassert the hegemony of the human subject by defining community as a precondition of knowledge which transcends both material and historical contexts, that is,

> a community that constitutes the world from transcendental perspectives. This would be the subject of the process of learning and inquiry that is itself involved in a self-formative process until the point in time at which a definitive and complete knowledge of reality is attained. But it is this very subject that Peirce cannot conceive. It falls through his fingers because he applies the pragmatist criterion of meaning to the concepts of both mind *and* matter. Here a hidden but unyielding positivism finally prevails. (1968/1971: 135)

Although Habermas's (1968/1971) reading of Peirce is based on the problematic *Collected Papers* (1931–58), even that text will not support his interpretation of Peirce's phenomenology and semiotics as language-based, positivistic conceptions of the object of inquiry. Habermas inverts, but cannot transcend the dualism of "mind *and* matter" which the pragmatic maxim ("criterion of meaning") was an admittedly rudimentary attempt to address. As it turns out, this is the first in a series of dualistic inversions that can be read as Habermas's projection onto Peirce, and some later theorists, of several classic dilemmas as part of his quest for some incorrigible foundation of philosophy as well as politics.

Like other scholars of Continental and Logos training, Habermas evidently finds it difficult to comprehend Peirce's starting point, namely, that signs are of multiple kinds, so that verbal language is not the basis of all cognition and action. Habermas even suggests that the three categories of Peirce's phenomenology "were derived likewise from linguistic functions" (1968/1971: 103). The implication, according to Habermas, is the following:

> Peirce [...] approached the problem immediately on the level of his linguistic concept of reality. For if reality is defined by the totality of possible true statements, and if these statements are symbolic representations, then why should the structure of reality not be elucidated in relation to the structure of language? (p. 102)

While this is clearly an untenable exegesis, the rest of Habermas's argument is revealing for its misconception of semiotics. Referring to Peirce's concept of the sign as a quality, Habermas's key point is that,

> The concept of quality is supposed to accomplish two incompatible purposes: To account for the moment of immediacy in singular sensations on the one hand and yet include an elementary representative function on the other. The attempt to derive this 'quality' from the logic of language must fail. Either quality corresponds to the substratum of the sign and is not iconic, or it retains its image character, in which case it must be classified as a representative symbol and is no longer immediate. (p. 106)

The inconsistency, however, only arises within a logic privileging verbal language. It may be true that the logic of language "does not suffice to explain how thought processes transform *the presymbolic influx of information content*. [...] This layer of immediate qualities goes beyond the concept of reality derived from the logic of language" (p. 107; emphasis added). But it is Habermas's own implicit premise, namely, that signs are either symbols or "presymbolic influx," which produces inconsistency. Peirce's logic, in contradistinction, is a general semiotics. The notion that humans necessarily first grasp a presymbolic influx of information and next transform it into linguistic signs is compatible with a dualistic philosophy centered in verbal language, but not with triadic semiotics. The absence of references in Habermas's text to the role of Peirce's interpretant in this respect is especially puzzling.

By coupling the logic of language with Peirce's counterfactual definition of reality as the consensus of the scientific community in the last instance, one might conclude that Peirce's "philosophy of science can be understood as the attempt to elucidate the *logic of scientific progress*" (Habermas, 1968/1971: 94).

Habermas, therefore, sums up his criticism of Peirce as a variety of his general critique of positivism:

> By carrying out a cumulative process of inquiry according to rules of a logic that objectifies reality from the point of view of technical control, the community of investigators performs a synthesis. But if this synthesis falls under the operational-ist concept of 'mind' and is dissolved objectivistically into a series of empirical events, then what remains is nothing but universal matters of fact existing in themselves and the combinations of signs through which these matters of fact are represented. (pp. 136–7)

The alternative for Habermas is a philosophy of science which reinstates the human subject as the privileged source of knowledge about reality and, crucially, as the reformer of reality. The hidden agenda (explicit in, for example, Habermas, 1981/1984, 1981/1987) is that of transcendental hermeneutics, as developed further by Karl-Otto Apel (1981), which assumes the primacy of the subject-to-subject relation over the subject-to-object relation in all forms of inquiry. The subject of transcendental hermeneutics is a positively defined consciousness, introspecting, interacting directly with other subjects, and intervening into the objects of inquiry. As such, it is incompatible with the differentiated, discursive subject that can be retrieved from Peircean semiotics, and it is more abstract and ahistorical than even Peirce's ideal scientific community. Against this background, it is ironic that Habermas should accuse Peirce of returning to a philosophy of consciousness, namely, the historical idealism of Hegel. Habermas thus argues that, "the identity of concept and object (*Sache*), which Peirce had first derived from a methodological conception of truth and thus understood as an *interpretation of the fact of scientific progress*, can only be justified in terms of an idealism that is not unlike Hegel's" (Habermas, 1968/1971: 111).

Transcendental hermeneutics represents a return to a philosophy of consciousness, a turn away both from the philosophy of language in twentieth-century thought, and from an interdisciplinary philosophy of signs. Despite Habermas's claim in his theory of communicative action to extend the linguistic turn to ethics and politics, to "start from the structure of linguistic expressions rather than from speakers' intentions" (Habermas, 1981/1984: 275), I want to argue that the theory implies a dualism of transcendental minds facing contingent natural and cultural realities, effectively returning the politics of communication to foundationalism rather than fallibilism.

Transcendental communities

Concluding his 1971 critique of Peirce, Habermas notes that "it is possible to think in syllogisms, but not to conduct a dialogue in them" (p. 137). The ambition of the theory of communicative action (Habermas, 1981/1984, 1981/1987) is to specify the ideal conditions of dialogue in science and, by analogy, in the political process.[3] Whereas Habermas draws substantially on the work of George Herbert Mead, the rest of the pragmatist tradition is not central to the theory as such, which presents a synthesis of classic and modern social theory with a critical inflection. In polemical summary, the theory of communicative action (TCA) hypostatizes Habermas's (1962/1989) historical account of the democratic potential of the public sphere in the form of an *a priori*, normative theory of communication.

While a detailed analysis of TCA falls outside the present argument (see Thompson, 1984), it is important to realize its roots in Habermas's comprehensive ontology of social life. The most basic distinction (corresponding structurally to Giddens' [1984] distinction between social integration and system integration) is made in phenomenological terms between the lifeworld and the system world, that is, on the one hand, the unmediated, authentic aspects of human experience and interaction and, on the other hand, their institutionalized, rationalized form in modern society. 'Communicative action' serves to produce mutual understanding in the terms of the lifeworld as part of an 'ideal speech situation,' and as such it is not structured by any ulterior purposes arising from the system world. Habermas does suggest that the two worlds are complementary sides of social reality. As noted by his translator, "the 'ideal speech situation' is *not* the image of a concrete form of life," but a counterfactual concept which enables research "to identify empirically the actually existing possibilities for embodying rationality structures in concrete forms of life" (McCarthy in Habermas, 1981/1984: 405–6). Nevertheless, the counterfactual communicative situation is made to serve as an absolute criterion, not only for establishing what communicative practices are possible, but also for evaluating certain practices as preferable in a specific social and historical context.[4]

Habermas supports his general argument with typologies of both social practices and discursive forms. A distinction is made, first, between three types of practice, that is, instrumental, strategic, and communicative action, which are later subdivided as elements of an inclusive typology of social action (Habermas, 1981/1984: 333):

> We call an action oriented to success *instrumental* when we consider it under the aspect of following technical rules of action and assess the efficiency of an intervention into a complex of circumstances and events. We call an action oriented to success *strategic* when we consider it under the aspect of following rules of rational choice and assess the efficacy of influencing the decisions of a rational opponent. Instrumental actions can be connected with and subordinated to social interactions of a different type – for example, as the 'task elements' of social roles; strategic actions are social actions by themselves. By contrast, I shall speak of *communicative* action whenever the actions of the agents involved are coordinated not through egocentric calculations of success but through acts of reaching understanding. In communicative action participants are not primarily oriented to their own individual successes; they pursue their individual goals under the condition that they can harmonize their plans of action on the basis of common situation definitions. (Habermas, 1981/1984: 285–6)

While instrumental and strategic action go together, being oriented toward (respectively material and social) success, communicative action, oriented toward insight and consensus, is Habermas's main consideration. Under a rubric of concealed strategic action, Habermas is particularly concerned about 'systematically distorted communication' as a source of social and personal pathologies, which he opposes to conscious deception or propaganda. A primary example of systematically distorted communication, to Habermas, is the mass media serving to legitimate the dominant social order.

Now, Habermas recognizes that his theory will hold

> only if it can be shown that the use of language with an orientation to reaching understanding is the *original mode* of language use, upon which indirect understanding, giving something to understand or letting something be understood, and the instrumental use of language in general are parasitic. In my view, Austin's distinction between illocutions and perlocutions accomplishes just that. (Habermas, 1981/1984: 288)

However, far from lending hard linguistic support to the understanding of some varieties of interpersonal and mass communication as ideal forms of social interaction, Austin's (1962: chaps 8–9) theory of speech acts serves to analytically distinguish different aspects or levels of *all* speech acts.

Austin's (1962) key distinction, between "illocutionary acts (the act performed *in* saying something) and perlocutionary acts (the act performed *by* saying something)" (Thompson, 1984: 295), is employed by Habermas to refer to different categories of action. Whereas perlocutions intend some ulterior purpose, according to Habermas illocution has no such orientation toward future action, the distinguishing feature being its present, ideal intentionality. In my reading (see also Alexander, 1991), however, Austin was quite clear about the reciprocity between illocution and perlocution, and about the possible range of perlocutionary effects on the recipient, regardless of the speaker's concrete intention: ·

> The perlocutionary act may be either the achievement of a perlocutionary object (convince, persuade) or the production of a perlocutionary sequel. Thus the act of warning may achieve its perlocutionary object of alerting and also have the perlocutionary sequel of alarming, and an argument against a view may fail to achieve its object but have the perlocutionary sequel of convincing our opponent of its truth ('I only succeeded in convincing him'). What is the perlocutionary object of one illocution may be the sequel of another. (Austin, 1962: 118)

By contrast, Habermas offers the following definitions:

> Thus I count as communicative action those linguistically mediated interactions in which all participants pursue illocutionary aims, and *only* illocutionary aims, with their mediating acts of communication. On the other hand, I regard as linguistically mediated strategic action those interactions in which at least one of the participants wants with his speech acts to produce perlocutionary effects on his opposite number. Austin did not keep these two cases separate as different types of interaction, because he was inclined to identify acts of communication, that is, acts of reaching understanding, with the interactions coordinated by speech acts. He didn't see that acts of communication or speech acts function as a coordinating mechanism for *other* actions. (Habermas, 1981/1984: 295)

While Habermas may want to stipulate a theory of privileged communicative interaction, it is not supported by Austin's original typology and thus fails in Habermas's own terms. Perhaps the most farreaching implication of speech-act theory, as elaborated in later empirical and theoretical research on the

pragmatics of communication (van Dijk, 1985), is that all language use is a
form of social action which articulates the intentions and purposes of agents.
Like the scientific communities examined so revealingly by Habermas
(1968/1971), other social formations have knowledge interests that are negotiated and enacted in their communicative practices. Communication cannot
transcend its social context definitively. The irony of Habermas's position is
that, in order to arrive at his theory of ideal communicative action, Habermas
performs a strategic interpretation of Austin.[5]

What Habermas develops, then, is a last-ditch articulation of the Logos tradition. Asking "Where is meaning?", Habermas's implied answer is that
meaning is inherent in certain natural conditions for language use. It is the original mode of language use that would make possible not only an incorrigible
understanding of other individuals, but also the development and legitimation
of certain fundamental principles of human community. Even if neither the
introspective subject nor the structure of the language system could be considered reliable guides to the nature of reality, Habermas proposes to deduce the
specific rules of interaction that would constitute a forum where communicative
reason might at last guide human understanding and social action.[6]

Austin and Habermas have each performed half a pragmatist turn. Austin
identified language use as action without examining its social contexts outside
of a few ideal-typical situations; his material was the language of textbook
examples. Habermas has addressed the social contexts of communication, but
from an *a priori*, normative position that misconceives the forms of language.
In the end, Habermas's theory of communicative action is at a loss to explain
why any human would want to arrive at an understanding with others about
something in the world, except as an aspect of their being already in and
engaging each other in relation to that world. His *maximalist* theory of communication rights has little practical relevance for the contexts in which
choices in the politics of communication must be made, because it neglects
almost entirely how communication will be terminated in action. This issue –
the relationship between communication and action, between time-out and
time-in culture, and between the ends and the end of communication – is the
main challenge for a minimalist, pragmatist theory of communication.

The end of communication

Erro, ergo sum

While Peirce's position on scientific communities and realism has been referred
to as "logical socialism" (Fisch, 1984: xxviii), no specific politics of communication follows from the writings of Peirce. Most of the implications of
pragmatism, like those of other social theory, must be worked out in non-
scientific genres and fora. Nevertheless, pragmatism refocuses theoretical
attention on an end-of-communication perspective. The answer to the question 'how to make a social difference through communication' must address
the question 'how to end communication.'

Whereas basic communication theories such as Lasswell (1948/1966) and Jakobson (1960/1981) address questions of who, says what, in which medium and code, to whom, in what context, and with what effects, the normative theories of communication ask who is permitted to communicate, about what, with whom, in which medium, to what extent, emphasizing rights rather than results. A pragmatist theory of communication would want to examine, in addition, who participates in transforming communication into action, in what sectors and institutions of society, with what basis in everyday life, by what form of consensus concerning criteria and procedures, and with what consequences for the structuration of society. In the perspective of 'communication rights,' these questions reemphasize a *minimalist* conception of communication: the making of discursive and interpretive difference is an enabling condition of making a social difference, which may ensure that other social rights are enacted in practice. Communication is a semiotic means to a social end.

Future research on these issues can serve to question and recontextualize the prevailing forms of communication in society, in keeping with a critical knowledge interest, with reference to both contemporary and historical cases.[7] And research from the end-of-communication perspective is long overdue. Recontextualization, however, only takes effect in the long run, and only through a double hermeneutic which relates scientific and other social practices in specific contexts of influence that rely on non-scientific genres. In this respect, mass communication research resembles its object, being an institutionalized form of social reflexivity with an uncertain outcome. Science is, moreover, fallible and offers no permanent foundation for researchers in search of a political platform. A recognition of these social conditions of research makes for a less reassured, but more realistic and relevant understanding of the mission of a politics of communication. Mass communication research thus cannot offer *a priori* principles concerning ideal regulatory frameworks, diversity of content, or levels of audience competence, but it can contribute to a differentiated understanding of how the general relationship between time-out and time-in culture, between meaning and action, might be restructured in the future. Both in communication and science, establishing the conditions of and obstacles to social action, the *cogito* of pragmatism is fallibilism: *erro, ergo sum.*

Surplus meaning

I conclude with a brief essay reflecting on the limits of the mass media as institutions-to-think-with, hence shifting the discourse from theoretical analysis to a genre of cultural criticism. Semiosis remains subject to determination in the first instance, and cultural criticism traditionally monitors the nature of this determination, reasserting the public concern that semiosis may be overdetermined by economy or ideology, and thus also contributing to the agenda of research. Different aspects of social semiosis may be described with reference to a category of surplus (Jensen, 1988b).

The modern mass media operate according to general principles of commodity production. The distinctive feature of commodity production during industrial capitalism is commonly said, in the Marxist tradition, to be the generating of *surplus value*. Critical studies of capitalist economy, accordingly, have been founded on

> the discovery of surplus value. It was shown that the appropriation of unpaid labour is the basis of the capitalist mode of production, and of the exploitation of the worker that occurs under it; that even if the capitalist buys the labour power of his labourer at its full value as a commodity on the market he yet extracts more value from it than he paid for, and that in the ultimate analysis this surplus value forms those sums of value from which are heaped up the constantly increasing masses of capital in the hands of the possessing classes. The genesis of capitalist production and the production of capital were both explained. (Engels, 1880/1959: 130)

Surplus value thus characterizes a specific economic practice; it is both a characteristic of the form of production and its concrete product, which is accumulated as capital. Surplus value is the end result of, as well as a precondition for, industrial capitalism, being what the economic system generates in order to sustain itself.

It should be emphasized that surplus value is both a quantitative and a qualitative feature of material production. While surplus value is defined as an excess quantity that is appropriated from the activity of production, it is also a constitutive element of the *process* which affects both the material forms and social uses of the commodities. At the systemic level of mass communication, advertising has been said to contribute to a pervasive form of commodity aesthetics (Haug, 1971; see also Schudson, 1984), and the corporate organization of film companies, publishing houses, newspapers, and other media institutions further shapes the predominant textual genres, the prototypical case being the television series. Even audiences can be said to participate indirectly in the production of surplus value as they perform the act of reception for advertisers as well as programmers (Smythe, 1977).

Signs, subjects, and social structures are, to a degree, structurally related phenomena. Marcuse (1955), accordingly, drew an analogy between industrial capitalist production and its characteristic social psychology. Basing himself on a Freudian framework, Marcuse distinguishes between that basic repression which is necessary for the social constitution of an individual and the *surplus repression* that follows from historical factors:

> [...] while any form of the reality principle demands a considerable degree and scope of repressive control over the instincts, the specific historical institutions of the reality principle and the specific interests of domination introduce *additional* controls over and above those indispensable for civilized human association. These additional controls arising from the specific institutions of domination are what we denote as surplus-repression. For example, the modifications and deflections of instinctual energy necessitated by the perpetuation of the monogamic-patriarchal family, or by the hierarchical division of labor, or by public control over the individual's private existence are instances of surplus-repression pertaining to the institutions of a *particular* reality principle. (Marcuse, 1955: 37–8)

Surplus repression thus characterizes the interaction between the individual and a specific social structure during socialization. It is the end result of, as well as a precondition for, the successful integration of individuals in contemporary industrial capitalist societies, being what a dominant social-psychological configuration generates in order to sustain itself.

Again, the qualitative aspect of repression does not come out in Marcuse's account, which rather conceives of surplus repression as an excess above some fundamental, anthropological level of repressive control. By contrast, I note that repression is always already a social structure, so that surplus repression may be thought of as a specific form of consciousness that is associated with a particular historical setting and social context.

I introduce the concept of *surplus meaning* to characterize certain features of contemporary meaning production as it arises from the reception and social uses of mass communication. Surplus meaning may reassert the limits of the social imagination and, thus, of social action and change. It is the end result of, as well as a precondition for, the discursive reproduction of a specific social system; it represents a social reality that is premised on particular reality principles and principles of material production. Also surplus meaning comprises both a qualitative and quantitative aspect. While indicating a static conception of social reality as a product, it equally refers to the process of negotiating meaning according to particular generative principles, a specific form of social semiosis.

It is the process of semiosis which constitutes a necessary condition of reflexivity in various political and scientific fora, but which may be seen to reiterate particular configurations of meaning as common sense. Surplus meaning may promote hegemony (Gramsci, 1971), "a sense of absolute because experienced reality beyond which it is very difficult for most members of the society to move, in most areas of their lives" (Williams, 1977: 110). One example is the polysemy of reception that I discussed in Chapter 5: the ambiguity in the social definition of television news suggests that the news genre is overrated as a political resource and endowed with a surplus of meaning. The super-themes (Chapters 7 and 9), further, represent highly generalized configurations of meaning beyond which a substantial part of the audience may find it difficult to reflect.

Surplus meaning is a heuristic concept reminding media users and researchers alike that the media make a difference, in part, by consolidating the society that is and has been. Social semiotics can make a difference by exploring the forms of communication and society that might be.

NOTES

Chapter 1 Introduction: From structuralism through poststructuralism to pragmatism

1. For an excellent historical overview, see Beniger (1986), who avoids the rhetoric, common also in the scientific literature, promising great political and cultural benefits from the 'information society' to the general public. By contrast, Beniger examines these new technologies as ambivalent social resources which enable both increased control over individuals through centralized information and new cultural forms that may transform the relations of control. See also Jensen (forthcoming) for an analysis of previous studies and a research agenda addressing the audience perspective on the information society.

2. As I go on to clarify below, a distinction should be made between the semio*logy* of Saussure and the semio*tics* of Peirce, although 'semiotics' often refers to work from both traditions. Furthermore, while some purist Peirce scholars insist on semio*tic* in the singular, I prefer the nomenclature of semiotics by analogy to disciplines such as linguistics and economics.

3. Similar arguments, emphasizing the continuity of social developments in the modern period and insisting on material, institutional, and technological structures as conditions of an apparently self-generating aesthetics of surfaces, have been offered by other scholars (see especially Berman, 1982, and Huyssen, 1986). Further, Jameson (1991) presents detailed examples to support his argument that postmodernism is the cultural logic of 'late' capitalism. Recently, Giddens (1990) has made a tactical use of the concept of postmodernity to suggest that while we still live in an ambivalent modernity, an alternative, optimistic post-modernity, taking us beyond the institutional contradictions and material limitations of modernity, is conceivable.

4. Structuralism in the wider sense has affected human, social, as well as natural sciences during the twentieth century. In Jean Piaget's definition, structuralism assigns attributes of wholeness, transformation, and self-regulation to the structures being studied (Hawkes, 1977: 16). Much work in the humanities and in anthropology over the last three decades has interpreted entire cultures and societies as discourses in order to discover deep structures of their mythologies, and ultimately of human culture (Barthes, 1957/1973; Lévi-Strauss, 1963). By analogy, critical social science has examined the deep structures of social institutions under industrial capitalism, their discursive articulation, and historical change (Althusser, 1977; Foucault, 1972). Moreover, research in a structuralist vein has taken verbal language as the model for theories concerning film, television, and photography. Benveniste (1985) makes the general argument that verbal language is the interpreting system *par excellence* because, unlike other semiotic systems, it will serve to explain its own structure and meaning. A major contribution to semiological research on the 'language' of film was the work of Christian Metz (1974). The primacy of verbal language has been challenged by recent cognitive film theory (Bordwell, 1985; Branigan, 1992), and I return to problems in the semiotics of visual communication in Chapter 10.

5. Whereas a detailed examination of either hermeneutics or phenomenology falls outside this study, I suggest that key analytical procedures, such as phenomenological reduction and the hermeneutic interpretation of a textual horizon of expectations, prove difficult to apply in any systematic fashion to issues of contemporary culture. I go on to argue in Chapters 2 and 3 that current theories of culture and communication especially require concepts and methods for examining communication as a contextualized social practice. For a survey and discussion of hermeneutics and phenomenology relating to textual research, see Eagleton (1983: chap. 2).

6. While I return to Peirce's semiotics, it is interesting to note that Barthes thus hinted at a chain of semiosis, but assumed that the second and final link was securely fastened in a homogenizing ideology. Whereas Peirce (1955: 299) described Kant as "a somewhat confused pragmatist", Barthes could be described as a somewhat confused (Peircean) semiotician. (In his later works, Barthes took a further step in the direction of Peircean semiosis, reformulating denotation as the final element in a chain of connotations (1970: 13–16). I owe this point to Peter Larsen.)

7. In fairness, it should be recalled that not only is the concept of a code central to Jakobson's (1960/1981) communicative model, but he also repeatedly advocated the notion of dynamic semiosis found in Peirce, as noted by Johansen (1993: 222–44). Johansen (1993) himself develops a Peircean model of communication, combining the constituents of other basic models with Peirce's triadic sign model, as elaborated below. One problem of Johansen's model, however, is that it still implies a static conception of communicators, contexts, and interpretations which does not do justice to the sequence of interpretants and their embeddedness in social contexts of action.

Chapter 2 Semiotic action: Recovering pragmatism

1. Peirce never completed a *magnum opus* definitively stating his theories and their implications for science and society. A new standard edition, *Writings of Charles S. Peirce: A Chronological Edition* (Peirce, 1982ff.), is currently being published by Indiana University Press; the majority of the thirty planned volumes are still in preparation. This edition ultimately will replace the *Collected Papers* (1931–58), whose thematic principles of editing have been widely criticized, but which remains a key reference. Recently, the first volume of a compact two-volume edition, *The Essential Peirce* (Peirce, 1992), was published by the editing team behind the chronological edition. Other useful collections are the reprints of Peirce (1955) and Peirce (1958). Some of the most insightful studies of Peirce can be found in Fisch (1986a) and Apel (1981), who place his ideas in their philosophical and historical contexts. For introductions to Peirce, see Hookway (1985), Skagestad (1981), and Murphey (1961); for biography, see Brent (1993).

2. This section relies substantially on Clarke's (1990) anthology, which places major Western philosophers in a perspective of semiotics. Further, I draw on Eco (1984) and Lobkowicz (1967), who account respectively for the concept of signs and of practice in the history of ideas preceding pragmatism.

3. The next few lines of the text run as follows: "It stands for that object, not in all respects, but in reference to a sort of idea, which I have sometimes called the *ground* of the representamen. 'Idea' is here to be understood in a sort of Platonic sense, very familiar in everyday talk; I mean in that sense in which we say that one man catches another man's idea, in which we say that when a man recalls what he was thinking at some previous time, he recalls the same idea, and in which when a man continues to think anything, say for a tenth of a second, in so far as the thought continues to agree with itself during that time, that is to have a *like* content, it is the same idea, and is not at each instant of the interval a new idea." Peirce thus signals an awareness that he may be accused of relapsing to a dualist, Platonic conception of signs. I take the theoretical point to be that the specific meaning of a sign must always be interpreted with reference to something else, as part of a relational structure, the three main constituents of which are sign, object, and interpretant, corresponding to the categories of Firstness, Secondness, and Thirdness in the ontology outlined below. The reference to the *Collected Papers* (Peirce, 1931–58), or CP, follows the convention in Peirce scholarship of indicating the volume number before, and the paragraph number after, a period. References to other editions indicate year of publication and page number.

4. Chapter 3 presents a critical discussion of social-scientific concepts and terminologies regarding the levels and processes of social structuration. In the present context, I rely on the standard distinction between 'macrosocial,' institutionalized structures and 'microsocial,' individualized action in context.

5. Especially psychologists and humanists were singled out for criticism. In correspondence late in life, Peirce explained the shortcomings of philosophy by noting that "all the humanists were no better than *littérateurs*, with the total lack of ratiocinative power which I had seen in the literary

men whom I had personally known. Such fools! On the intellectual level of the wine-tasters of Bordeaux" (1958: 418).

6. I can only note in passing the contribution of W.V.O. Quine to pragmatism as logical inquiry. His work has challenged major premises of Anglo-American philosophy of language and theory of science, arriving at something like a logical nihilism through a behaviorist inflection of pragmatism. For overview and discussion, see West (1989: chap. 5) and Johansen (1993: chap. 5).

7. "Less attention, I suppose, is paid to philosophy in the United States than in any other country of the civilized world. [...] So, of all the countries in the world, America is the one where the precepts of Descartes are least studied and best followed. No one should be surprised at that" (Tocqueville, 1848/1966: 429). Since Alexis de Tocqueville, the United States has often been referred to as a culture of pragmatism in which political and economic pragmatism helps to explain the rise of a philosophical pragmatism (West, 1989; White, 1973). The ambiguity of the term follows from a history of ideas premised on a dichotomy of theory, being propositions with universal, even eternal relevance, versus practice in its historical contexts. Lobkowicz (1967) traces this history from Aristotle through Duns Scotus and Kant to Marx, who was the first to claim that "man can transform himself by transforming the material world" (p. 139). Peircean pragmatism offers a framework for reinterpreting that history.

8. The fallibilism of Peirce differs from the falsificationism of Popper, to which I return in Chapter 9. In sum, Peirce suggested that even the procedures and criteria of scientific falsification do not constitute a solid foundation, substituting for this essentialist metaphor that of a cable whose mutually supporting fibers make up a relational structure (CP 5.265).

Chapter 3 Meaningful society: Recontextualizing social science

1. The account is based primarily on the summary statement in Giddens (1984) (see also Giddens, 1990, and 1991). Critical anthologies with responses by Giddens include Held and Thompson (1989) and Bryant and Jary (1991). Among seminal influences on structuration theory have been the phenomenological sociology of Schütz (1973), the symbolic interactionism of Goffman (1974), and the cultural sociology of Bourdieu (1977, 1984). Whereas Giddens refers to (Saussurean) structuralism and poststructuralism as "dead traditions of thought" (1987: 73), he emphasizes the relevance of semiotics for social theory (1984: 31). Apart from sections on mass media in Giddens' (1989) textbook, however, the media are treated especially in the context of other social phenomena, notably the reorganization of time and space during modernization and globalization. For further application of structuration theory to mass communication, see Thompson (1990).

2. Contrary to a traditional reading of Weber, via Talcott Parsons, as a "value-free sociologist of social action" (Turner, 1991b: xxvi) who would explain capitalism with reference to spiritual values rather than material causes, Weber in fact stressed the contingent and conflictual aspects of social life. Recent research has described Weber as a theorist of modernity equally employing cultural and material, interpretive and structural categories of analysis (see Schroeder, 1992; Turner, 1991b). The dual emphasis is also explained, in part, by Weber's private dilemma of whether to pursue politics or science, applied or basic social science. Punning on the title of Veblen's *The Theory of the Leisure Class*, Bershady speculates that the grand theories developed by a sequence of early German social scientists grow out of "the leisure of the theory class" (1991: 76), the financial privileges promoting a particular academic culture.

3. It is striking that, just as Weber preached interpretive sociology, but practiced structural explanation, Durkheim's works preached objectivist sociology, but most interestingly practiced the interpretation of, for example, religion and suicide as social categories. For a selection, see Durkheim (1972), including the introduction by Giddens (1972) that suggests the turn of the latter from appreciation to critique especially of a Durkheimian understanding of structure as 'constraint' (Giddens, 1984: 169–74).

4. Despite differences between Parsons and Merton, I assume that "both together can be taken as the founders of the school of theory known as structural-functionalism" (Berger and Berger, 1976: 49). Parsons has recently been rehabilitated as a theorist of modernity, in part for his

contribution to establishing sociology as a discipline, in part for his empirical studies (Robertson and Turner, 1991). Yet, it remains striking that pragmatism, including Mead, Park, and Dewey, played practically no role in Parsons' theory of (American) society, and in his theory of science. "Perhaps the critical issue in Parsons' failure to engage with pragmatic philosophy was his neglect of the important work of Charles Peirce, who has in any case only very recently been taken seriously by social scientists" (Robertson and Turner, 1991: 6).

5. Another version of the social-organism metaphor in current social science is the systems theory of Niklas Luhmann, which in effect does away with reflexive social agents at the theoretical level of analysis and instead conceives societies as self-organizing systems (for example, Luhmann, 1987). I return in Chapter 10 to related problems in the semiotic systems theory of René Thom.

6. The work of Pierre Bourdieu on social organization, individual agency, and culture is another major contribution to studies of the everyday (Bourdieu, 1977, 1984), and his category of *habitus* might be compatible with the pragmatist notion of belief as a predisposition to act. While a detailed analysis of Bourdieu's work falls outside this volume, I pursue Giddens' meta-theoretical strategy, in part, because of the problematic theoretical categories in Bourdieu. For one thing, while 'cultural capital' can be operationalized in empirical studies, the metaphor tends to obfuscate the status and explanatory value of findings, as in the call for analysis of all material as well as symbolic goods, including smiles, through economic calculation (Bourdieu, 1977: 178). The collapsed dualism makes the analysis less informative, and could be replaced by an explicitly triadic conception of society. For another thing, the key categories of doxa, orthodoxy, and heterodoxy only partly emerge from the anthropological context of Kabylia, but are treated as a complete taxonomy and transferred to modern social contexts (Bourdieu, 1977: 159–97).

7. The everyday has also been a center of attention in recent media studies (Moores, 1993; Silverstone, 1994), not least in the inherently political debate concerning the relative power of media and audiences. As noted by Drotner (1994), the most familiar, optimistic position in communication studies is represented by Michel de Certeau (1984). He has characterized ordinary people as resourceful producers of their own culture who appropriate or poach the modern means of communication for their own ends through 'tactics' – "an art of the weak" (p. 37) – that is contrasted with the 'strategies' of the powers that be. The opposite, pessimistic perspective has been developed by Henri Lefebvre (1984). He refers to everyday life as "modernity's unconscious" (p. 117), a historically residual domain persisting in the face of "the Bureaucratic Society of Controlled Consumption," whose fragmented totality and cybernetic control infrastructure Lefebvre considers terroristic. In this society, the role of ordinary people is said to be the consumption of goods and, increasingly, of signs in a media environment that makes symbols into signals and art into displays. For a nuanced discussion of the power of media and audiences in everyday contexts, see Schudson (1987).

8. Another perspective on socialization as a civilizing process in everyday contexts comes from the work of Norbert Elias, who defies categorization because of a unique, sometimes idiosyncratic, conception of human civilization simultaneously in an evolutionary and a historical perspective. For his ideas regarding the role of language and communication in the constitution of society, see Elias (1989).

9. In the present context, I leave aside the questions concerning the identities of Volosinov and Bakhtin. See the translators' discussion in the general introduction to Volosinov (1929/1973).

10. Generative models have at least two different sources. First, the transformational-generative (TG) grammar of Noam Chomsky (1965) provided a precise model of how the transformation of one deep structure of language may generate various surface structures. While the formalist TG grammar gave little attention to language as a discursive practice in social context (see Halliday, 1978; Potter and Wetherell, 1987), the underlying model has proven a productive heuristic device in both linguistics and computer science (see Jensen, 1991a). Second, twentieth-century structuralism in social-scientific and humanistic research was built on the general premise that social, psychological, and cultural phenomena constitute deep-structural systems (Chapter 1). The challenge for current research is to identify the principles of the generative processes reproducing such systems.

Chapter 4 A new theory of mass communication: Constituents of social semiotics

1. Interdisciplinary theory development requires not only goodwill, but good reference works. Handbooks of mass communication research still focus on either quantitative (Berger and Chaffee, 1987) or qualitative traditions (Jensen and Jankowski, 1991). For interdisciplinary first aid, humanistic scholars may turn to *Statistics: A Spectator Sport* (Jaeger, 1990), which provides an introduction to principles informing the quantitative mainstream of social science; social scientists may turn to the conceptual framework laid out in *Keywords* (Williams, 1983) and to introductions to discourse analysis (for example, Potter and Wetherell, 1987).

2. Research debates on the definition of culture are notorious and too numerous to even reference here. I rely particularly on the framework of Raymond Williams (see especially Williams, 1977), who described culture simultaneously as a 'structure of feeling' and as a vehicle of social power. Further, I draw on the historical overviews in Fink (1988) and Martin-Barbero (1993: chap. 1). For a recent approach to culture as social practice, see Willis (1990).

3. I interpret the duality of culture as a subdivision of the 'medium' of triadic society, as discussed in Chapter 3. The two aspects of culture bear witness to two historically specific, interrelated conceptions of the place of the medium within social structuration.

4. In *How Institutions Think* (1987), Mary Douglas has offered one version of the argument that social institutions serve to process meaning, internally and externally. By contrast to Douglas's Durkheimian conception of meaning as an experience of 'the sacred' in the life of any society or organization, I pursue a Weberian analysis of meaning as performative in the context of modern societies.

5. Also in theoretical terms, it can be argued that the two aspects of culture, while related to the organization of time, space, as well as agency, are distinguished primarily by their orientation toward time. Time-out culture is characterized by an emphasis on reflective semiosis during a specified period of time; time-in culture is characterized by concurrent semiosis orienting other social action. In addition, time-out culture may or may not occur in a separate locale, a space-out, such as a theater or cinema. In a historical perspective, much contemporary cultural practice is characterized by a specific integration between time-out and time-in culture, between mass communication and other forms of social interaction in the same time and space, for example through the genre of advertising and the prevalence of intertextuality in general.

6. Before 1989, Habermas's early work was available to Anglophone researchers in articles, regularly reprinted (for example, Habermas, 1991b). The argument in 1962 was based on the historical development of political democracies in Western Europe, and Habermas himself explicitly warned against applying the model to the different cultural conditions in the United States (Habermas, 1962/1989: 267, note 65). However, several studies of American mass media have suggested its relevance here, as well (Jensen, 1987a; Schiller, 1981; Tuchman, 1978). In fact, Habermas (1962/1989: chaps 20–3) recognizes this implicitly by relying extensively on US examples, particularly regarding the era of corporate capitalism. For critical analyses of Habermas's public-sphere work, see Calhoun (1992), which includes a response by Habermas, Curran (1991), and Thompson (1990). Whereas Habermas's (1962/1989) model takes the nation state as its point of departure, the current transnationalization of states and societies, not least via the public-sphere media, calls for a revised framework in further research. For the present argument, I note the relative persistence of the nation state both as an institutional and as a discursive fact.

7. Compared to Fiske's (1987) useful distinction between 'primary texts' (for example, a new feature movie), 'secondary texts' (for example, advertising for the movie), and 'tertiary texts' (for example, audience conversations or public debate about the movie), my argument emphasizes that the ranking applies at the methodological, not at the theoretical level. Mass media discourses are 'primary' only in the sense that empirical communication studies must explain the specific contribution of media to the social production of meaning. (The three types constitute what Fiske [1987] calls 'vertical intertextuality,' as opposed to 'horizontal intertextuality,' which is the thematic, mostly incidental, reference of one media text to another. In Chapter 7, I examine intertextuality as a structural feature of contemporary media environments, and I return in Chapter 10 to intertextuality as a constitutive aspect of human cognition.) My distinction between

the theoretical and methodological levels of analysis further recognizes media discourses as structured meaning potentials, as opposed to the 'empty-text' argument of Fish (1979), which assumes radical polysemy, even while I emphasize the origins of both media discourses and audiences in larger social contexts of action. (On the difficulties of conceptualizing the textual and contextual determinations of polysemy, see Mortensen and Ytreberg, 1991.)

8. The main point of Negt and Kluge (1972/1993) in this respect was that the communications sector of culture is constrained by a pervasive logic of commodity production, which is itself reinforced through the practices of culture and communication. Hence, explanations of the dominant forms of communication under industrial capitalism could be extrapolated from that logic. The problem with this neo-Marxist argument, widespread in European communication studies of the 1970s and 1980s, is that it neglects both the reality of human agency and the structuring role of the 'medium' in actual triadic societies.

9. The model serves both an organizing and a heuristic purpose (McQuail and Windahl, 1981: 2). This and other models, particularly in Chapter 3, can be defined semiotically as iconic representations of a structure of conceptual relations (see Peirce, 1985: 12). The configuration of words as icons indicates *that a relation exists* between the concepts; it is the verbal articulation of the concepts that serves to specify the *nature* of the relations, in the models and with further details in the text. The models thus are complex signs, comprising iconic, indexical, and symbolic elements.

10. The analytical constituents correspond to the analytical level of discourse in Figure 4.4 where materials – 'data' – about the everyday discourses that enter into mass communication are collected and categorized.

11. The model of methodological constituents has been presented in detail in Jensen (1986) and (1987b), with an emphasis on the problems and potentials of previous research. While emphasizing theoretical and meta-theoretical implications here, I summarize the four elements of the model as a background to the empirical studies in Chapters 5–8. I note that, apart from the internationally most influential Anglo-American works, the turn to qualitative reception studies is noticeable in several cultural settings and research traditions, with important contributions being published in French (Wolton, 1992), German (Baacke and Kübler, 1987), Spanish (González, 1990; Orozco-Gómez, 1992), the Scandinavian languages (Carlsson, 1988), and in other contexts.

12. Under a heading of 'gratifications obtained,' uses-and-gratifications research has also proposed to study the audience experience of media contents. As I have argued elsewhere (Jensen, 1987b), the design of such studies, in effect repeating the public-opinion profiles of gratifications-sought studies, does not allow for valid inferences about the audience experience of specific contents. Different problematics call for different methodologies; reception studies and gratifications studies are complementary approaches, each with an independent explanatory value.

Chapter 5 The politics of polysemy: Context constituents of social semiotics

1. This chapter focuses on findings concerning reception. For other findings from the study, regarding news as a social institution and the genre varieties of American television news, see Jensen (1986: chaps 3 and 4).

2. For responses by John Fiske and Horace Newcomb both to these criticisms regarding populism in communication theory and to the prospects for social semiotics, presented in an earlier publication (Jensen, 1991c), see Fiske (1991) and Newcomb (1991). In essence, Fiske still finds the greatest explanatory value in the Saussurean semiological tradition, whereas Newcomb finds no new explanatory value in Peircean semiotics, compared with the cultural-forum model (Newcomb and Hirsch, 1984) and other current mid-level theories of mass communication. Because I agree with both authors that theories must be evaluated historically on their merits, I do not comment on specific disagreements, but offer further substantiation of social semiotics in this volume.

3. Chapters 8 and 9 return to the general discussion of different methodologies for different purposes of research. In the present study relying on individual interviews, my premise was, first, that respondents would be able and used to individually offering arguments about the content and

relevance of news stories, since this is a familiar aspect of everyday conversation as well as a consensual political ideal. Second, interviews about each program with one representative from each socioeconomic group were conducted within a twenty-four hour cycle, before the next broadcast of the program, to ensure a measure of ecological validity. Third, the service staff, while being less familiar with the interview context than the academic staff, would at least be familiar with the university setting, by contrast to a sample off the street. The data are available for further analysis at the University of Aarhus, Denmark (Jensen, 1986).

4. The contradictory social definition of news helps to explain the popularity of sensationalist journalism. Gripsrud (1992), for one, has suggested that the melodramatic qualities of such news provide audiences with a mediation between public political principles (as articulated by the socalled 'quality' press as well as much national television news) and the moral principles of personal life. Drawing on the work of Peter Brooks (1976) about classic melodrama on the stage and in literature, Gripsrud notes that "Brooks regards the melodrama as 'a sense-making system' [...] in the desacralized modern society emerging from the French Revolution. God was no longer the ultimate signified, the meaning behind every phenomenon. Everything was in principle debatable, no meaning was absolutely guaranteed. Melodrama was a textual machine designed to cope with the threatening black hole God left after Him when he returned to His heaven: it was constructed to demonstrate the existence of an underlying universe of absolute forces and values, moral forces and values. The melodramatic is, therefore an expressionist aesthetic, striving to *externalize* what is underneath the chaotic and uncertain surface of modern existence. [...] Melodrama was didactic drama, designed to teach the audience a lesson. Today's popular press also teaches the audience a lesson, every day. It says that what the world (the news) is really about, is *emotions*, fundamental and strong: love, hate, grief, joy, lust and disgust. [...] If the world looks incomprehensibly chaotic, it is only on the surface. Underneath, it's the same old story" (1992: 86–9). Hence, while sensationalist journalism is sometimes taken as a symptom of the cultural and moral bankruptcy of its readers, it is rather evidence of a particular historical condition of political communication, as well as a commentary, from the reception perspective, on the bankruptcy of traditional news ideals and institutions. I return in Chapters 7 and 9 to another interpretive strategy – the construction of 'super-themes' – that audiences rely on to mediate between traditional, 'serious' news coverage and everyday life.

Chapter 6 Television futures: Audience constituents of social semiotics

1. I return in Chapter 11 to the place of knowledge interests within the rest of Habermas's philosophical system. Although Habermas offers one of the most comprehensive and sophisticated conceptions of the relationship between science, communication, and society, he stops short, I suggest, of the pragmatist epistemology that is implied by the concept of knowledge interests. In the present chapter, I examine the concept of knowledge interests as a necessary component of social semiotics.

2. I refer to the cultural-forum model of Newcomb and Hirsch (1984), here and elsewhere, as one alternative to the more common transmission or ritual models which offers a preliminary specification of the pragmatist concept of communities, even though the cultural-forum model may overstate the efficacy of the media in monitoring other social institutions. See the critique in Jensen (1991c) and the response by Newcomb (1991), as well as my critical discussion of John Fiske's work in Chapter 5 and the response in Fiske (1991).

Chapter 7 Reception as flow: Media constituents of social semiotics

1. John Fiske's *Television Culture* (1987) remains the most significant statement of this position. For a timely and well-argued critique of what is termed "the new revisionism" of reception studies, see Curran (1990). Responding to the critique, Morley (1992) has noted that while it remains important not to overstate the social power of audiences, the new reception studies represented a necessary step in the history of research, transcending the dominant text-centrism of much work during the 1960s and 1970s as well as differentiating the understanding of reception processes.

2. The flow feature of television increasingly is found in other cultural contexts, as well, particularly the semi-commercial television systems of Western Europe. The design of the present study has later been used to examine Danish television audiences, this time including household interviews about the flow experience as well as a quantitative component examining different viewer types. (See the findings in Jensen et al., 1994.)

3. In his theoretical analysis of the reception of film and television, Ellis (1982) has suggested that whereas the cinema context mobilizes the concentrated 'gaze' of the spectator, television typically attracts only the intermittent 'glance' of the viewer. Such a distracted mode of reception may lead to a relatively selective decoding and to the interpretation of several discrete segments as belonging to the 'same' message.

4. A majority of the households in the sample had two or more television sets. However, the diaries and questionnaire responses suggested that joint viewing of programs remained common. The recordings, together with the diaries, offer insight into the viewer flows that were available for viewing in the households. Survey evidence also supports the conclusion that joint viewing, while decreasing as the number of household sets increases, still accounts for a large proportion of all television viewing (Bower, 1985: 111).

5. Since the ratio of changes was taken, following the 'new viewer' argument, as the measure of relative control, the duration of each segment in the viewer flow was not singled out for analysis.

6. The category of super-themes is discussed in greater detail in Chapter 9 as an example of theory development in qualitative reception studies. In Chapter 10, I go on to examine the status of super-themes in the perspective of general communication theory and theory of science.

7. I emphasize that the set of social spheres suggested by the super-themes is different from Habermas's (1962/1989) model of spheres, as presented in Chapter 4. The television genres at this time of day develop perspectives on the rest of social reality from a point of view inside the home, which produces the dichotomy of 'private' and 'public' domains. The private domain here corresponds to Habermas's intimate sphere, whereas the public domain, referring to the entire natural and supernatural universe, comprises the other spheres of Habermas's model. The public-sphere model may serve as a second-order, analytical representation of the first-order, partial model expressed in the super-themes.

Chapter 8 Discourses of research: Analytical constituents of social semiotics

1. Most socalled 'ethnographic' studies in mass communication research fall short of the traditional requirements regarding the duration, intensity, and holism of the *ethnography* within anthropology. As noted by Lull, "ethnography has become an abused buzz-word in our field" (1988b: 242). In a wider sense, however, *ethnographic methods*, being multi-method, triangulated research designs typically combining observation, interview, and records, are applied quite legitimately within social sciences and cultural studies for "the analysis of multiply structured contexts of action, aiming to produce a rich descriptive and interpretive account of the lives and values of those subject to investigation" (Morley and Silverstone, 1991: 149–50). General introductions to ethnographic research can be found, from the perspective of anthropology, in Ellen (1984) and, from the perspective of other social sciences, in Hammersley and Atkinson (1983).

2. While the study of verbal language, emerging from the Logos tradition (Chapter 1), thus offers a heuristic model of qualitative research as currently practiced, I return in Chapter 10 to the problems posed by major semiotic forms that do not lend themselves to analysis in the categories of verbal language, especially visual, analog communication.

3. Whereas communication is the inescapable condition of interviewing, this may be taken as either a strength or a weakness of the data produced. The traditional survey interview seeks to eliminate as far as possible the elements of interaction, ideally registering the respondent's ideas or perceptions prior to the interview session. By contrast, depth interviewing relies on interaction to probe the respondent's positions. The record of the qualitative interview, then, includes not only articulated positions, but also the process that makes possible a later assessment of the information given. See further Chapter 4 on the methodological constituents of reception analysis.

4. An interface between grammatical and pragmatic analysis of communication, and between social science and semiotics, is the socalled 'case grammar' (Fillmore, 1968, 1977) that informs the study of these 'missing agentives.' Case grammar identifies deep-structural cases such as Agentive, Objective, Instrumentative, and Locative in order to establish the implicit logic of sentences. In pragmatic terms, the cases suggest what social roles are assigned to the participants in communication and to the other social agents referred to in its discourse. In social science, such issues have been addressed from Mead to Goffman, but with little specific analysis of language structures. In semiotics, Peirce developed a logic of relations reminiscent of the categories of case grammar, but with little attention to their social embedding.

Chapter 9 The epistemology of communication: Abduction and the logic of qualitative research

1. I owe the terminology of apartheid versus imperialism, referring to segregation and domination as the Scylla and Charybdis of interdisciplinary research, to my former teacher and colleague, Hans Hauge, who credited the point to Roman Jakobson (personal communication, circa 1980). I have been unable to locate the reference in Jakobson's writings.

2. I emphasize that my critique of Karl Erik Rosengren's work under a heading of 'imperialism' only reflects a professional disagreement on the means, and perhaps the ends, of mass communication research. I have benefited, in many contexts, from Karl Erik's scholarly scope and personal generosity, including his comments to drafts of this book.

3. In a later article, Searle (1990) has confronted the argument that socalled 'neural networks,' having a structure similar to that of the brain, are more likely to produce valid simulations of the human mind. Instead of the Chinese room, Searle here proposes the image of a "Chinese gym," a hall full of monolingual, English-speaking persons, in which these people "would carry out the same operations as the nodes and synapses in a connectionist architecture [...]" (Searle, 1990: 22). Searle's position and the possible counterarguments, however, are unchanged. I return in Chapter 10 to the relationship between neural networks (parallel distributed processing systems) and semiotic networks.

4. Peirce presented the three basic syllogisms in one article of a series published in the *Popular Science Monthly* in 1878. The title of the particular article, 'Deduction, Induction, and Hypothesis,' indicates that Peirce in some cases used the term 'hypothesis,' in other cases the term 'abduction'; I retain the latter term by analogy to deduction and induction.

5. This explanation of why it was Darwin and his time that came to advance the theory of evolution is a second abduction, arguably made possible (third abduction) by the contemporary context of science that assumes a close link between the history of ideas and the history of scientific institutions.

6. A more systematic variation on the basic syllogism would produce the following abduction: These beans are white / All the beans from this bag are white // These beans are from this bag. As elaborated below, in abduction the phenomenon to be explained serves as the first premise, the hypothetical rule serves as the second premise, leading in the conclusion to the application of the hypothetical rule to the phenomenon. I owe this point and other helpful comments regarding logic to Søren Kjørup.

7. Peirce further associated different experiential qualities with each form of inference. "We may say, therefore, that [abduction] produces the *sensuous* element of thought, and induction the *habitual* element. As for deduction, [...] this may be considered as the logical formula for paying attention, which is the *volitional* element of thought, and corresponds to the nervous discharge in the sphere of physiology" (Peirce, 1986: 337–8). While the concrete relations stipulated between logic, physiology, and psychology now appear dubious, the point remains that logical inference manifests itself as human forms of experience and action, as interpretive and social difference.

8. Overcoded abduction can be understood as the outcome of socialization into a specific semiotic system, a culture. To know the potential meaning of a sign is be able to perform overcoded abduction. While Schillemans (1992: 266) compares Eco's overcoded abduction to Peirce's deduc-

tion, for conceptual clarity I reserve the different terms for the three canonical forms of inference in Peirce's original article.

9. I owe the terminology of horizontal extrapolation and vertical generalization to Grethe Skylv.

10. Brinberg and McGrath (1985) offer a lucid and systematic account of validity in different types of empirical research. Interestingly, what the authors call the three domains of research (substantive, methodological, conceptual) are comparable to the object, sign, and interpretant of Peirce's basic triad.

11. After finishing the manuscript for this volume, I was made aware (by Svein Østerud) of the brief reference to abduction as a stage in the research process by Denzin (1989: 109–11). While noting the role of abduction in 'naturalistic inquiry,' however, Denzin tends to conceive of abduction as a preliminary inference, to be followed by "rigorous" deduction and inductions establishing "causal processes" (p. 100). My argument has been that, beyond the development of hypotheses and theory, abduction also has independent explanatory value as a constitutive element of empirical qualitative research.

Chapter 10 The ontology of communication: Another guess at the riddle

1. Traditionally, ontology has been conceived as a subdivision of metaphysics, which, following the agenda set by Aristotle, has been a 'first philosophy' addressing basic distinctions such as essence and existence, necessary and contingent existence, and particulars and universals. For overviews, see especially Hancock (1972); also MacIntyre (1972) and Walsh (1972). Though often associated with religion and the occult, and pursued by deductive reasoning, since Kant "metaphysical ideas, such as an ultimate subject or a first cause, do have a *regulative use* in encouraging us never to be satisfied with what we actually know at any given time" (Hancock, 1972: 297; emphasis added). A similar, procedural conception is found in Peirce, who took metaphysics to be an observational science developing first, but fallible premises. Below, drawing on Husserl's distinction between formal and material ontology, I develop the argument that Peirce's categories of Firstness, Secondness, and Thirdness constitute a general or formal ontology, to be complemented by domain-specific ontologies as part of an interdisciplinary theory of communication. Today, interdisciplinary fields such as cognitive science, anthropology, and communication research have taken over, in part, the role of philosophy in reflecting upon the metaphysical premises of science.

2. Cognitive science is founded on the analogy between computers and the human mind, both defined as information-processing systems. While there are disagreements concerning the nature of the analogy (see Searle's Chinese-room example and references in Chapter 9), connectionism, also known as parallel distributed processing, explores certain homologies between machine architecture and the structure of the human mind that may be tested through computer programs. Experimental evidence suggests that a connectionist structure is needed to explain, first, the number and variety of mental operations that humans can perform within a given period, and, second, humans' mobilization of vast amounts of implicit knowledge in these operations. As noted in a recent overview by Carley and Kaufer (1993) presenting a typology of semantic networks, very similar arguments have been made in other fields, including literary and cultural studies, whose concept of intertextuality goes back to Bakhtin's (1981) analysis of multiple meanings, or 'heteroglossia,' in the discourse of the novel. (For theory and empirical studies on connectionism, see McClelland et al., 1986, and Rumelhart et al., 1986.)

3. The distinction between formal and regional-material ontology, while informing much philosophical work on metaphysics, was elaborated by Edmund Husserl as part of his phenomenology. See the overview in Wolf (1984); also Claesges (1984). The categories of Firstness, Secondness, and Thirdness constitute the most general level of Peirce's phenomenology, and are comparable to Husserl's formal ontology. However, Husserl took both forms of ontology as establishing the *a priori* premises of further inquiry, including empirical research in different material domains. By contrast, I take Peirce to conceive of both forms of ontology as fallible: the categories must remain "a guess at the riddle," even while serving as procedural assumptions in empirical research.

4. Another interpretation is to see either signs as such or their range as evolutionary limitations, that is, as distinctive features of *homo sapiens* rather than ontological universals in all possible worlds. The extent to which different phases of philosophy and science have reiterated similar problems of epistemology and ontology without solving them is supporting evidence for this interpretation, even if such recurring problems might also be attributed to historical limitations of research. The validity of the evolutionary explanation of philosophical failure is, in the nature of the matter, undecidable.

5. Much socalled 'new science,' blending natural science with social and human sciences, not least psychology, illustrates other problems of interdisciplinary research. A prominent example is Capra's (1983) "exploration of the parallels between modern physics and Eastern mysticism." While his "parallels" refer to some of the *signs* that are employed by both Eastern and Western thought, and which describe the universe as a dynamic whole and the thinker-researcher as a constitutive element of that whole, it is not clear in what sense the methods of observation or the 'theoretical concepts' may be compatible. It is only at an inordinately high level of abstraction that the principle of complementarity, developed in atomic physics to suggest how "the interaction between the objects and the measuring instruments [...] forms an integral part of the phenomena" (Bohr, 1958: 72), can be said to underlie the contemplative self-knowledge of religious mysticism. The problem again is the direct parallel being made between the constituents of one regional ontology and those of another. In the field of communications, a recent volume exploring the interfaces between Eastern and Western communication theory (Kincaid, 1987), while addressing classic epistemological and ontological issues, ultimately produces few concrete insights.

Chapter 11 The politics of communication: How to make a difference

1. The polemical form of Rorty's philosophy is illustrated in the following description of his own encounter with foundationalist philosophy: "In 1951, a graduate student who (like myself) was in the process of learning about, or being converted to, analytic philosophy could still believe that there were a finite number of distinct specifiable problems to be resolved – problems which any serious analytic philosopher would agree to be *the* outstanding problems. For example, there was the problem of the counterfactual conditional, the problem of whether an 'emotive' analysis of ethical terms was satisfactory, Quine's problem about the nature of analyticity, and a few more. These were problems which fitted nicely into the vocabulary of the positivists. They could be seen as the final, proper formulation of problems which had been seen, as in a glass darkly, by Leibniz, Hume, and Kant. Further, there was agreement on what a solution to a philosophic problem looked like – e.g. Russell on definite descriptions, Frege on meaning and reference, Tarski on truth. In those days, when my generation was young, all of the conditions for a Kuhnian 'normal' problem-solving discipline were fulfilled" (Rorty, 1982: 215; quoted in Bernstein, 1991: 331). This condition is contrasted with the current scene: "The best hope for an American philosopher is Andy Warhol's promise that we shall *all* be superstars, for approximately fifteen minutes apiece" (Rorty, 1982: 215).

2. While crediting Peirce as the person who gave pragmatism its name, and who inspired James, Dewey, and others to develop the position (Rorty, 1982: 161), Rorty has denounced Peirce's pragmatism with special reference to his notion of the ideal end of inquiry, even if "Peirce was moving in the right direction" (Rorty, 1991a: 131). As noted in Chapter 2, however, both the counterfactual conception of consensus in 'the last instance' and the pragmatist understanding of belief as a predisposition to act implies a different sort of realism than the straw-man Rorty sets up. It is not the case, for instance, that Peirce had committed himself to the position that "'There are rocks' is linked by a relation of correspondence – accurate representation – to the way the world is" (Rorty, 1991a: 129); rather this fact has the status of law and habit as articulated by an interpretant. In a meticulous analysis of Rorty's references to Peirce, Haack (1993) has shown that Rorty's framing of Peirce as a foundationalist philosopher cannot be justified.

3. *The Theory of Communicative Action*, originally published in German in 1981 (the first volume in English in 1984, the second in 1987), is the fullest account of Habermas's normative theory of communication and society. I focus here on Volume 1, which most specifically addresses issues pertaining to mass communication.

4. Counterfactual arguments address the conditions of existence (Chapter 2), that is, what would have been the case under specified circumstances, and what may thus be the case in the future. By assuming that, because a certain form of communication is possible, it is also desirable, even ideal, Habermas problematically derives an 'ought' from an 'is.' Curiously, in his critique of instrumental rationality and positivism, Habermas (1968/1971) makes the opposite assumption, namely, that what is physically, humanly, or socially possible, may be far from desirable.

5. In recent debates concerning TCA, Habermas tends to restate his positions, rather than engaging his critics in a reflective form of communicative action. See the critical essays in Honneth and Joas (1991) and the response by Habermas (1991a), especially his restatement of communicative and strategic action (pp. 241–2). Unlike Rortyan cannibalism, however, Habermas's action is strategic for a purpose, assuming that philosophy may still make a difference to society.

6. Habermas's (1981/1984, 1981/1987) emphasis on an original mode of communication underlying actual interaction, recalls another modernist theme, namely, the aesthetic of ruptures. The assumption has been that a particular, innovative aesthetic form will enable its audience to break on through to the other side of the representation to gain fresh insight into reality. This aesthetic has been central to debates on cultural quality, offering a contrast to the aesthetic of much popular culture. Again, it remains unclear how the aesthetic rupture would relate to subsequent social action, specifically why it would be superior to popular-cultural conventions as a cultural resource. (On modernism and aesthetics, see Berman, 1982, and Huyssen, 1986.)

7. Much work in the politics of communication has served to specify the issues and options in the context of contemporary Western mass media, not least in the debate over electronic media as a 'public service' (for overviews, see Golding and Murdock, 1991; McQuail, 1992). The issues may be summed up in an ABC of communication policy (Jensen, 1986: chap. 15). A stands for *access*. Although the main restriction on public access to most media as cultural resources stems from their definition as private enterprises, furthermore the structure of, for instance, political communication does not anticipate public participation as a constitutive element of the democratic process. B stands for *balance*, which points beyond notions of 'fairness' to questions of the affirmative representation of groups, issues, genres, as well as the variety of the total spectrum of available information in the whole media environment. C stands for *critical comprehension*. The issue is how to establish educational and other institutional contexts for meta-communication (Chapters 6 and 8) on the media.

References

Aarsleff, H. (1982). *From Locke to Saussure*. London: Athlone Press.

Abrams, M. et al. (eds) (1962). *The Norton Anthology of English Literature*. Vol. 2. New York: Norton.

Ainslie, P. (ed.) (1988). 'The new TV viewer'. *Channels of Communication*, September: 53–62.

Alexander, J. (1987). 'Action and its environments'. In J. Alexander, B. Giesen, R. Münch, and N. Smelser (eds), *The Micro–Macro Link*. Berkeley: University of California Press.

Alexander, J. (1991). 'Habermas and critical theory: Beyond the Marxian dilemma?'. In A. Honneth and H. Joas (eds), *Communicative Action: Essays on Jürgen Habermas's 'The Theory of Communicative Action'*. Cambridge, MA: MIT Press.

Alexander, J. and Giesen, B. (1987). 'From reduction to linkage: The long view of the micro–macro link'. In J. Alexander, B. Giesen, R. Münch, and N. Smelser (eds), *The Micro–Macro Link*. Berkeley: University of California Press.

Altheide, D. (1976). *Creating Reality*. Beverly Hills, CA: Sage.

Althusser, L. (1971). 'Ideology and ideological state apparatuses'. In *Lenin and Philosophy and Other Essays*. London: New Left Books.

Althusser, L. (1977). *For Marx*. London: Verso.

Anderson, J.A. and Meyer, T. (1988). *Mediated Communication: A Social Action Perspective*. Newbury Park, CA: Sage.

Ang, I. (1985). *Watching Dallas*. London: Methuen.

Ang, I. (1991). *Desperately Seeking the Audience*. London: Routledge.

Antaki, C. (ed.) (1988). *Analysing Everyday Explanation*. London: Sage.

Apel, K.-O. (1981). *Charles S. Peirce: From Pragmatism to Pragmaticism*. Amherst: University of Massachusetts Press.

Arndt, H. (1979). 'Some neglected types of speech function: The principles of functional classification'. In T. Pettersson (ed.), *Papers from the 5th Scandinavian Conference of Linguistics*. Stockholm: Almqvist and Wiksell.

Arnheim, R. (1974). *Art and Visual Perception*. Berkeley: University of California Press.

Austin, J. (1962). *How to Do Things with Words*. London: Oxford University Press.

Baacke, D. and Kübler, H. (eds) (1987). *Qualitative Medienforschung: Konzepte und Erprobungen*. [Qualitative media research: Concepts and explorations.] Tübingen: Niemeyer.

Bakhtin, M.M. (1981). *The Dialogic Imagination*. Austin: University of Texas Press.

Barthes, R. (1970). *S/Z*. Paris: Seuil.

Barthes, R. (1973) *Mythologies*. London: Paladin. (Orig. publ. 1957.)

Barthes, R. (1984a). *Elements of Semiology*. New York: Hill and Wang. (Orig. publ. 1964.)

Barthes, R. (1984b). 'Rhetoric of the image'. In *Image, Music, Text*. London: Fontana. (Orig. publ. 1964.)

Barton, D. and Ivanic, R. (eds) (1991). *Writing in the Community*. Newbury Park, CA : Sage.

Barwise, P. and Ehrenberg, A. (1988). *Television and Its Audience*. London: Sage.

Bateson, G. (1972). *Steps to an Ecology of Mind*. London: Paladin.

Baudrillard, J. (1988). *Selected Writings*. Cambridge: Polity Press.

Bazerman, C. (1988). *Shaping Written Knowledge*. Madison: University of Wisconsin Press.

Bazerman, C. (1993). 'A contention over the term *Rhetoric*'. In T. Enos and S. Brown (eds), *Defining the New Rhetorics*. Newbury Park, CA: Sage.

Bechtel, R., Achelpohl, C., and Akers, R. (1972). 'Correlates between observed behavior and questionnaire responses on television viewing'. In E. Rubinstein, G. Comstock, and J. Murray (eds), *Television and Social Behavior. Vol. 4: Television in Day-to-Day Life: Patterns of Use*. Washington, DC: Government Printing Office.

Belson, W. (1968). *The Impact of Television*. London: Crosby, Lockwood and Son.

Beniger, J. (1986). *The Control Revolution*. Cambridge, MA: Harvard University Press.

Beniger, J. (1988). 'Information and communication: The new convergence'. *Communication Research*, 15 (2): 198–218.

Beniger, J. (1990). 'Who are the most important theorists of communication?'. *Communication Research*, 17 (5): 698–715.

Benjamin, W. (1977). 'The work of art in the age of mechanical reproduction'. In J. Curran, M. Gurevitch, and J. Woollacott (eds), *Mass Communication and Society*. London: Edward Arnold.

Bennett, T. and Woollacott, J. (1987). *Bond and Beyond*. London: Methuen.

Benveniste, E. (1985). 'The semiology of language'. In H. Innis (ed.), *Semiotics: An Introductory Anthology*. Bloomington: Indiana University Press.

Berelson, B. (1952). *Content Analysis in Communications Research*. Glencoe, IL: Free Press.

Berger, C. and Chaffee, S. (eds) (1987). *Handbook of Communication Science*. Newbury Park, CA: Sage.

Berger, J. (1972). *Ways of Seeing*. Harmondsworth: Penguin.

Berger, P.L. and Berger, B. (1976). *Sociology: A Biographical Approach*. Harmondsworth: Penguin.

Berger, P.L. and Luckmann, T. (1966). *The Social Construction of Reality*. London: Allen Lane.

Berman, M. (1982). *All That Is Solid Melts into Air: The Experience of Modernity*. London: Verso.

Bernstein, R. (1966). *John Dewey*. Atascadero, CA: Ridgeview.

Bernstein, R. (1986). *Philosophical Profiles*. Cambridge: Polity Press.

Bernstein, R. (1991). *The New Constellation*. Cambridge: Polity Press.

Bershady, H. (1991). 'Practice against theory in American sociology: An exercise in the sociology of knowledge'. In R. Robertson and B. Turner (eds), *Talcott Parsons: Theorist of Modernity*. London: Sage.

Bertaux, D. (ed.) (1981). *Biography and Society*. Beverly Hills, CA: Sage.

Biltereyst, D. (1991). 'Resisting American hegemony: A comparative analysis of domestic and US fiction'. *European Journal of Communication*, 6 (4): 469–97.

Blumler, J. (1979). 'The role of theory in uses and gratifications studies'. *Communication Research*, 6 (1): 9–36.

Blumler, J. and Katz, E. (eds) (1974). *The Uses of Mass Communications*. Beverly Hills, CA: Sage.

Bogart, L. (1980). 'Television news as entertainment'. In P.H. Tannenbaum (ed.), *The Entertainment Functions of Television*. Hillsdale, NJ: Lawrence Erlbaum.

Bohr, N. (1958). *Atomic Physics and Human Knowledge*. New York: Wiley.

Bordwell, D. (1985). *Narration in the Fiction Film*. London: Methuen.

Bordwell, D. (1989). *Making Meaning*. Cambridge, MA: Harvard University Press.

Bourdieu, P. (1977). *Outline of a Theory of Practice*. Cambridge: Cambridge University Press.

Bourdieu, P. (1984). *Distinction*. Cambridge, MA: Harvard University Press.

Bower, R.T. (1985). *The Changing Television Audience in America*. New York: Columbia University Press.

Branigan, E. (1992). *Narrative Comprehension and Film*. London: Routledge.

Brannigan, A. (1981). *The Social Basis of Scientific Discoveries*. Cambridge: Cambridge University Press.

Brent, J. (1993). *Charles Sanders Peirce: A Life*. Bloomington: Indiana University Press.

Brinberg, D. and McGrath, J. (1985). *Validity and the Research Process*. Newbury Park, CA: Sage.

Brodkey, L. (1987). *Academic Writing as Social Practice*. Philadelphia: Temple University Press.

Brooks, P. (1976). *The Melodramatic Imagination*. New Haven, CT: Yale University Press.

Browne, N. (1987). 'The political economy of the television (super)text'. In H. Newcomb (ed.), *Television: The Critical View*. 4th edn. New York: Oxford University Press.

Bruner, J. (1986). *Actual Minds, Possible Worlds*. Cambridge, MA: Harvard University Press.

Bryant, C. and Jary, D. (eds) (1991). *Giddens' Theory of Structuration: A Critical Appreciation.* London: Routledge.

Bunge, M. (1980). *The Mind–Body Problem: A Psychobiological Approach.* Oxford: Pergamon.

Calhoun, C. (ed.) (1992). *Habermas and the Public Sphere.* Cambridge, MA: MIT Press.

Cantril, H. (1940). *The Invasion from Mars.* Princeton: Princeton University Press.

Capra, F. (1983). *The Tao of Physics: An Exploration of the Parallels between Modern Physics and Eastern Mysticism.* London: Fontana.

Carey, J.W. (1989). *Communication as Culture.* Boston: Unwin Hyman.

Carley, K. and Kaufer, D. (1993). 'Semantic connectivity: An approach for analyzing symbols in semantic networks'. *Communication Theory,* 3 (3): 183–213.

Carlsson, U. (ed.) (1988). 'Reception analysis in Danish media research'. *The Nordicom Review,* 1.

Carroll, P. and Noble, D. (1977). *The Free and the Unfree: A New History of the United States.* Harmondsworth: Penguin.

Certeau, M. de (1984). *The Practice of Everyday Life.* Berkeley: University of California Press.

Chambers, I. (1986). *Popular Culture: The Metropolitan Experience.* London: Methuen.

Chomsky, N. (1965). *Aspects of the Theory of Syntax.* Cambridge, MA: MIT Press.

Claesges, U. (1984). 'Ontologie, formale und materiale'. [Ontology, formal and material.] In J. Ritter and Karlfried Gründer (eds), *Historiches Wörterbuch der Philosophie.* [Historical dictionary of philosophy.] Vol. 6. Basel: Schwabe & Co.

Clarke, D.S. (1990). *Sources of Semiotic.* Carbondale: Southern Illinois University Press.

Clifford, J. and Marcus, G.E. (eds) (1986). *Writing Culture: The Poetics and Politics of Ethnography.* Berkeley: University of California Press.

Clough, P. (1992). *The End(s) of Ethnography.* Newbury Park, CA: Sage.

Colapietro, V. (1989). *Peirce's Approach to the Self.* Albany: State University of New York Press.

Comstock, G., Chaffee, S., Katzman, N., McCombs, M., and Roberts, D. (1978). *Television and Human Behavior.* New York: Columbia University Press.

Corner, J., Richardson, K., and Fenton, N. (1990). *Nuclear Reactions.* London: John Libbey.

Coulthard, M. and Montgomery, M. (eds) (1981). *Studies in Discourse Analysis.* London: Routledge and Kegan Paul.

Coward, R. and Ellis, J. (1977). *Language and Materialism.* London: Routledge and Kegan Paul.

Crigler, A. and Jensen, K.B. (1991). 'Discourses of politics: Talking about public issues in the United States and Denmark'. In P. Dahlgren and C. Sparks (eds), *Communication and Citizenship.* London: Routledge.

Crystal, D. and Davy, D. (1969). *Investigating English Style.* London: Longman.

Culler, J. (1975). *Structuralist Poetics.* London: Routledge & Kegan Paul.

Culler, J. (1981). *The Pursuit of Signs.* Ithaca, NY: Cornell University Press.

Curran, J. (1990). 'The "new revisionism" in mass communication research: A reappraisal'. *European Journal of Communication,* 5 (2–3): 135–64.

Curran, J. (1991). 'Mass media and democracy: A reappraisal'. In J. Curran and M. Gurevitch (eds), *Mass Media and Society.* London: Edward Arnold.

Dahlmüller, G., Hund, W., and Kommer, H. (1973). *Kritik des Fernsehens.* [Critique of television.] Darmstadt: Luchterhand.

Dayan, D. and Katz, E. (1987) 'Televised ceremonial events'. In A.A. Berger (ed.), *Television in Society.* New Brunswick, NJ: Transaction Books.

Day-Lewis, S. (1989). *One Day in the Life of Television.* London: Grafton.

Deleuze, G. (1986). *Cinema 1: The Movement-Image.* Minneapolis: University of Minnesota Press.

Deleuze, G. (1989). *Cinema 2: The Time-Image.* London: Athlone Press.

Dennett, D. (1982). 'Comments on Rorty'. *Synthèse,* 53: 349–56.

Denzin, N. (1989). *The Research Act.* 3rd edn. Englewood Cliffs, NJ: Prentice Hall.

Denzin, N. and Lincoln, Y. (eds) (1994). *Handbook of Qualitative Research.* Thousand Oaks, CA: Sage.

Derrida, J. (1976) *Of Grammatology.* Baltimore, MD: Johns Hopkins University Press. (Orig. publ. 1967.)

210   *The social semiotics of mass communication*

Dewey, J. (1927). *The Public and Its Problems*. New York: Holt.
Donohue, G., Olien, C., and Tichenor, P. (1987). 'Media access and knowledge gaps'. *Critical Studies in Mass Communication*, 4 (1): 87–92.
Douglas, M. (1987). *How Institutions Think*. London: Routledge & Kegan Paul.
Dreyfus, H. (1979). *What Computers Can't Do*. Rev. edn. New York: Harper & Row.
Drotner, K. (1994). 'Ethnographic enigmas: "The everyday" in recent media studies'. *Cultural Studies*, 8(2): 341–57.
Durkheim, É. (1972). *Selected Writings*. Cambridge: Cambridge University Press.
Durkheim, É. (1982). *The Rules of Sociological Method*. 2nd edn. New York: Free Press. (Orig. publ. 1901.)
Eagleton, T. (1983). *Literary Theory: An Introduction*. Minneapolis: University of Minnesota Press.
Eco, U. (1976). *A Theory of Semiotics*. Bloomington: Indiana University Press.
Eco, U. (1984). *Semiotics and the Philosophy of Language*. London: Macmillan.
Eco, U. (1985). 'The semantics of metaphor'. In R. Innis (ed.), *Semiotics: An Introductory Anthology*. Bloomington: Indiana University Press.
Eco, U. (1987). *The Role of the Reader*. London: Hutchinson.
Egebak, N. (1972). *Fra tegnfunktion til tekstfunktion*. [From sign function to text function.] Copenhagen: Berlingske Leksikon Bibliotek.
Elias, N. (1989). 'The symbol theory: An introduction'. *Theory, Culture and Society*, 6: 169–217, 339–83, 499–537.
Ellen, R.F. (ed.) (1984). *Ethnographic Research: A Guide to General Conduct*. New York: Academic Press.
Ellis, J. (1982). *Visible Fictions*. London: Routlege and Kegan Paul.
Engels, F. (1959). 'Socialism: Utopian and scientific'. In L. Feuer (ed.) *Marx and Engels: Basic Writings in Politics and Philosophy*. London: Fontana. (Orig. publ. 1880.)
Enos, T. and Brown, S. (eds) (1993). *Defining the New Rhetorics*. Newbury Park, CA: Sage.
Eysenck, M.W. and Keane, M.T. (1990). *Cognitive Psychology: A Student's Handbook*. London: Lawrence Erlbaum.
Featherstone, M. (ed.) (1991). 'A special issue on Georg Simmel'. *Theory, Culture & Society*, 8 (3).
Fejes, F. (1984). 'Critical communications research and media effects: The problem of the disappearing audience'. *Media, Culture & Society*, 6: 219–32.
Fielding, N. and Lee, R. (eds) (1991). *Using Computers in Qualitative Research*. London: Sage.
Fillmore, C.J. (1968). 'The case for case'. In E. Bach and R.T. Harms (eds), *Universals in Linguistic Theory*. New York: Holt, Rinehart, Winston.
Fillmore, C.J. (1977). 'The case for case reopened'. In P. Cole and J. Sadock (eds), *Syntax and Semantics. Vol. 8: Grammatical Relations*. New York: Academic Press.
Fink, H. (1988). 'Et hyperkomplekst begreb: Kultur, kulturbegreb og kulturrelativisme'. [A hypercomplex concept: Culture, concepts of culture, and cultural relativism.] In H. Fink and H. Horstbøll (eds), *Kulturbegrebets kulturhistorie*. [A cultural history of the concept of culture.] Aarhus, Denmark: Aarhus University Press.
Fisch, M. (1984). 'Introduction'. In C.S. Peirce, *Writings of Charles S. Peirce*. Vol. 2. Bloomington: Indiana University Press.
Fisch, M. (1986a). *Peirce, Semeiotic, and Pragmatism*. Bloomington: Indiana University Press.
Fisch, M. (1986b). 'Introduction'. In C.S. Peirce, *Writings of Charles S. Peirce*. Vol. 3. Bloomington: Indiana University Press.
Fish, S. (1979). *Is There a Text in This Class? The Authority of Interpretive Communities*. Cambridge, MA: Harvard University Press.
Fish, S. (1989). *Doing What Comes Naturally*. Oxford: Clarendon Press.
Fiske, J. (1986). 'Television: Polysemy and popularity'. *Critical Studies in Mass Communication*, 3 (4): 391–407.
Fiske, J. (1987). *Television Culture*. London: Methuen.
Fiske, J. (1991). 'Semiological struggles'. In J. Anderson (ed.), *Communication Yearbook*. Vol. 14. Newbury Park, CA: Sage.
Fiske, J. and Hartley, J. (1978). *Reading Television*, London: Methuen.

References   211

Foucault, M. (1972). *The Archaeology of Knowledge*. London: Tavistock.

Fowler, R., Hodge, B., Kress, G., and Trew, T. (1979). *Language and Control*. London: Routledge & Kegan Paul.

Galbraith, J.K. (1967). *The New Industrial State*. New York: Signet.

Gans, H. (1979). *Deciding What's News*. New York: Pantheon.

Garner, R. (1971). '"Presupposition" in philosophy and linguistics'. In C. Fillmore and T. Langendoen (eds), *Studies in Linguistic Semantics*. New York: Holt, Rinehart, Winston.

Geertz, C. (1973). 'Thick description'. In *The Interpretation of Cultures*. New York: Basic Books.

Gerbner, G. (ed.) (1981). 'The living McLuhan'. *Journal of Communication*, 31 (3): 116–99.

Gerbner, G. and Gross, L. (1976). 'Living with television: The violence profile'. *Journal of Communication*, 26 (3): 173–99.

Gerth, H. and Mills, C. Wright (1991). 'Introduction: The man and his work'. In M. Weber, *From Max Weber: Essays in Sociology*. London: Routledge. (Orig. publ. 1948.)

Giddens, A. (1972). 'Introduction: Durkheim's writings in sociology and social philosophy'. In É. Durkheim, *Selected Writings*. Cambridge: Cambridge University Press.

Giddens, A. (1984). *The Constitution of Society*. Berkeley: University of California Press.

Giddens, A. (1987). *Social Theory and Modern Sociology*. Cambridge: Polity Press.

Giddens, A. (1989). *Sociology*. Cambridge: Polity Press.

Giddens, A. (1990). *The Consequences of Modernity*. Cambridge: Polity Press.

Giddens, A. (1991). *Modernity and Self-Identity*. Cambridge: Polity Press.

Giere, R. (1988). *Explaining Science: A Cognitive Approach*. Chicago: University of Chicago Press.

Gilbert, G. and Mulkay, M. (1984). *Opening Pandora's Box: A Sociological Analysis of Scientists' Discourse*. Cambridge: Cambridge University Press.

Ginzburg, C. (1989). 'Clues: Roots for an evidential paradigm'. In *Clues, Myths, and the Historical Method*. Baltimore, MD: Johns Hopkins University Press.

Gitlin, T. (1978). 'Media sociology: The dominant paradigm'. *Theory and Society*, 6: 205–253.

Gitlin, T. (1983). *Inside Prime Time*. New York: Pantheon.

Glaser, B.G. and Strauss, A.L. (1967). *The Discovery of Grounded Theory: Strategies for Qualitative Research*. Chicago: Aldine.

Goffman, E. (1974). *Frame Analysis: An Essay on the Organization of Experience*. Cambridge, MA: Harvard University Press.

Golding, P. and Murdock, G. (1991). 'Culture, communications, and political economy'. In J. Curran and M. Gurevitch (eds), *Mass Media and Society*. London: Edward Arnold.

Gombrich, E.H. (1960). *Art and Illusion*. Princeton: Princeton University Press.

González, J. (ed.) (1990). *Estudios sobre las culturas contemporaneas*, 4 (10).

Goodman, N. (1976). *Languages of Art*. 2nd edn. Indianapolis, IN: Hackett Publishing Co.

Goodman, N. (1978). *Ways of Worldmaking*. Indianapolis, IN: Hackett Publishing Co.

Gorbman, C. (1987). *Unheard Melodies*. Bloomington: Indiana University Press.

Gorden, R. L. (1969). *Interviewing: Strategy, Techniques and Tactics*. Homewood, IL: Dorsey Press.

Graber, D. (1984). *Processing the News: How People Tame the Information Tide*. New York: Longman.

Gramsci, A. (1971). *Selections from the Prison Notebooks*. New York: International Publishers.

Gray, A. (1987). 'Reading the audience'. *Screen*, 28 (3): 24–36.

Green, M. (1991). 'Media, education, and communities'. In K.B. Jensen and N.W. Jankowski (eds), *A Handbook of Qualitative Methodologies for Mass Communication Research*. London: Routledge.

Greenfield, P. (1985). *Mind and Media*. Cambridge, MA: Harvard University Press.

Greimas, A.J. (1966). *Semantique structurale*. [Structural semantics.] Paris: Larousse.

Greimas, A.J. and Courtés, J. (1982). *Semiotics and Language: An Analytical Dictionary*. Bloomington: Indiana University Press.

Grice, H.P. (1975). 'Logic and conversation'. In P. Cole and J. Morgan (eds), *Syntax and Semantics*. Vol. 3. New York: Academic Press.

Gripsrud, J. (1992). 'The aesthetics and politics of melodrama'. In P. Dahlgren and C. Sparks (eds), *Journalism and Popular Culture*. London: Sage.

Gripsrud, J. (1994). 'Moving images, moving identities: Text and context in the reception history of film and television'. In J. Gripsrud and K. Skretting (eds), *History of Moving Images: Reports from a Norwegian Project*. Oslo: The Research Council of Norway.

Gross, A. (1990). *The Rhetoric of Science*. Cambridge, MA: Harvard University Press.

Grossberg, L. (1988). 'Wandering audiences, nomadic critics'. *Cultural Studies*, 2: 377–91.

Haack, S. (1993). 'Philosophy/philosophy: An untenable dualism'. *Transactions of the Charles S. Peirce Society*, 29 (3): 411–26.

Habermas, J. (1971). *Knowledge and Human Interests*. Boston: Beacon Press. (Orig. publ. 1968.)

Habermas, J. (1984). *The Theory of Communicative Action*. Vol. 1. Boston: Beacon Press. (Orig. publ. 1981.)

Habermas, J. (1987). *The Theory of Communicative Action*. Vol. 2. Cambridge: Polity Press. (Orig. publ. 1981.)

Habermas, J. (1989). *The Structural Transformation of the Public Sphere*. Cambridge, MA: MIT Press. (Orig. publ. 1962.)

Habermas, J. (1991a). 'A reply'. In A. Honneth and H. Joas (eds), *Communicative Action: Essays on Jürgen Habermas's 'The Theory of Communicative Action'*. Cambridge, MA: MIT Press.

Habermas, J. (1991b). 'The public sphere'. In C. Mukerji and M. Schudson (eds), *Rethinking Popular Culture*. Berkeley: University of California Press.

Hacking, I. (1983). *Representing and Intervening*. Cambridge: Cambridge University Press.

Hacking, I. (1992). '"Style" for historians and philosophers'. *Studies in the History and Philosophy of Science*, 23 (1): 1–20.

Hall, S. (1973). 'Encoding and decoding in the television discourse'. Occasional Paper No. 7. Birmingham: Centre for Contemporary Cultural Studies.

Hall, S. (1980). 'Recent developments in theories of language and ideology: A critical note'. In S. Hall, D. Hobson, A. Lowe, and P. Willis (eds), *Culture, Media, Language*. London: Hutchinson.

Hall, S. (1983). 'The problem of ideology – Marxism without guarantees'. In B. Matthews (ed.), *Marx: A Hundred Years On*. London: Lawrence & Wishart.

Halliday, M. (1973). *Explorations in the Functions of Language*. London: Edward Arnold.

Halliday, M. (1978). *Language as Social Semiotic*. London: Longman.

Halliday, M. and Hasan, R. (1976). *Cohesion in English*. London: Longman.

Halloran, J., Elliott, P., and Murdock, G. (1970). *Demonstrations and Communications: A Case Study*. Harmondsworth: Penguin.

Hammersley, M. (1989). *The Dilemma of Qualitative Method: Herbert Blumer and the Chicago Tradition*. London: Routledge.

Hammersley, M. and Atkinson, P. (1983). *Ethnography: Principles and Practice*. London: Tavistock.

Hancock, R. (1972). 'History of metaphysics'. In P. Edwards (ed.), *The Encyclopedia of Philosophy*. Vol. 5. New York: Macmillan.

Harvey, D. (1989). *The Condition of Postmodernity*. Oxford: Basil Blackwell.

Haug, W. (1971). *Kritik der Warenästhetik*. [A critique of commodity aesthetics.] Frankfurt: Suhrkamp.

Haugeland, J. (1985). Semantic engines: An introduction to mind design . In J. Haugeland (ed.), *Mind Design*. Cambridge, MA: MIT Press.

Hauser, A. (1951). *The Social History of Art*. Vols 1–4. New York: Vintage.

Havelock, E. (1963). *Preface to Plato*. Oxford: Basil Blackwell.

Hawkes, T. (1977). *Structuralism and Semiotics*. London: Methuen.

Heeter, C. and Greenberg, B. (1988). *Cableviewing*. Norwood, NJ: Ablex.

Heim, M. (1987). *Electric Language*. New Haven, CT: Yale University Press.

Held, D. and Thompson, J. (eds) (1989). *Social Theory of Modern Societies: Anthony Giddens and His Critics*. Cambridge: Cambridge University Press.

Hesse, M. (1963). *Models and Analogies in Science*. London: Sheed and Ward.

Hobson, D. (1980). 'Housewives and the mass media'. In S. Hall, D. Hobson, A. Lowe, and P.

Willis, (eds), *Culture, Media, Language*. London: Hutchinson.

Hobson, D. (1982). *Crossroads: The Drama of a Soap Opera*. London: Methuen.

Hodge, R. and Kress, G. (1988). *Social Semiotics*. Cambridge: Polity Press.

Hofstadter, D. (1979). *Gödel, Escher, Bach: An Eternal Golden Braid*. Harmondsworth: Penguin.

Höijer, B. (1990). 'Studying viewers' reception of television programs: Theoretical and methodological considerations'. *European Journal of Communication*, 5 (1): 29–56.

Holzer, H. (1973). *Kommunikationssoziologie*. [Sociology of communication.] Hamburg: Rowohlt.

Honneth, A. and Joas, H. (eds) (1991). *Communicative Action: Essays on Jürgen Habermas's 'The Theory of Communicative Action'*. Cambridge, MA: MIT Press.

Hookway, C. (1985). *Peirce*. London: Routledge.

Horton, D. and Wohl, R. (1956). 'Mass communication and para-social interaction'. *Psychiatry*, 19: 215–29.

Houser, N. (1986). 'Introduction'. In C.S. Peirce, *Writings of Charles S. Peirce*. Vol. 4. Bloomington: Indiana University Press.

Hughes, R. (1981). *The Shock of the New*. New York: Alfred A. Knopf.

Huyssen, A. (1986). *After the Great Divide*. London: Macmillan.

Hyman, H. (1954). *Interviewing in Social Research*. Chicago: University of Chicago Press.

Innis, R. (ed.) (1985). *Semiotics: An Introductory Anthology*. Bloomington: Indiana University Press.

Jaeger, R. (1990). *Statistics: A Spectator Sport*. 2nd edn. Newbury Park, CA: Sage.

Jakobson, R. (1981). 'Linguistics and poetics'. In *Selected Writings*. Vol. 3. The Hauge: Mouton. (Orig. publ. 1960.)

James, W. (1981). *The Principles of Psychology*. Vol. 1. Cambridge, MA: Harvard University Press. (Orig. publ. 1890.)

Jameson, F. (1991). *Postmodernism, Or, The Cultural Logic of Late Capitalism*. London: Verso.

Jankowski, N. and Wester, F. (1991). 'The qualitative tradition in social science inquiry: Contributions to mass communication research'. In K.B. Jensen and N. W. Jankowski (eds), *A Handbook of Qualitative Methodologies for Mass Communication Research*. London: Routledge.

Jensen, K.B. (1986). *Making Sense of the News*. Aarhus, Denmark: Aarhus University Press.

Jensen, K.B. (1987a). 'News as ideology: Economic statistics and political ritual in television network news'. *Journal of Communication*, 37 (1): 8–27.

Jensen, K.B. (1987b). 'Qualitative audience research: Toward an integrative approach to reception'. *Critical Studies in Mass Communication*, 4 (1): 21–36.

Jensen, K.B. (1988a). 'News as social resource'. *European Journal of Communication*, 3 (3): 275–301.

Jensen, K.B. (1988b). 'Surplus meaning: Outline of a social theory of media reception'. *SPIEL: Siegener Periodicum zur Internationalen Empirischen Literaturwissenschaft*, 7 (2): 293–311.

Jensen, K.B. (1991a). 'Humanistic scholarship as qualitative science: Contributions to mass communication research'. In K.B. Jensen and N.W. Jankowski (eds), *A Handbook of Qualitative Methodologies for Mass Communication Research*. London: Routledge.

Jensen, K.B. (1991b). 'Reception analysis: Mass communication as the social production of meaning'. In K.B. Jensen and N.W. Jankowski (eds), *A Handbook of Qualitative Methodologies for Mass Communication Research*. London: Routledge.

Jensen, K.B. (1991c). 'When is meaning? Communication theory, pragmatism, and mass media reception'. In J. Anderson (ed.), *Communication Yearbook*. Vol. 14. Newbury Park, CA: Sage.

Jensen, K.B. (1991d). *News of the World: The Reception and Social Uses of Television News around the World. A Project Outline*. Paris: UNESCO.

Jensen, K.B. (forthcoming). 'Print cultures and visual cultures: A research agenda on new media environments'. In J. Stappers (ed.), *Approaches to Mass Communication*. London: Sage.

Jensen, K.B. and Rosengren, K.E. (1990). 'Five traditions in search of the audience'. *European Journal of Communication*, 5 (2–3): 207–38.

Jensen, K.B. and Jankowski, N.W. (eds) (1991). *A Handbook of Qualitative Methodologies for Mass Communication Research*. London: Routledge.

Jensen, K.B., Schrøder, K., Stampe, T., Søndergaard, H., and Topsøe-Jensen, J. (1994). 'Super flow, channels flows, and audience flows: A study of viewers' reception of television as flow'. *The Nordicom Review*, 2/1994: 1–13.

Jhally, S. and Lewis, J. (1992). *Enlightened Racism: The Cosby Show, Audiences, and the Myth of the American Dream*. Boulder, CO: Westview Press.

Joas, H. (1993). *Pragmatism and Social Theory*. Chicago: University of Chicago Press.

Johansen, J. Dines (1985). 'Prolegomena to a semiotic theory of text interpretation'. *Semiotica*, 57 (3–4): 225–88.

Johansen, J. Dines (1993). *Dialogic Semiosis*. Bloomington: Indiana University Press.

Johnson, M. (1987). *The Body in the Mind*. Chicago: University of Chicago Press.

Jungk, R. and Müllert, N. (1981). *Zukunftwerkstätten*. [Workshops on the future.] Hamburg: Hoffmann und Campe.

Katz, E. and Lazarsfeld, P. (1955). *Personal Influence*. Glencoe, IL: Free Press.

Katz, E., Gurevitch, M., and Haas, H. (1973). 'On the use of mass media for important things'. *American Sociological Review*, 38: 164–81.

Katz, E., Adoni, H., and Parness, P. (1977). 'Remembering the news'. *Journalism Quarterly*, 54 (2): 231–9.

Kincaid, D.L. (ed) (1987). *Communication Theory: Eastern and Western Perspectives*. San Diego, CA: Academic Press.

Kinder, M. (1984). 'Music video and the spectator: Television, ideology, and dream'. *Film Quarterly*, 38: 2–15.

Kirk, J. and Miller, M. (1986). *Reliability and Validity in Qualitative Research*. Beverly Hills, CA: Sage.

Kracauer, S. (1953). 'The challenge of qualitative content analysis'. *Public Opinion Quarterly*, 16 (2): 631–42.

Kubey, R. and Csikszentmihalyi, M. (1990). *Television and the Quality of Life*. Hillsdale, NJ: Lawrence Erlbaum.

Kuhn, T. (1970). *The Structure of Scientific Revolutions*. Rev. edn. Chicago: University of Chicago Press.

Kuklick, B. (1977). *The Rise of American Philosophy, Cambridge, Massachusetts, 1860–1930*. New Haven, CT: Yale University Press.

Kvale, S. (1987). 'Validity in the qualitative research interview'. *Methods*, 1: 37–72.

Kvale, S. (ed.) (1989). *Issues of Validity in Qualitative Research*. Lund, Sweden: Studentlitteratur.

Lacan, J. (1977). *The Four Fundamental Concepts of Psychoanalysis*. Harmondsworth: Penguin.

Lang, K. and Lang, G.E (1953). 'The unique perspective of television and its effect: A pilot study'. *American Sociological Review*, 18: 3–12.

Lang, K. and Lang, G.E. (1985). 'Method as master, or mastery over method'. In M. Gurevitch and M. Levy (eds), *Mass Communication Review Yearbook*. Vol. 5. Beverly Hills, CA: Sage.

Larsen, P. (1991). 'Textual analysis of fictional media content'. In K.B. Jensen and N.W. Jankowski (eds), *A Handbook of Qualitative Methodologies for Mass Communication Research*. London: Routledge.

Lasswell, H. (1966). 'The structure and function of communication in society'. In B. Berelson and M. Janowitz (eds), *Reader in Public Opinion and Communication*. Glencoe, IL: Free Press. (Orig. publ. 1948.)

Latour, B. (1987). *Science in Action*. Milton Keynes: Open University Press.

Lauretis, T. de (1984). *Alice Doesn't*. Bloomington: Indiana University Press.

Leech, G. (1974). *Semantics*. Harmondsworth: Penguin.

Leech, G. (1983). *Principles of Pragmatics*. London: Longman.

Leech, G. and Svartvik, J. (1975). *A Communicative Grammar of English*. London: Longman.

Lefebvre, H. (1984). *Everyday Life in the Modern World*. New Brunswick, NJ: Transaction Publishers.

Lévi-Strauss, C. (1963). *Structural Anthropology*. New York: Penguin.

Levy, M. (1977). 'Experiencing television news'. *Journal of Communication*, 27 (4): 112–17.

Levy, M. (ed.) (1992). 'Communication scholarship and political correctness'. *Journal of Communication*, 42 (2): 56–149.

Levy, M. and Gurevitch, M. (eds) (1994). *Defining Media Studies.* New York: Oxford University Press.

Lewis, J. (1985). 'Decoding television news'. In P. Drummond and R. Paterson (eds), *Television in Transition.* London: British Film Institute.

Lewis, J. (1991). *The Ideological Octopus: An Exploration of Television and Its Audience.* New York: Routledge.

Lichtblau, K. (1991). 'Causality or interaction? Simmel, Weber and interpretive sociology'. In M. Featherstone (ed.), 'A special issue on Georg Simmel'. *Theory, Culture & Society*, 8 (3): 33–62.

Liebes, T. and Katz, E. (1990). *The Export of Meaning.* New York: Oxford University Press.

Lindlof, T. (1988). 'Media audiences as interpretive communities'. In J. Anderson (ed.), *Communication Yearbook.* Vol. 11. Newbury Park, CA: Sage.

Lindlof, T. and Anderson, J. (1988). 'Problems in decolonizing the human subject in qualitative audience research'. Paper presented to the 16th Congress of the International Association for Mass Communication Research, Barcelona, Spain, July 24–9, 1988.

Livingstone, S. (1990). *Making Sense of Television.* Oxford: Pergamon.

Lobkowicz, N. (1967). *Theory and Practice: History of a Concept from Aristotle to Marx.* Notre Dame, IN: University of Notre Dame Press.

Lowe, D. (1982). *History of Bourgeois Perception*, Chicago: University of Chicago Press.

Lowery, S. and DeFleur, M. (1988). *Milestones in Mass Communication Research: Media Effects.* 2nd edn. New York: Longman.

Luhmann, N. (1987). 'The evolutionary differentiation between society and interaction'. In J. Alexander, B. Giesen, R. Münch, and N. Smelser (eds), *The Micro–Macro Link.* Berkeley: University of California Press.

Lull, J. (1980). 'The social uses of television'. *Human Communication Research*, 6: 197–209.

Lull, J. (ed.) (1986). *Popular Music and Communication.* Newbury Park, CA: Sage.

Lull, J. (ed.) (1988a). *World Families Watch Television.* Newbury Park, CA: Sage.

Lull, J. (1988b). 'Critical response: The audience as nuisance'. *Critical Studies in Mass Communication*, 5: 239–43.

Lyotard, J.-F. (1984). *The Postmodern Condition.* Minneapolis: University of Minnesota Press.

McChesney, R. (1993). 'Critical communication research at the crossroads'. *Journal of Communication*, 43 (4): 98–104.

McClelland, J., Rumelhart, D., and the PDP Research Group (1986). *Parallel Distributed Processing. Vol. 2: Psychological and Biological Models.* Cambridge, MA: MIT Press.

McCombs, M. and Shaw, D.L. (1972). 'The agenda-setting function of mass media'. *Public Opinion Quarterly*, 36: 176–87.

McCombs, M. and Shaw, D. (1977). *The Emergence of American Political Issues: The Agenda-Setting Function of the Press.* St. Paul, MN: West Publishing Company.

McGuigan, J. (1992). *Cultural Populism.* London: Routledge.

MacIntyre, A. (1972). 'Ontology'. In P. Edwards (ed.), *The Encyclopedia of Philosophy.* Vol. 5. New York: Macmillan.

McLuhan, M. (1962). *The Gutenberg Galaxy.* Toronto: University of Toronto Press.

McLuhan, M. (1964). *Understanding Media.* New York: McGraw-Hill.

McQuail, D. (1983). *Mass Communication Theory: An Introduction.* London: Sage.

McQuail, D. (1987). *Mass Communication Theory: An Introduction.* 2nd edn. London: Sage.

McQuail, D. (1992). *Media Performance.* London: Sage.

McQuail, D., Blumler, J., and Brown, J. (1972). 'The television audience: A revised perspective'. In D. McQuail (ed.), *Sociology of Mass Communication.* Harmondsworth: Penguin.

McQuail, D. and Windahl, S. (1981). *Communication Models for the Study of Mass Communications.* London: Longman.

Mancini, P. (1990). 'Selective reception and super-themes in decoding television news'. Paper presented to the conference of the International Communication Association, Dublin, Ireland, June 24–9 1990.

Marcus, G. and Fischer, M. (1986). *Anthropology as Cultural Critique.* Chicago: University of Chicago Press.

Marcuse, H. (1955). *Eros and Civilization.* Boston: Beacon Press.

Margolis, J. (1986). *Pragmatism Without Foundations*. Oxford: Blackwell.
Martin-Barbero, J. (1993). *Communication, Culture and Hegemony*. London: Sage.
Masterman, L. (1985). *Teaching the Media*. London: Comedia.
Mead, G.H. (1934). *Mind, Self, and Society*. Chicago: University of Chicago Press.
Merton, R.K. (1968). *Social Theory and Social Structure*. Enlarged edn. New York: Free Press.
Merton, R. and Kendall, P. (1955). 'The focused interview'. In P. Lazarsfeld and M. Rosenberg (eds), *The Language of Social Research*. Glencoe, IL: Free Press.
Messaris, P. (1993). 'Visual "literacy": A theoretical synthesis'. *Communication Theory*, 3 (4): 277–94.
Metz, C. (1974). *Language and Cinema*. The Hague: Mouton.
Metz, C. (1982). *The Imaginary Signifier*. Bloomington: Indiana University Press.
Meyrowitz, J. (1985). *No Sense of Place*. New York: Oxford University Press.
Miles, M.B. and Huberman, A.M. (1994). *Qualitative Data Analysis*. 2nd edn. London: Sage.
Miller, D.C. (1991). *Handbook of Research Design and Social Measurement*. 5th edn. Newbury Park, CA: Sage.
Mishler, E. (1986). *Research Interviewing: Context and Narrative*. Cambridge, MA: Harvard University Press.
Modleski, T. (1984). *Loving with a Vengeance*. New York: Routledge.
Moores, S. (1988). '"The box on the dresser": Memories of early radio and everyday life'. *Media, Culture and Society*, 10 (1): 23–40.
Moores, S. (1993). *Interpreting Audiences: The Ethnography of Media Consumption*. London: Sage.
Morley, D. (1980). *The 'Nationwide' Audience*. London: British Film Institute.
Morley, D. (1986). *Family Television*. London: Comedia.
Morley, D. (1992). 'Introduction'. In *Television, Audiences, and Cultural Studies*. London: Routledge.
Morley, D. and Silverstone, R. (1991) 'Communication and context: Ethnographic perspectives on the media audience'. In K.B. Jensen and N.W. Jankowski (eds), *A Handbook of Qualitative Methodologies for Mass Communication Research*. London: Routledge.
Morris, C. (1964). *Signification and Significance*. Cambridge, MA: MIT Press.
Morris, C. (1971). *Writings on the General Theory of Signs*. The Hague: Mouton.
Morris, C. (1985). 'Signs and the act'. In H. Innis (ed.), *Semiotics: An Introductory Anthology*. Bloomington: Indiana University Press.
Morris, M. (1990). 'Banality in cultural studies'. In P. Mellencamp (ed.), *Logics of Television*. Bloomington: Indiana University Press.
Mortensen, F. (1977). 'The bourgeois public sphere: A Danish mass communications research project'. In M. Berg, P. Hemanus, and J. Ekecrantz (eds), *Current Theories in Scandinavian Mass Communication*. Grenaa, Denmark: GMT.
Mortensen, J. and Ytreberg, E. (1991). 'Polysemy and the interpretation of texts – A philosophical assessment of the cultural studies tradition'. In H. Rønning and K. Lundby (eds), *Media and Communication: Readings in Methodology, History, and Culture*. Oslo: Norwegian University Press.
Mukerji, C. and Schudson, M. (eds) (1991). 'Introduction'. In C. Mukerji and M. Schudson (eds), *Rethinking Popular Culture*. Berkeley: University of California Press.
Murphey, M. (1961). *The Development of Peirce's Philosophy*. Cambridge, MA: Harvard University Press.
Murphy, J. (1990). *Pragmatism: From Peirce to Davidson*. Boulder, CO: Westview Press.
Nash, W. (1990). *The Writing Scholar*. Newbury Park, CA: Sage.
Negt, O. and Kluge, A. (1993). *Public Sphere and Experience*. Minneapolis: University of Minnesota Press. (Orig. publ. 1972.)
Nelson, J., Megill, A., and McCloskey, D. (eds) (1987). *The Rhetoric of the Human Sciences*. Madison: University of Wisconsin Press.
Neuman, W. R. (1989). 'Parallel content analysis: Old paradigms and new proposals'. In G. Comstock (ed.), *Public Communication and Behavior*. Vol. 2. Orlando, FL: Academic Press.
Newcomb, H. (1988). 'One night of prime time: An analysis of television's multiple voices'. In J.

Carey (ed.), *Media, Myths, and Narratives*. Beverly Hills, CA: Sage.

Newcomb, H. (1991). 'The search for media meaning'. In J. Anderson (ed.), *Communication Yearbook*. Vol. 14. Newbury Park, CA: Sage.

Newcomb, H. and Hirsch, P. (1984). 'Television as a cultural forum: Implications for research'. In W. Rowland and B. Watkins (eds), *Interpreting Television*. Beverly Hills, CA: Sage.

Nielsen, A.C. (1988). *Nielsen Report on Television*. Northbrook, IL: Nielsen Media Research.

Nielsen, A.C. (1989). *Nielsen Report on Television*. Northbrook, IL: Nielsen Media Research.

Nielsen, K. (1993). 'Peirce, pragmatism, and the challenge of postmodernism'. *Transactions of the Charles S. Peirce Society*, 29 (4): 513–60.

NIMH (National Institute of Mental Health) (1982). *Television and Behavior*. Vols 1–2. Washington, DC: Government Printing Office.

Ogden, C.K. and Richards, I.A. (1946). *The Meaning of Meaning*. 8th edn. New York: Harcourt, Brace & World. (Orig. publ. 1923.)

Olsen, E. and Skougaard, M. (eds) (1993). *Dagbogen 2. september*. [The diary of September 2.] Copenhagen: Nationalmuseet, Danmarks Radio.

Ong, W. (1982). *Orality and Literacy*. London: Methuen.

Orozco-Gómez, G. (ed.) (1992). *Hablan los televidentes*. Lomas de Santa Fé, Mexico: Universidad Iberoamericana.

Paivio, A. (1986). *Mental Representation: A Dual-Coding Approach*. New York: Oxford University Press.

Palmgreen, P., Wenner, L., and Rayburn, J. (1980). 'Relations between gratifications sought and obtained: A study of television news'. *Communication Research*, 7 (2): 161–92.

Park, R.E. (1940). 'News as a form of knowledge'. *American Journal of Sociology*, 45: 669–86.

Parsons, T. (1951). *The Social System*. Glencoe, IL: Free Press.

Pearson, R. and Uricchio, W. (eds) (1991). *The Many Lives of the Batman*. New York: Routledge.

Peirce, C.S. (1931–58). *Collected Papers*. Vols 1–8. Cambridge, MA: Harvard University Press.

Peirce, C.S. (1955). *Philosophical Writings of Peirce*. New York: Dover.

Peirce, C.S. (1958). *Selected Writings*. New York: Dover.

Peirce, C.S. (1985). 'Logic as semiotic: The theory of signs'. In H. Innis (ed.), *Semiotics: An Introductory Anthology*. Bloomington: Indiana University Press.

Peirce, C.S. (1986). *Writings of Charles S. Peirce*. Vol. 3. Bloomington: Indiana University Press.

Peirce, C.S. (1992). *The Essential Peirce*. Vol. 1. Bloomington: Indiana University Press.

Pelfrey, R. (1985). *Art and Mass Media*. New York: Harper & Row.

Perelman, C. (1979). *The New Rhetoric and the Humanities*. Dordrecht, The Netherlands: Reidel.

Peters, J.D. (1989). 'John Locke, individualism, and the origin of communication'. *Quarterly Journal of Speech*, 75 (4): 387–99.

Pfaffenberger, B. (1988). *Microcomputer Applications in Qualitative Research*. London: Sage.

Piepe, A., Emerson, M., and Farnborough, J. (1975). *Television and the Working Class*. Westmead: Saxon House.

Piepe, A., Crouch, S., and Emerson, M. (1978). *Mass Media and Cultural Relationships*. Westmead: Saxon House.

Pingree, S., Hawkins, R., Johnsson-Smaragdi, U., Rosengren, K., and Reynolds, N. (1991). 'Television structures and adolescent viewing patterns: A Swedish–American comparison'. *European Journal of Communication*, 6: 417–40.

Polkinghorne, D. (1988). *Narrative Knowing and the Human Sciences*. Albany: State University of New York Press.

Popper, K. (1972). *Conjectures and Refutations*. London: Routledge, Kegan & Paul.

Postman, N. (1985). *Amusing Ourselves to Death*. New York: Viking.

Potter, J. and Wetherell, M. (1987). *Discourse and Social Psychology*. London: Sage.

Prado, C. (1987). *The Limits of Pragmatism*. Atlantic Highlands, NJ: Humanities Press International.

Press, A. (1991). *Women Watching Television*. Philadelphia: University of Pennsylvania Press.

Radway, J. (1984) *Reading the Romance: Women, Patriarchy, and Popular Literature*. Chapel Hill: University of North Carolina Press.

Radway, J. (1988). 'Reception study: Ethnography and the problems of dispersed audiences and nomadic subjects'. *Cultural Studies*, 2 (3): 359–76.

Ragin, C. (1987). *The Comparative Method*. Berkeley: University of California Press.

Richards, J. and Sheridan, D. (eds) (1987). *Mass Observation at the Movies*. London: Routledge & Kegan Paul.

Robertson, R. and Turner, B. (1991). 'An introduction to Talcott Parsons: Theory, politics, and humanity'. In R. Robertson and B. Turner (eds), *Talcott Parsons: Theorist of Modernity*. London: Sage.

Robinson, J.P. and Levy, M. (1986). *The Main Source*. Beverly Hills, CA: Sage.

Rochberg-Halton, E. (1986). *Meaning and Modernity*. Chicago: University of Chicago Press.

Rogers, E. and Storey, J. (1987). 'Communication campaigns'. In C. Berger and S. Chaffee (eds), *Handbook of Communication Science*. Beverly Hills, CA: Sage.

Roper, Inc. (1985). *Public Attitudes toward Television and Other Mass Media in a Time of Change*. New York: Roper.

Rorty, A. (ed.) (1966). *Pragmatic Philosophy*. New York: Doubleday.

Rorty, R. (ed.) (1967). *The Linguistic Turn*. Chicago: University of Chicago Press.

Rorty, R. (1979). *Philosophy and the Mirror of Nature*. Princeton: Princeton University Press.

Rorty, R. (1982). *Consequences of Pragmatism*. Minneapolis: University of Minnesota Press.

Rorty, R. (1989). *Contingency, Irony, and Solidarity*. Cambridge: Cambridge University Press.

Rorty, R. (1991a). *Philosophical Papers. Vol. 1: Objectivity, Relativism, and Truth*. Cambridge: Cambridge University Press.

Rorty, R. (1991b). *Philosophical Papers. Vol. 2: Essays on Heidegger and Others*. Cambridge: Cambridge University Press.

Rosengren, K. (1985). 'Communication research: One paradigm or four?'. In E. Rogers and F. Balle (eds), *The Media Revolution in America and Western Europe*. Norwood, NJ: Ablex.

Rosengren, K. (1993). 'From field to frog ponds'. *Journal of Communication*, 43 (3): 6–17.

Rosengren, K. (forthcoming). 'Substantive theories and formal models: Their role in research on individual media use'. To be published in proceedings from the conference, 'The Viewer as TV Director: Understanding Individual Patterns of Exposure and Interpretation', Hamburg, Germany, October 23–4 1992.

Rosengren, K., Wenner, L., and Palmgreen, P. (eds) (1985). *Media Gratifications Research: Current Perspectives*. Beverly Hills, CA: Sage.

Rosenthal, S. (1986). *Speculative Pragmatism*. LaSalle, IL: Open Court.

Rumelhart, D., McClelland, V.J., and the PDP Research Group (1986). *Parallel Distributed Processing. Vol. 1: Foundations*. Cambridge, MA: MIT Press.

Sallach, D. (1974). 'Class domination and ideological hegemony'. In G. Tuchman (ed.), *The TV Establishment*. Englewood Cliffs, NJ: Prentice Hall.

Salthe, S. (1985). *Evolving Hierarchical Systems*. New York: Columbia University Press.

Saussure, F. de (1959) *Course in General Linguistics*. London: Peter Owen. (Orig. publ. 1916.)

Scannell, P. (1988). 'Radio Times: The temporal arrangements of broadcasting in the modern world'. In P. Drummond and R. Paterson (eds), *Television and Its Audience*. London: British Film Institute.

Schillemans, S. (1992). 'Umberto Eco and William of Baskerville: Partners in abduction'. *Semiotica*, 92 (3–4): 259–85.

Schiller, D. (1981). *Objectivity and the News*. Philadelphia: University of Pennsylvania Press.

Schlesinger, P., Dobash, R., Dobash, R., and Weaver, C. (1992). *Women Viewing Violence*. London: British Film Institute.

Schrøder, K. (1994). 'Audience semiotics, interpretive communities and the "ethnographic turn" in media research'. *Media, Culture & Society*, 16 (2): 337–47.

Schroeder, R. (1992). *Max Weber and the Sociology of Culture*. London: Sage.

Schudson, M. (1978). *Discovering the News*. New York: Basic Books.

Schudson, M. (1984). *Advertising, the Uneasy Persuasion*. New York: Basic Books.

Schudson, M. (1987). 'The new validation of popular culture: Sense and sentimentality in academia'. *Critical Studies in Mass Communication*, 4 (1): 51–68.

Schudson, M. (1991). 'Historical approaches to communication studies'. In K.B. Jensen and

N.W. Jankowski (eds), *A Handbook of Qualitative Methodologies for Mass Communication Research*. London: Routledge.

Schütz, A. (1973). 'On multiple realities'. In *Collected Papers. Vol. 1: The Problem of Social Reality*. The Hague: Martinus Nijhoff.

Searle, J. (1969). *Speech Acts*. London: Cambridge University Press.

Searle, J. (1981). 'Mind, brains, and programs'. In D. Hofstadter and D. Dennett (eds), *The Mind's I*. Harmondsworth: Penguin.

Searle, J. (1990). 'Is the brain's mind a computer program?'. *Scientific American*, January: 20–5.

Sebeok, T. (1985). 'Zoosemiotic components of human communication'. In H. Innis (ed.), *Semiotics: An Introductory Anthology*. Bloomington: Indiana University Press.

Sebeok, T. and Umiker-Sebeok, J. (1983). '"You know my method": A juxtaposition of Charles S. Peirce and Sherlock Holmes'. In U. Eco and T. Sebeok (eds), *The Sign of Three*. Bloomington: Indiana University Press.

Sennett, R. (1974). *The Fall of Public Man*. Cambridge: Cambridge University Press.

Seymour-Ure, C. (1989). 'Prime ministers' reaction to television: Britain, Australia, and Canada'. *Media, Culture & Society*, 11(3): 307–25.

Shannon, C. and Weaver W. (1949). *The Mathematical Theory of Communication*. Urbana: University of Illinois Press.

Sheriff, J. (1987). *The Fate of Meaning*. Princeton: Princeton University Press.

Siebert, F., Peterson, T., and Schramm, W. (1956). *Four Theories of the Press*. Urbana: University of Illinois Press.

Silverstone, R. (1994). *Television and Everyday Life*. London: Routledge.

Simons, H.W. (ed.) (1989). *Rhetoric in the Human Sciences*. London: Sage.

Singer, M. (1984). *Man's Glassy Essence: Explorations in Semiotic Anthropology*. Bloomington: Indiana University Press.

Skagestad, P. (1981). *The Road of Inquiry*. New York: Columbia University Press.

Smythe, D. (1977). 'Communication: Blindspot of Western Marxism'. *Canadian Journal of Political and Social Theory*, 1: 1–27.

Snow, C.P. (1964). *The Two Cultures and a Second Look*. Cambridge: Cambridge University Press.

Spigel, L. (1992). *Make Room for TV*. Chicago: University of Chicago Press.

Stearn, G. (ed.) (1967). *McLuhan: Hot & Cool*. New York: Signet.

Svennevig, M. (1986). 'The viewer viewed'. Paper presented to the International Television Studies Conference, London.

Szalai, A. (ed.) (1972). *The Use of Time*. The Hague: Mouton.

Terkel, S. (1974). *Working*. New York: Random House.

Thibault, P. (1991). *Social Semiotics as Praxis*. Minneapolis: University of Minnesota Press.

Thom, R. (1985). 'From the icon to the symbol'. In R. Innis (ed.), *Semiotics: An Introductory Anthology*. Bloomington: Indiana University Press.

Thompson, J. (1984). *Studies in the Theory of Ideology*. Cambridge: Polity Press.

Thompson, J. (1990). *Ideology and Modern Culture*. Cambridge: Polity Press.

Thompson, P. (1978). *The Voice of the Past*. London: Oxford University Press.

Tichenor, P., Olien, C., and Donohue, G. (1970). 'Mass media flow and differential growth in knowledge'. *Public Opinion Quarterly*, 34 (2): 159–70.

Tocqueville, A. de (1966). *Democracy in America*. New York: Harper & Row. (Orig. publ. 1848.)

Todorov, T. (1968). 'Le grammaire du récit'. [The grammar of narrative.] *Langages*, 12: 94–102.

Tomaselli, K. and Shepperson, A. (eds) (1991a). 'Popularising semiotics'. Theme issue of *Communication Research Trends*, 11 (2).

Tomaselli, K. and Shepperson, A. (eds) (1991b). 'Popularising semiotics (continued)'. Theme issue of *Communication Research Trends*, 11 (3).

Toulmin, S. (1958). *The Uses of Argument*. Cambridge: Cambridge University Press.

Tuchman, G. (1978). *Making News: A Study in the Construction of Reality*. New York: Free Press.

Turing, A. (1981). 'Computing machinery and intelligence'. In D. Hofstadter and D. Dennett (eds), *The Mind's I*. Harmondsworth: Penguin. (Orig. publ. 1950.)

Turkle, S. (1984). *The Second Self: Computers and the Human Spirit*. New York: Simon & Schuster.

Turner, B. (1991a). 'Neofunctionalism and the "new theoretical movement": The post-Parsonian rapprochement between Germany and America'. In R. Robertson and B. Turner (eds), *Talcott Parsons: Theorist of Modernity*. London: Sage.

Turner, B. (1991b). 'Preface to the new edition'. In M. Weber, *From Max Weber: Essays in Sociology*. London: Routledge.

Turner, V. (1967). 'Betwixt and between: The liminal period of *Rites de Passage*'. In *The Forest of Symbols*. Ithaca: Cornell University Press.

van Dijk, T.A. (1977). *Text and Context: Explorations in the Semantics and Pragmatics of Discourse*. London: Longman.

van Dijk, T.A. (ed.) (1985). *Handbook of Discourse Analysis*. Vols 1–4. London: Academic Press.

van Dijk, T.A. (1988). *News as Discourse*. Hillsdale, NJ: Lawrence Erlbaum.

van Dijk, T.A. (1991). 'The interdisciplinary study of news as discourse'. In K.B. Jensen and N.W. Jankowski (eds), *A Handbook of Qualitative Methodologies for Mass Communication Research*. London: Routledge.

Van Maanen, J. (1988). *Tales of the Field*. Chicago: University of Chicago Press.

Volosinov, V.N. (1973). *Marxism and the Philosophy of Language*. New York: Seminar Press. (Orig. publ. 1929.)

Volosinov, V.N. (1985). 'Verbal interaction'. In H. Innis (ed.), *Semiotics: An Introductory Anthology*. Bloomington: Indiana University Press.

Walsh, W.H. (1972). 'The nature of metaphysics'. In P. Edwards (ed.), *The Encyclopedia of Philosophy*. Vol. 5. New York: Macmillan.

Weber, M. (1964). *The Theory of Social and Economic Organization*. New York: Free Press.

Weber, M. (1991). *From Max Weber: Essays in Sociology*. London: Routledge. (Orig. publ. 1948.)

West, C. (1989). *The American Evasion of Philosophy: A Genealogy of Pragmatism*. Madison: University of Wisconsin Press.

White, M. (1973). *Pragmatism and the American Mind*. New York: Oxford University Press.

Williams, R. (1974). *Television: Technology and Cultural Form*. London: Fontana.

Williams, R. (1977). *Marxism and Literature*. London: Oxford University Press.

Williams, R. (1983). *Keywords*. London: Fontana.

Willis, P. (1990). *Common Culture*. Milton Keynes: Open University.

Winograd, T. and Flores, F. (1986). *Understanding Computers and Cognition*. Norwood, NJ: Ablex.

Wittgenstein, L. (1958). *Philosophical Investigations*. London: Macmillan.

Wolf. U. (1984). 'Ontologie'. [Ontology.] In J. Ritter and Karlfried Gründer (eds), *Historiches Wörterbuch der Philosophie*. [Historical dictionary of philosophy.] Vol. 6. Basel: Schwabe and Co.

Wollen, P. (1972). *Signs and Meaning in Cinema*. Bloomington: Indiana University Press.

Wolton, D. (ed.) (1992). 'À la recherche du public'. *Hermes*, 11–12.

Index

DATE DUE

THE SOCIAL SEMIOTICS
OF MASS COMMUNICATION

To Grethe

THE SOCIAL SEMIOTICS
OF MASS COMMUNICATION

Klaus Bruhn Jensen

SAGE Publications
London • Thousand Oaks • New Delhi

First published 1995

SAGE Publications Ltd
6 Bonhill Street
London EC2A 4PU

SAGE Publications Inc
2455 Teller Road
Thousand Oaks, California 91320

SAGE Publications India Pvt Ltd
32, M-Block Market
Greater Kailash – I
New Delhi 110 048

British Library Cataloguing in Publication data

A catalogue record for this book is
available from the British Library

ISBN 0-8039-7809-X
ISBN 0-8039-7810-3 (pbk)

Library of Congress catalog card number 95-067894

Typeset by M Rules
Printed in Great Britain at the University Press, Cambridge

Contents

Acknowledgments

During the ten years of research within media studies, communication theory, and theory of science that inform this volume, I have accumulated many professional and personal debts, and I would like to acknowledge the main ones associated with the present publication. I first had the opportunity to concentrate on the works of Charles Sanders Peirce and other pragmatists during 1988–9 when I was on a leave of absence from the University of Copenhagen, supported financially by the American Council of Learned Societies and spent at the Annenberg School of Communications, University of Southern California; I remain indebted to those institutions for the right aid at the right moment. I am especially grateful to the anonymous respondents who gave generously of their time to make possible the studies reported in Chapters 5, 6, 7, and 9. Colleagues, students, and collaborators have helped me to clarify the ideas and positions developed in the following pages. For comments to earlier drafts of this volume, I would like in particular to thank Hans Arndt, Henrik Dahl, Peter Dahlgren, Erik Arne Hansen, Søren Kjørup, Finn Olesen, Karl Erik Rosengren, Grethe Skylv, and Svein Østerud.

Earlier versions of some chapters have been published in different contexts. Part of Chapter 1 first appeared in the 1992 issue of *Sekvens*, the yearbook of the Department of Film and Media Studies, University of Copenhagen. Certain key arguments in Chapter 4 were originally presented in 'When is meaning? Communication theory, pragmatism, and mass media reception,' in J. Anderson (ed.), *Communication Yearbook*, Vol. 14, Newbury Park, CA: Sage, 1991. Chapter 5 was published as 'The politics of polysemy: Television news, everyday consciousness, and political action,' *Media, Culture & Society*, 12 (1), 1990; Chapter 6 as 'Television futures: A social action methodology for studying interpretive communities,' *Critical Studies in Mass Communication*, 7 (2), 1990 (used by permission of the Speech Communication Association); and Chapter 7 as 'Reception as flow: The "new television viewer" revisited,' *Cultural Studies*, 8 (2), 1994. One section of Chapter 8 appeared as 'The past in the future: Problems and potentials of historical reception studies,' *Journal of Communication*, 43 (4), 1993; another part of Chapter 8 as 'Discourses of interviewing: Validating qualitative research findings through textual analysis,' in S. Kvale (ed.), *Issues of Validity in Qualitative Research*, Lund, Sweden: Studentlitteratur,1989.

For permission to reproduce figures, I am grateful to the following publishers: Indiana University Press for Figures 1.1, 10.2 and 10.3; Oxford University Press for Figure 4.2; Larousse, Paris for Figure 8.3; The MIT Press for Figure 10.1; and Lawrence Erlbaum Associates Ltd., Hove, UK for Figure 10.5.

Klaus Bruhn Jensen
Copenhagen

PART I
SOURCES OF SOCIAL SEMIOTICS